COLLUSION

Luke Harding is a journalist, writer, and award-winning foreign correspondent with the *Guardian*. Between 2007 and 2011, he was the *Guardian*'s Moscow bureau chief. The Kremlin expelled him from the country in the first case of its kind since the Cold War.

He is the author of five previous non-fiction books: *A Very Expensive Poison: The Assassination of Alexander Litvinenko and Putin's War with the West*, *The Snowden Files: The Inside Story of the World's Most Wanted Man*, *Mafia State: How One Reporter Became an Enemy of the Brutal New Russia*, *WikiLeaks: Inside Julian Assange's War on Secrecy*, and *The Liar: The Fall of Jonathan Aitken* (the last two co-written with David Leigh).

Two have been made into Hollywood movies. Dreamworks' *The Fifth Estate*, based on *WikiLeaks*, was released in 2013. Director Oliver Stone's biopic *Snowden*, adapted from *The Snowden Files*, appeared in 2016. A stage version of *Poison* is forthcoming. His books have been translated into thirty languages. Luke lives near London with his wife, the freelance journalist Phoebe Taplin, and their two children.

"Harding is a brave, assiduous and energetic journalist. A former Moscow correspondent who was expelled from the country in 2011, he is well placed to offer an important perspective." *Sunday Times*

"You and I are

it's real. An

Collusion is

Mark Haddon, on Twitter @mark_haddo

"Amazing research and brilliantly collated." John Le Carré

"Meticulously, scrupulously researched, leaves no room for doubt . . . Putin comes across as a deeply nasty piece of work, Trump a blundering idiot." Richard Dawkins

"Harding at his best. He has sleuthed the Russia–Trump connections with exceptional skill. A fine read and a great contribution to the public domain." Professor Robert Service, University of Oxford

"Harding presents the facts, traces their genesis, does not make bold assumptions, does not give any space to conspiracies of any kind, but succeeds in giving substance to what we know through the analysis of the past." Robert Saviano, *L'Espresso*

"Harding's analysis of Steele's claims is thorough, fascinating, fast-paced and lively, embedded in a chronological account of the madness we've all been living through for the past aeon . . . I sincerely hope this book will be the first of many that will do that scrutiny for us." *Observer*

"It's hard to follow all the allegations and denials in the press. Better to settle down with this book by Luke Harding . . . Harding has found numerous sources who claim that the Kremlin has been courting Trump since 1987. He therefore scrutinises dealings between Trump and various Russian associates, pointing out their connections with Putin and seeing patterns in the flow of money into Trump properties. Harding has not only done the legwork, he can explain what it all means." *Herald*

COLLUSION

How Russia Helped Trump
Win the White House

LUKE HARDING

First published by Guardian Faber in 2017

Guardian Faber is an imprint of Faber & Faber Ltd,
Bloomsbury House, 74–77 Great Russell Street,
London WC1B 3DA

This paperback edition first published in 2018

Guardian is a registered trademark of
Guardian News & Media Ltd,
Kings Place, 90 York Way, London N1 9GU

Printed and bound by CPI Group (UK) Ltd, Croydon, CR0 4YY

A CIP record for this book
is available from the British Library

ISBN 978-1-78335-150-3

2 4 6 8 10 9 7 5 3 1

CONTENTS

	Prologue: Meeting	3
1	The End of History Not	15
2	I Think He's an Idiot	42
3	Publish and Be Damned	64
4	Hack	89
5	General Misha	115
6	He Does Bastards	140
7	Tuesday Night Massacre	171
8	Collusion	212
9	Thraldom	248
10	From Russia with Cash	272
11	The Strange Case of the German Bank	299
	Epilogue	323
	Notes on Sources	339
	Thanks	341
	Index	343

COLLUSION

Meeting

December 2016
Grosvenor Gardens, London SW1

Victoria station in London. A mixture of shabby and genteel. There's a railway terminus, a bus station, and—a little further on—a triangular park. Here you can find a statue of the French World War I hero Marshal Ferdinand Foch sitting on a horse. Written on the plinth are Foch's words: "I am conscious of having served England . . ." Someone has added in black pen: "by murdering thousands."

It's a zone of arrivals and departures. Around Foch are brown benches splattered white with pigeon droppings and tall plane trees. There are tourists, commuters, and the odd hirsute bum, sipping from a can of lager and muttering. The man who owns this prime slice of real estate is the Duke of

Westminster. He's Britain's wealthiest aristocrat.

Keep going and you reach a row of tall neoclassical houses, done in French Renaissance style. This is Grosvenor Gardens. The street looks onto the back wall of a world-famous residence, Buckingham Palace. With a bit of pluck and a long ladder you might vault directly into Her Majesty's private back garden. Its fir trees, poking into the grey London skyline, are visible to commoners. The Queen's lake is unseen.

Some of the houses here announce their inhabitants: PR firm, Japanese restaurant, language school. But at number 9–11 Grosvenor Gardens there's no clue as to who or what is inside. Two pillars frame an anonymous black front door. There's a closed-circuit TV sign. No names on the door buzzer. Above, three floors of offices.

If you enter and turn right, you find yourself in a modest ground-floor suite: a couple of bare rooms painted ivory white, a medium-sized colour map of the world fixed to one wall, white blinds just above street level on high windows. There are computers, and a newspaper, too: a copy of *The Times*. The impression is of a small, discreet, professional operation.

The office is home to a British firm, Orbis Business Intelligence Ltd. Orbis's website says it's a "leading corporate intelligence consultancy." It adds, vaguely: "We provide senior decision-makers with strategic insight, intelligence and investigative services. We then work with clients to implement strategies which protect their interests worldwide."

Decoded, Orbis is in the non-state spying business. It spies for commercial clients—delving into the secrets of individuals and institutions, governments and international organizations. London is the global capital of private intelligence. "A tough sector," in the words of one former British spy, who worked in it for a year before landing a job with a large corporation. There are more than a dozen such firms, staffed mostly by former intelligence officers specializing in foreign know-how.

This isn't quite the world of classic espionage or James Bond. But it's not far from it.

The man who runs Orbis is called Christopher Steele. Steele and his business partner Christopher Burrows are Orbis's directors. Both are British. Steele is fifty-two; Burrows a little older, fifty-eight. Their names don't appear on Orbis's public material. Nor is there mention of their former careers. A pair of bright younger graduates work alongside them. They form a small team.

Steele's office gives few clues as to the nature of his under-cover work.

There's only one hint.

Lined up near the director's desk are nesting Russian dolls, or *matryoshki*. A souvenir from Moscow. They feature Russia's great nineteenth-century writers: Tolstoy, Gogol, Lermontov, Pushkin. The dolls are hand-painted and have the names of the authors written towards the base in florid Cyrillic characters. The upper-case *T* of Tolstoy resembles a swirling Greek Pi.

In the tumultuous days of 2016, the dolls were as good a metaphor as any for the astonishing secret investigation Steele had recently been asked to do. It was an explosive assignment: to uncover the Kremlin's innermost secrets with relation to one Donald J. Trump, to unnest them one by one, like so many dolls, until the truth was finally revealed. Its conclusions would shake the American intelligence community and cause a political earthquake not seen since the dark days of President Richard Nixon and Watergate.

Steele's findings were sensational, and the resulting dossier would in effect accuse President-elect Trump of the gravest of crimes: collusion with a foreign power. That power was Russia. The alleged crime—vehemently denied, contested, and in certain key respects unprovable—was treason. The new US president designate was, it was whispered, a traitor.

To find a plot that crazy, you had to turn to fiction: Richard Condon's *The Manchurian Candidate*, about a Soviet–Chinese operation to seize the White House. Or a largely forgotten thriller by the writer Ted Allbeury, *The Twentieth Day of January*. In this one, Moscow recruits a young American during the 1968 Paris student riots who goes on to greater things. Like Steele, Allbeury was a former British intelligence officer.

Until his work was brought blindingly into the light, Steele was unknown. Unknown, that is, beyond a narrow circle of US and UK government intelligence insiders and Russia experts. That was the way he preferred it.

The year 2016 was an extraordinary historical moment. First, Brexit, Britain's shock decision to leave the European Union. Then, to the surprise—and dismay—of many Americans, not to mention others around the world, Donald J. Trump was unexpectedly elected that November as the United States' forty-fifth president.

The campaign that got him to the White House had been rancorous, divisive, and mean-spirited. Looming above the campaign was this single and scarcely believable accusation: a foreign leader traditionally seen as an enemy of the United States had secretly helped Trump in his against-the-odds presidential campaign—maybe even nudging him across the line to victory. Trump, went the claim, was the Kremlin's candidate.

He was a puppet of Putin, whom top Republicans had previously regarded as a cold-eyed KGB villain—"a murderer and a thug," according to John McCain, the Republican senator from Arizona. Someone who wished America ill.

At this point, the accusation of collusion with Moscow stuck for two reasons. First, there was Trump's own curious behaviour on the campaign trail. Faced with claims that Russia was hacking Democratic emails, and leaking them to damage his rival, Hillary Clinton, Trump publicly urged Moscow to keep going.

At a July 2016 press conference in Florida, he said this:

"Russia, if you're listening, I hope you're able to find the thirty thousand emails that are missing. I think you will probably be rewarded mightily by our press. Let's see if that happens."

As a Clinton aide pointed out, this was a straightforward appeal to a foreign power to commit espionage against a political opponent. Was this Trump opportunism? Or something more co-ordinated, more sinister?

Few doubted that the emails released via WikiLeaks in June and October 2016 hurt the Democratic candidate. In themselves, they weren't especially scandalous. To an unscrupulous adversary like Trump, however, they were a present, a great gift: an opportunity to grab the media cycle by the neck and to shake home the message of "Crooked Hillary." Also relevant was the fact that Moscow had stolen Republican National Committee emails, too. Only it hadn't published them.

Second, how to explain Trump's flattering praise of Putin? In the febrile months leading up the November 8, 2016 vote, Trump had lambasted not only Clinton and Obama but also his Republican party rivals, *Saturday Night Live*, the "failing"

New York Times, the US media in general—his favourite enemy—and Meryl Streep. And others. It was a long list.

Russia's president, by contrast, was lauded as "very smart." Putin was, practically, the only person on the planet to escape Trump's sweeping invective, delivered in semi-literate exclamatory style via Twitter, at a time when most sane people were in bed. Trump was willing to verbally assault anyone who queried his behaviour—anyone but his friend Putin.

The budding Trump–Putin friendship couldn't merely be explained by personal chemistry; they hadn't—it appeared—met. Sure, there were ideological similarities: a contempt for international bodies such as the UN and a dislike of the European Union. And, you might argue, Christian-inflected white nationalism. But this wasn't quite enough. It was as if there were a strange fealty at work, an unexplained factor, an invisible hand, a missing piece of the puzzle. Trump didn't praise any other foreign leader in quite the same way. Or as often. His obeisance to Putin would continue even as he ascended to office.

These two issues—the promotion of Russia's hacked emails and the praise of Putin—raised a remarkable question. Had Putin somehow been *blackmailing* the candidate? If not, how to explain Trump's infatuation? If yes, blackmailing how, exactly?

There were plenty of rumours, of course. Some of them had reached my newspaper, the *Guardian*. In the lead-up to the US presidential election, and in the feverish and dumbfounding period afterwards, investigative journalists on both sides of the Atlantic were pursuing a number of leads. This was a difficult, frustrating, and tantalizing business. There were doubts about sources. Some of the dirt on Trump came from people close to the Clinton campaign, people with an axe to grind.

Nevertheless, this was, we realized, potentially the most important US political story in a generation. If Trump had indeed conspired with Russia, not only publicly but perhaps covertly, too, via undisclosed back-channels, that looked like treachery. It was Watergate all over again.

But this time around, the "burglars" weren't low-level Nixon operatives. They weren't even Americans. According to the CIA and the FBI, they were anonymous hackers working for Putin's spy agencies. The cash paying their salaries was Russian—and possibly American. They didn't bust into the DNC using lock picks, surgical gloves, and bugging equipment, like their 1972 counterparts.

Instead, they penetrated the DNC's computer networks—an ingress by the brute method of thousands of phishing emails. The operation, the FBI would conclude, was simple and inexpensive. It was devastatingly effective. And perhaps proof that America's political systems were more vulnerable to shadowy electronic forces than anyone had thought.

Meanwhile, Trump hadn't exactly helped our efforts to establish the truth. Breaking with all precedent, he'd refused to disclose his tax returns. His global real estate empire was hidden behind a network of several hundred opaque companies. Visualized as a graphic, Trump's corporate holdings looked like a giant exploding puffball.

Was Trump a multibillionaire, as he flamboyantly claimed? Or was he in fact broke and over-leveraged, owing large sums of money to banks abroad? What financial ties, if any, did he have to foreign governments? What might be said of his family, in particular the future president's powerful son-in-law, Jared Kushner?

In December 2016, Nick Hopkins, a *Guardian* colleague, and I went to see Chris Steele to ask him these and other questions. Hopkins is the paper's investigations editor. He had met Steele previously and knew of his expertise on Russia. This was my expertise, too. From 2007 to 2011, I spent four years in Russia as the *Guardian*'s Moscow bureau chief, until I was put in an airport cell and deported from the country. This, I am sure, was as a result of some of my less flattering reports on Vladimir Putin.

It was a Thursday afternoon, two and a half weeks before Christmas. London's streets were crowded and hectic with shoppers. We travelled by underground from the *Guardian*'s office near King's Cross. At Victoria station we got out and walked the short distance to Grosvenor Gardens—past Marshal Foch and his entourage of pigeons.

We buzzed the front door of Orbis. They decided to let us in. Steele greeted us. He was of medium height, dressed in a regular suit, with once-black hair now mostly grey, friendly in manner but with an edge of reserve that was entirely understandable.

Journalists and spies have traditionally viewed each other with suspicion. In some respects, they are engaged in the same trade: cultivating sources, collecting and sifting information, separating fact from fiction. Both write for an audience. A newspaper's audience is anybody with an Internet connection. Spies write for a small official circle, cleared for secrets. Often, I imagine, the product is the same. The spies have one advantage. They receive material obtained from state eavesdropping and secret sources.

Steele had agreed to chat over four o'clock tea. By this point his investigation had not made worldwide headlines. He had not yet removed himself from the public eye, so the three of us returned to the street and looked for a spot to grab a cup of tea.

We tried Balls Brothers—a café and wine bar, its green awnings overlooking Lower Grosvenor Garden. A waitress told us they had no space: the tables were reserved for Christmas office parties. We wandered across the road into a pub, the Shakespeare, its name marked in letters of black against gold. A portrait of the bard himself hung above the entrance.

We found a tucked-away table. I went to the bar and came back with drinks: beer for Steele, Coke for Nick, pot of tea for me. The decor had a railway theme, publicity for the Great Western Railway. There were old black-and-white photos of men in flat caps reading in a carriage and young women splashing in the sea at a beach.

Steele was someone who liked being in the shadows, away from publicity or fuss. In the world of corporate intelligence, the fewer people who knew what you were doing the better. Invisible was good. Reporters (they knew things, but could be indiscreet and on occasion treacherous) were a necessary evil.

"Have you heard of me?" he asked.

I confessed I hadn't.

I knew most people in town who were focused on Russia, but not Steele.

"Good," he said. "That's how I like it."

Steele's reticence was a matter of professional custom. First, he was a former spy. Second, he was bound by the rules of commercial confidentiality. He wasn't going to say anything about his clients. There was no hint he had been involved in what was the single most important investigation in decades. Besides, those who investigated, criticized, or betrayed Putin often met with disastrous ends.

One critic was Alexander Litvinenko. Litvinenko was a former FSB officer who fled Russia in 2000 after exposing corruption at the top of his organization. (Two years earlier Putin had personally fired him.) In exile in London, Litvinenko denounced Russia's president in books and articles. His friends warned him that nothing good would come of this.

In 2003, MI6 recruited Litvinenko as an occasional expert on Russian organized crime. Litvinenko advised British and Spanish intelligence. His thesis was later cited in leaked US diplomatic cables out of Madrid. It said the Kremlin, its well-resourced spy agencies, and the Russian mafia had merged. In effect, they formed a single criminal entity, a mafia state.

Litvinenko's reward was a radioactive cup of tea, delivered to him by two Russians in a London hotel bar. The hotel, the Millennium, is next to the US embassy on Grosvenor Square, in an area familiar to Russian spies. If the CIA officers stationed there had peered out of their third-floor window on November 1, 2006, they might have seen Litvinenko's assassins, Dmitry Kovtun and Andrei Lugovoi, walk through the hotel's revolving door. A UK public inquiry found Putin "probably approved" this operation.

I had spent a decade investigating the Litvinenko assassination, and Steele had also followed the case closely. He hadn't met Litvinenko, but he led MI6's subsequent investigation into this unprecedented murder. Steele concluded it was a plot authorized at the highest levels of Russian power. The poison was polonium—a rare, lethal, and highly radioactive isotope. Once it is ingested, death is certain. In Litvinenko's case, it took more than three weeks of suffering.

Not knowing the powder keg Steele was sitting on, we had come to talk to him about the Trump–Russia investigation we were quietly carrying out since the US election. We had two leads. One was intriguing and at this point speculative: that Russia had covertly financed Trump's campaign. We knew many of the alleged details. There was no proof. We had no primary source. If proof did exist, it was well hidden.

The other lead was more solid. We had documentary evidence that high-ranking Russian bureaucrats and well-connected insiders had laundered $20 billion. The scheme was ingenious—its trail involving British lawyers, Moldovan judges, a Latvian bank, and limited companies registered in London. The cash had gone everywhere, some of it through US accounts with banks like JP Morgan Chase and Wells Fargo. Most of the beneficiaries remained a mystery.

Cash had been hidden offshore. The scheme had been partly used for political operations abroad. It illustrated the porousness of the US banking system, pores open to Russian money. And if you could launder money into New York, you could, presumably, spend it on covert hacking. On anything you wished for.

Steele listened more than he talked. He wouldn't confirm that our stories were correct, though he implied we were on the right track.

He offered parallel lines of inquiry.

"You need to look at the contracts for the hotel deals and land deals that Trump did. Check their values against the money Trump secured via loans," Steele told us.

This, it seemed, was a reference to Trump's former home in Florida. Trump had bought the mansion in 2004 for $41 million. Four years later, he sold it to a Russian oligarch for $95 million. Even allowing for inflation, for the repainting Trump said he'd carried out on the property, for the allure of the Trump brand, and for the whims of a very rich man seeking to invest in the United States, this seemed an extraordinary profit.

"The difference is what's important," Steele said.

Another theme of the election campaign was Trump's relations with women. This had come to the fore after the emergence of a 2005 recording. On it Trump bragged about the privileges of being "a star." One perk: when he met beautiful women he could simply "grab them by the pussy." Trump apologized for this. He insisted the women who alleged sexual harassment were liars—Jezebels motivated not by justice but by politics.

To our surprise, Steele implied that Trump and sex was an interesting line of inquiry. He gave no details.

Steele wasn't going to tell us much. Nevertheless, it appeared he might confirm—or trash—information we'd acquired from elsewhere. For an investigative journalist this was helpful.

After forty-five minutes it was time for Steele to go.

The situation had a distinct Watergate echo. Our mission was now clear: follow the sex and the money.

We left separately, determined to keep our investigation going. Then things got a whole lot bigger.

Two days later, Steele's work would land on Obama's desk, but its beginnings were decades in the making.

1

The End of History Not

1990–2016

Moscow–London–Washington

> The greatest geopolitical
> catastrophe of the twentieth century.
> —VLADIMIR PUTIN,
> on the break-up of the USSR

Moscow, summer 1991. Mikhail Gorbachev was in power. Official relations with the West may have softened, but the KGB still assumed all Western embassy workers were spooks.

The KGB goons assigned to them were easy to spot. They had a method. Sometimes they pursued targets on foot, sometimes in cars. The officers charged with keeping tabs on Western diplomats were never subtle.

One of their specialities was breaking into Moscow apartments. The owners were away, of course. The KGB team would leave a series of clues—stolen shoes, women's tights knotted together, cigarette butts stomped out and left demonstratively on the floor. Or a surprise turd in the toilet, waiting in grim ambush. The message, crudely put, was this: We are the masters here! We can do what the fuck we please!

The KGB kept watch on all foreigners, especially American and British ones. The UK mission in Moscow was under close observation. The embassy was a magnificent mansion built in the 1890s by a rich sugar merchant, on the south bank of the Moskva River. It looks directly across to the Soviet Kremlin. The view was dreamy: a grand palace, gold church domes, and medieval spires topped with revolutionary red stars.

One of those whom it routinely surveilled was a twenty-seven-year-old diplomat, newly married to his wife, Laura, on his first foreign posting, and working as a second secretary in the chancery division.

In this case, the KGB's suspicions were right.

The "diplomat" was a British intelligence officer. His workplace was a grand affair: chandeliers, reception rooms with mahogany panelling, gilt-framed portraits of the Queen and other royals hanging from the walls. His desk was in the embassy library, surrounded by ancient books. Three colleagues were neighbours. The officer's actual employer was an invisible entity back in London—SIS, the Secret Intelligence Service.

The officer was Christopher Steele. Steele arrived in Moscow via the usual establishment route for upwardly mobile British spies: the University of Cambridge. Cambridge had produced some of MI6's most talented Cold War officers. A few of them— it turned out to great embarrassment—had secret second jobs with the KGB. The joke inside MI6 was that only those who had never visited the Soviet Union would wish to defect.

Steele studied social and political sciences at Girton College. His views were centre-left; he and his elder sister were the first generation of his family to go to university. Steele's paternal grandfather was a miner from Pontypridd, in south Wales; his great-uncle died in a pit accident. These were the years of Prime Minister Margaret Thatcher, whose implacable opposition to the striking coal workers killed the industry. Steele wrote for the student newspaper, *Varsity*. He became president of the Cambridge Union, a debating society dominated by well-heeled and well-connected young men and women.

It's unclear who recruited Steele. Traditionally, certain Cambridge tutors were rumoured to identify promising SIS candidates. Whatever the route, Steele's timing was good. After three years at MI6, he was sent to the Soviet Union in April 1990, soon after the fall of the Berlin Wall and the collapse of the communist bloc across Eastern Europe.

It was a tumultuous time. Steele had a front-row seat to history. Seventy years after the Bolshevik revolution, the red empire was crumbling. The Baltic states had revolted against Soviet power; their own national authorities were governing in parallel with Moscow. The Soviet Russian republic had elected a democratic president—Boris Yeltsin. There were queues; food was scarce.

There was still much to enjoy. Like other expatriates, the Steeles visited the Izmailovsky craft market, next to an imperial park where Peter the Great's father, Tsar Alexei, had established a model farm. Here you could buy lacquered boxes, patchwork quilts, furry hats, and Soviet kitsch. Steele acquired samovars, carpets from central Asia, a papier mâché Stalin mask, and the Tolstoy doll set—price $150—that adorned his later office.

Much of the Soviet Union was off-limits to diplomats. Steele was the embassy's "internal traveller" and visited newly accessible cities. One of them was Samara, a wartime Soviet capital. There, he became the first foreigner to see Stalin's underground bunker. Instead of Lenin, he found dusty portraits of Peter the Great and the imperial commander Mikhail Kutuzov—proof, seemingly, that Stalin was more nationalist than Marxist.

On the weekends, Steele took part in soccer matches with a group of expats in a Russian league. In one game, he played against the legendary Soviet Union striker Oleh Blokhin, who scored from the halfway line.

The atmosphere was optimistic. It appeared to Steele that the country was shifting markedly in the right direction. Citizens once terrified of interacting with outsiders were ready to talk. The KGB, however, found nothing to celebrate in the USSR's tilt towards freedom and reform. That August, seven apparatchiks staged a coup while Gorbachev was vacationing in Crimea.

Most of the British embassy was away. Steele was home and at his second-floor apartment in Gruzinsky Pereulok. He left the apartment block, turned right, and walked ten minutes into town. Crowds had gathered outside the White House, the seat of government; thus far the army hadn't moved against them.

From fifty yards away, Steele watched as a snowy-haired man in a suit climbed on a tank and—reading from notes brushed by the wind—denounced the coup as cynical and illegal. This was a defiant Yeltsin. Steele listened as Yeltsin urged a general strike. And, fist clenched, told his supporters to remain strong.

The coup failed, and a weakened Gorbachev survived. The putschists—the leading group in all the main Soviet state and party institutions—were arrested. In the West, and in the United States in particular, many concluded that Washington had won the Cold War. And that, after decades of ideological struggle, liberal democracy had triumphed.

Steele knew better. Three days after the coup, surveillance on him resumed. His colleagues in Hungary and Czechoslovakia reported that after revolutions there the secret police vanished, never to come back. But here were the same KGB guys, with the same familiar faces. They went back to their old routines of bugging, apartment break-ins, and harassment.

The regime changed. The system didn't.

By the time Steele left Moscow in April 1993 the Soviet Union had gone. A new country led by Yeltsin had replaced it: the Russian Federation. The KGB had been dissolved.

But its officers hadn't exactly disappeared. They loathed the United States still and were merely biding their time.

One mid-ranking former KGB spy unhappy about this state of affairs was Vladimir Putin. Putin had missed perestroika and glasnost, Gorbachev's reformist ideas, and had returned from provincial East Germany and Dresden. He was now carving out a political career in the new St Petersburg. He mourned the lost USSR. Its disappearance was "the greatest geopolitical catastrophe of the twentieth century."

A post-communist spy agency, the Federal Security Service, or FSB, had taken over the KGB's main functions. Back home, Steele would soon move into MI6's new purpose-built office— a large, striking postmodern pile of a building overlooking the River Thames. This gaudy Babylonian temple was hard to miss; in 1994, the government acknowledged MI6's existence. Staff called it Vauxhall Cross. The FSB would become its bitter adversary.

From London Steele continued to work on the new Russia. He was ambitious, keen to succeed, and keen to be seen to succeed. He was part of an SIS team.

And perhaps less posh than some of his upper-class peers. Steele's family was blue-collar. His father, Perris, and mother, Janet, from London, met when they worked at the UK Meteorological Office. Dad was forecaster to the military and Royal Air Force. The family lived on army bases in Aden, where Steele was born, on the Shetland Islands and—twice— in Cyprus. Steele's education had been varied. He went to a British forces school in Cyprus. He did sixth form at a college in Berkshire. He then spent a "seventh" or additional term at Wellington College, an elite private boarding school. There he sat the entrance exam for Cambridge.

Steele now moved in a small world of Kremlin specialists. There were conferences and seminars in university towns like Oxford; contacts to be made; émigrés to be met, lunched, charmed. In 1998 he got another posting—to the British embassy in Paris. He had a family: two sons and then a daughter, born in France, where Steele was officially "First Secretary Financial."

At this point his career hit a bump. In 1999 a list of MI6 officers was leaked online. Steele was one of them. He appeared next to Andrew Stafford and Geoffrey Tantum as "Christopher David Steele, 90 Moscow; dob 1964." His future business partner, Christopher Burrows, was blown, too. Burrows's entry reads: "82 East Berlin, 87 Bonn, 93 Athens, dob 1958."

The breach wasn't Steele's fault, but it had unfortunate consequences. As an exposed British officer he couldn't go back to Russia.

In Moscow the spies were staging a comeback. In 1998

Putin became FSB chief, followed by prime minister and, in 2000, president. By 2002, when Steele left Paris, Putin had consolidated his grip. Most of Russia's genuine political opposition had been wiped out, from parliament, public life, and the evening news.

The idea that Russia might slowly turn into a democracy or that history, as Francis Fukuyama put it, might be ending had proved a late-century fantasy. Rather, the United States' traditional nuclear-armed adversary was moving in an authoritarian direction.

At first George W. Bush and Tony Blair viewed Putin as a respectable ally in the war against terror. Russia's leader remained an enigma. As Steele knew better than most, obtaining information from inside the presidential administration was hard.

One former member of the US National Security Council described Putin as a "black box." "The Brits had slightly better assets than us. We had nothing. No human intelligence," the source said. And, with the focus on fighting Islamists, Russia was downgraded on the list of US–UK intelligence priorities.

By 2006 Steele held a senior post at MI6's Russia desk in London. There were ominous signs that Putin was taking Russia in an aggressive direction. The number of hostile Russian agents in the United Kingdom grew, surpassing Cold War levels. Steele tracked a new campaign of subversion and covert influence.

And then the two FSB assassins put a mini-nuclear poison in Litvinenko's teapot. It was an audacious operation, and a sign of things to come. One reason MI6 picked Steele to investigate was that—unlike colleagues who had known the victim—he wasn't emotionally involved. Steele's gloomy view of

Russia—that under Putin it was not only domestically repressive but also internationally reckless and revisionist—looked about right. Steele briefed government ministers. Some got it. Others couldn't believe Russian spies would carry out murder and mayhem on the streets of London.

All told, Steele spent twenty-two years as a British intelligence officer. There were some high points—he saw his years in Moscow as formative—and some low ones. Two of the diplomats with whom he shared a Moscow office, Tim Barrow and David Manning, went on to become ambassadors to the EU and the United States. But Steele didn't quite rise to the top, in what was a highly competitive service. Espionage might sound exciting, but the salary of a civil servant was ordinary. And in 2009 there was personal tragedy, when his wife died aged forty-three after a period of illness.

That same year Steele left MI6 and set up Orbis. Making the transition from government to the private sector wasn't easy. Steele and Burrows were now pursuing the same intelligence matters as before but without any of the support and peer review they had in their previous jobs. MI6's security branch would often ask an officer to go back to a source, or redraft a report, or remark, "We think it's interesting. We'd like to have more on this." This kept up quality and objectivity.

Steele and Burrows, by contrast, were out on their own, where success depended more on one's own wits. There was no more internal challenge. The people they had to please were corporate clients. The pay was considerably better.

The shabby environs of Victoria were a long way away from Washington and its bitterly contested US presidential election. So how did Steele come to be commissioned in the first place to research Trump and produce his devastating dossier?

At the same moment Steele said goodbye to official spying, another figure was embarking on a new career in the crowded field of private business intelligence. His name was Glenn Simpson. He was a former journalist.

Simpson was an alluring figure: a large, tall, angular, bear-like person who slotted himself easily onto a bar stool and enjoyed a beer or two. He was a good-humoured social companion who spoke in a nasal drawl. Behind small oval glasses was a twinkling intelligence. He excelled at what he did.

Simpson had been an illustrious *Wall Street Journal* correspondent. Based in Washington and Brussels, he had specialized in post-Soviet murk. He didn't speak Russian or visit the Russian Federation. This was deemed too dangerous. Instead, from out of the country, he examined the dark intersection between organized crime and the Russian state. Very often that meant the same thing.

One of Simpson's subjects was Semion Mogilevich, a Ukrainian-Russian mafia don and one of the FBI's ten most wanted individuals. Mogilevich, it was alleged, was behind a mysterious intermediary company, RosUkrEnergo (RUE), that imported Siberian natural gas into Ukraine. The profits were measured in billions of dollars.

Mogilevich wasn't someone a reporter might meet; he was more myth than man. He lived in Moscow—or was it Budapest? Seemingly, the Russian state and FSB harboured him. Simpson talked to US investigators. Over years, he built up a portfolio of contacts in Hungary, Israel, Cyprus. At home he knew individuals inside the Department of Justice—in particular its Organized Crime and Racketeering Section—the US Treasury, and elsewhere.

By 2009 Simpson decided to quit journalism, at a time when the media industry was in all sorts of financial trouble. He co-founded his own commercial research and political intelligence firm based in Washington, DC. Its name was Fusion GPS. Its website gave little away. It didn't even list an address or the downtown loft from where a team of analysts worked.

Fusion's research would be similar to what Simpson had done before. That meant investigating difficult corruption cases or the business activities of post-Soviet figures. There would still be a public interest dimension, only this time private clients would pay. Fusion was very good at what it did and—Simpson admitted—expensive.

In 2009 Simpson met Steele. They knew some of the same FBI people and shared expertise on Russia. Fusion and Orbis began a professional partnership. The Washington- and London-based firms worked for oligarchs litigating against other oligarchs. This might involve asset tracing—identifying large sums concealed behind layers of offshore companies.

Later that year Steele embarked on a separate and sensitive new assignment that drew on his knowledge of covert Russian techniques. And of soccer: in Moscow he had played in defence as a full-back. The client was the English Football Association, the FA. England was bidding to host the 2018 soccer World Cup. England's main rival was Russia. There were joint bids, too, from Spain and Portugal, and the Netherlands and Belgium. His brief was to investigate the eight other bidding nations, with a particular focus on Russia.

It was rumoured that the FSB had carried out a major influence operation, ahead of a vote in Zurich by the executive committee of FIFA, soccer's international governing body. A second vote was to take place at the same time for the 2022 World Cup. One of the countries bidding was the desert emirate of Qatar.

According to Steele, Putin was a reluctant backer of Russia's World Cup bid and only became engaged from mid-2010, when it appeared Moscow might lose. Putin then summoned a group of oligarchs. He instructed them to do whatever was necessary to achieve victory, including striking personal deals with FIFA voters.

Putin's method, Steele said, was unseen. "Nothing was written down. Don't expect me or anyone to produce a piece of paper saying please, X, bribe Y with this amount in this way. He's not going to do this." He added: "Putin is an ex-intelligence officer. Everything he does has to be deniable." The oligarchs were brought in to disguise the Kremlin's controlling role, Steele said, according to the *Sunday Times*.

Steele "lit the fuse" of something bigger, as one friend put it.

Steele discovered that FIFA corruption was global. It was a stunning conspiracy. He took the unusual step of briefing an American contact in Rome, the head of the FBI's Eurasia and Serious Crime Division. This led to a probe by US federal prosecutors. And to the arrest in 2015 of seven FIFA officials, allegedly connected to $150 million in kickbacks, paid on TV deals stretching from Latin America to the Caribbean. The United States indicted fourteen individuals.

By this point, of course, Russia had won its bid to host the World Cup. England—the country that invented soccer—scraped just two votes.

The episode burnished Steele's reputation inside the US intelligence community and the FBI. Here was a pro, a well-connected Brit, who understood Russian espionage and its subterranean tricks. Steele was regarded as credible.

Between 2014 and 2016, Steele authored more than a hundred reports on Russia and Ukraine. These were written for a private client but shared widely within the State Department and sent up to Secretary of State John Kerry and to Assistant Secretary of State Victoria Nuland, who was in charge of the US response to the Ukraine crisis. Many of Steele's secret sources were the same sources who would supply information on Trump.

One former State Department envoy during the Obama administration said he read dozens of Steele's reports on Russia. The envoy said that on Russia, Steele was "as good as the CIA or anyone."

Steele's professional reputation inside US agencies would prove important the next time he discovered alarming material, and lit the fuse again.

Trump's political rise in the autumn of 2015 and the early months of 2016 was swift and irresistible. The candidate was a human wrecking ball who flattened everything in his path, including the Republican Party's aghast, frozen-to-the-spot establishment. Marco Rubio, Jeb Bush, Ted Cruz—all were batted aside, taunted, crushed. Scandals that would have killed off a normal presidential candidate made Trump stronger. The media loved it. Increasingly, so did the voters.

Might anything stop him?

The front-runner was Jeb Bush, a son of one US president and brother of another. But as the campaign got under way Bush struggled. Trump dubbed the former Florida governor "low-energy." During the primaries, one of Trump's wealthy opponents, Paul

Singer, commissioned Fusion to investigate Trump. Singer was a New York hedge fund billionaire and Republican donor, and the backer of a conservative website, the Washington Free Beacon. Singer dropped out after Trump became the presumptive nominee. Senior Democrats seeking to elect Hillary took over the Trump contract. The new client was the Democratic National Committee. A lawyer working for Hillary's campaign, Marc E. Elias, retained Fusion and received its reports.

The world of private investigation was a morally ambiguous one—a sort of open market in dirt. Information on Trump was of no further use to Republicans, but it could be of value to Democrats, Trump's next set of opponents.

A little before this point, in early spring 2016, Simpson approached Steele, his friend and colleague. Steele started to scrutinize Paul Manafort, Trump's new campaign manager. From April Steele investigated Trump on behalf of the DNC, Fusion's anonymous client. All Steele knew at first was that the client was a law firm. He had no idea what he'd find. He later told David Corn, Washington editor of the magazine *Mother Jones*: "It started off as a general inquiry." Trump's organization owned luxury hotels around the world. Trump had, as far back as 1987, sought to do real estate deals in Moscow.

One obvious question for him, Steele said, was: "Are there business ties to Russia?"

Over time, Steele had built up a network of sources. He was fiercely possessive of them: who they were he would never say. A source might mean practically anybody. It could be someone famous: for example, a well-known foreign government official or diplomat with access to secret material. Or it could be someone obscure—a lowly chambermaid cleaning the penthouse suite and emptying the bins in a five-star hotel.

Normally an intelligence officer would debrief sources directly. Since Steele could no longer visit Russia, this had to be done by others or in third countries. There were intermediaries, subsources, operators—a sensitive chain. Only one of Steele's sources on Trump knew of Steele.

Steele put out his Trump–Russia query. He waited for answers. His sources started reporting back. The information was astonishing, "hair-raising." As he told friends, "For anyone who reads it, this is a life-changing experience."

Steele had stumbled upon a well-advanced conspiracy that went beyond anything he had discovered with Litvinenko or FIFA. It was the boldest plot yet. It involved the Kremlin and Trump. Their relationship, Steele's sources claimed, went back a long way. For at least the past five years Russian intelligence had been secretly cultivating Trump. This operation had succeeded beyond Moscow's wildest expectations. Not only had Trump upended political debate in the United States—raining chaos and confusion wherever he went and winning the nomination—but it was just possible that he might become the next president.

Which opened all sorts of intriguing options for Putin.

In June 2016 Steele typed up his first memo. He sent it to Fusion. It arrived via enciphered mail.

The headline read: "US Presidential Election: Republican Candidate Donald Trump's Activities in Russia and Compromising Relationship with the Kremlin."

It said:

Summary

- Russian regime has been cultivating, supporting and assisting TRUMP for at least 5 years. Aim, endorsed by

PUTIN, has been to encourage splits and divisions in the western alliance.

- So far TRUMP has declined various sweetener real estate business deals, offered him in Russia to further the Kremlin's cultivation of him. However he and his inner circle have accepted a regular flow of intelligence from the Kremlin, including on his Democratic and other political rivals.

- Former top Russian intelligence officer claims FSB has compromised TRUMP through his activities in Moscow sufficiently to be able to blackmail him. According to several knowledgeable sources, his conduct in Moscow has included perverted sexual acts which have been arranged/monitored by the FSB.

- A dossier of compromising material on Hillary CLINTON has been collated by the Russian Intelligence Services over many years and mainly comprises bugged conversations she had on various visits to Russia and intercepted phone calls rather than any embarrassing conduct. The dossier is controlled by Kremlin spokesman, PESKOV, directly on Putin's orders. However, it has not yet been distributed abroad, including to TRUMP. Russian intentions for its deployment still unclear.

The memo was sensational. There would be others, sixteen in all, sent to Fusion between June and early November 2016. At first, obtaining intelligence from Moscow went well. For around six months—during the first half of the year—Steele was able to make inquiries in Russia with relative ease. It got harder from late July as Trump's ties to Russia came under scrutiny. Finally, the lights went out. Amid a Kremlin cover-up, the sources went silent and information channels shut down.

If Steele's reporting was to be believed, Trump had been colluding with Russia. This arrangement was transactional, with both sides trading favours. It said Trump had turned down "various lucrative real estate development business deals in Russia," especially in connection with the 2018 soccer World Cup, hosted by Moscow.

But he'd been happy to accept a flow of Kremlin-sourced intelligence material, apparently delivered to him by his inner circle. That didn't necessarily mean the candidate was a KGB agent. It did signify, however, that Russia's leading spy agency had expended considerable effort in getting close to Trump—and, by extension, to his family, friends, close associates, and business partners, not to mention his campaign manager and personal lawyer.

On the eve of the most consequential US election for generations, one of the two candidates was compromised, Steele's sources claimed. The memo alleged Trump had unusual sexual proclivities. If true, this meant he could be blackmailed.

Steele's collaborators offered salacious details. It said that Russian intelligence had sought to exploit "TRUMP's personal obsessions and sexual perversion" during a trip to Moscow in 2013. The operation had allegedly worked. The tycoon had booked the presidential suite of the Ritz-Carlton hotel, "where he knew President and Mrs OBAMA (whom he hated) had stayed on one of their official trips to Russia."

There, the memo said Trump had deliberately "defiled" the Obamas' bed. A number of prostitutes "had performed a 'golden showers' (urination) show in front of him." The memo added: "The hotel was known to be under FSB control with microphones and concealed cameras in all the main rooms to record anything they wanted to."

There was another fascinating dimension to this alleged plot, of course categorically denied by Trump. According to Steele's sources, associates of Trump and Russian spies had held a series of clandestine meetings in central Europe, Moscow, and elsewhere. The Russians were very good at tradecraft. Nonetheless, could this be a trail that others might later detect?

Steele's sources offered one final piece of devastating information. They alleged that Trump's team had co-ordinated with Russia on the hacking operation against Clinton. And that the Americans had secretly co-paid for it.

Steele wrote up his findings in MI6 house style. The memos read like CX reports—classified SIS intelligence documents. They were marked CONFIDENTIAL/SENSITIVE SOURCE. The names of prominent individuals were in bold—TRUMP, PUTIN, CLINTON. The reports began with a summary. They offered supporting detail. Sources were anonymous. They were merely introduced in generic terms: "a senior Russian foreign ministry figure" or "a former top level Russian intelligence officer still active inside the Kremlin." They were given letters, starting with *A* and proceeding down the alphabet.

How certain was Steele that his sources had got it right and that he wasn't being fed misinformation? The matter was so serious, so important, so explosive, so far-reaching—this was an essential question.

As spies and former spies knew, the world of intelligence was non-binary. There were degrees of veracity. A typical CX report would include phrases like: "To a high degree of probability."

Intelligence could be flawed because humans were inherently unreliable. They forgot things. They got things wrong.

One of Steele's former Vauxhall Cross colleagues likened intelligence work to delicate shading. This twilight world wasn't black and white—rather it was a muted palette of greys, off-whites, and sepia tones, he told me. He said you could shade in one direction—more optimistically—or in another direction—less optimistically. Steele was generally in the first category.

Steele was adamant that his reporting was credible. One associate described him as sober, cautious, highly regarded, professional, and conservative. "He's not the sort of person who will pass on gossip. If he puts something in a report, he believes there is sufficient credibility in it," the associate said. The idea that Steele's work was fake or a cowboy operation or born of political malice was completely wrong, he added.

The dossier, Steele told friends, was a thoroughly professional job, using professional methods. And—significantly—based on sources who had proven themselves in other areas. Evaluating sources depended on a critical box of tools: what was a source's reporting record, was he or she credible, what was the motivation?

Steele recognized that no piece of intelligence was 100 percent right. According to friends, he assessed his work on the Trump dossier was 70 to 90 percent accurate. Over eight years, Orbis had produced scores of reports on Russia for private clients and others. A lot of this content was verified or "proven up." And, Steele said, "I've been dealing with this country for thirty years. Why would I invent this stuff?"

Meanwhile, others were confirming his alarming discoveries.

*

It is known as the Doughnut. This impregnable-looking building, hollow in the middle and with a security fence around
its circumference, is situated in Cheltenham, not far from the
Cotswolds. What it does is secret. Although, thanks to Edward
Snowden, the breathtaking scale of its mission is now better
known.

The Doughnut is a key part of British intelligence gathering. It is home to the Government Communications
Headquarters—the UK's eavesdropping agency. In 2013
Snowden revealed that GCHQ has the capacity to hoover up
most of the Internet: email traffic, browsing histories, text
messages, and other data, stolen in the billions from fibre optic
cables or via intercepts of mobile phones.

Snowden's leak also showed GCHQ's close relationship
with the NSA—the US National Security Agency. The two
agencies are practically indistinguishable. They are part of an
Anglo-Saxon spying alliance, Five Eyes. This encompasses the
United States, the United Kingdom, Canada, New Zealand,
and Australia. Collectively, these agencies can surveil the entire
planet.

On any day, their targets might include Taliban command-
ers in Afghanistan, the Iranian leadership, or the Stalinist her-
mit state of North Korea. GCHQ would routinely listen to
the conversations of known or suspected foreign intelligence
officers active in the United Kingdom and continental Europe.
Especially Russian ones.

In late 2015 GCHQ was carrying out standard "collection"
against Moscow targets. These were known Kremlin operatives
already on the grid. Nothing unusual here. Except that the
Russians were talking to people associated with Trump. The
precise nature of these exchanges has not been made public.

According to sources in the United States and the United Kingdom, these interactions formed a suspicious pattern. They continued through the first half of 2016. The intelligence was handed to the United States as part of a routine sharing of information. Other friendly spy agencies supplied similar Trump–Russia electronic material. According to one source, the countries involved included Germany, Estonia–Sweden, Poland, and Australia. A second source suggested that both the Dutch spy agency and the French General Directorate for External Security, or DGSE, were contributors as well.

The FBI and the CIA were slow to appreciate the extensive nature of these contacts between Trump's team and Moscow. This was in part due to institutional squeamishness—the law prohibits US agencies from examining the private communications of US citizens without a warrant.

The electronic intelligence suggested Steele was right. According to one account, the US agencies looked as though they were "asleep." "'Wake up! There's something not right here!' The BND [German intelligence], the Dutch, the DGSE, SIS were all saying this," one Washington-based source told me.

James Clapper, the director of national intelligence, later confirmed the stream of intelligence from Europe, declining to give details and adding: "It's sensitive." It included an early attribution from GCHQ that the perpetrators behind the DNC hack were Russian state operatives. And that it was carried out from Moscow by professional spies.

After an initially slow start Brennan used GCHQ information and tip-offs from other partners to launch a major inter-agency investigation.

Meanwhile, the FBI was receiving disturbing warnings from a separate direction—Steele.

At this point Steele's Fusion material was unpublished and unknown. Whatever the outcome of the election, it raised grave questions about Russian interference and the US democratic process. There was, Steele felt, overwhelming public interest in passing his findings to US investigators. The United States' multiple intelligence agencies had the resources to prove—or disprove—his discoveries. He realized these allegations were—as he put it to a friend—a "radioactive hot potato." He anticipated a hesitant response, at least at first.

In June Steele flew to Rome to brief his contact from the FBI, with whom he had co-operated over FIFA. His information started to reach the FBI in Washington. It had certainly arrived by the time of the Democratic National Convention in late July, when the website WikiLeaks first began releasing hacked Democratic emails. It was at this moment that FBI director James Comey opened a formal investigation into Trump–Russia.

In September Steele went back to Rome. There he met with an FBI team. It debriefed him. The FBI's response was one of "shock and horror," Steele said. After a few weeks, the bureau asked him to explain how he had compiled his reports and to give background on his sources. It asked him to send future copies.

Steele had hoped for a thorough and decisive FBI investigation. Instead, the bureau moved cautiously. It told him that it couldn't intervene or go public with material involving a presidential candidate. Then it went silent. Steele's frustrations grew. Glenn Simpson decided on an alternative course of action.

Later that month Steele had a series of off-the-record meetings with a small number of American journalists. They included the *New York Times*, the *Washington Post, Yahoo! News, The New Yorker*, and CNN. In mid-October he visited New York and met with reporters again. Comey then announced he was reopening an investigation into Clinton's use of a private email server. At this point, Steele's relationship with the FBI broke down. The excuse given by the bureau for saying nothing on Trump looked invalid. In late October, Steele spoke to David Corn via Skype.

The story was of "huge significance, way above party politics," Steele said. He believed Trump's own Republicans "should be aware of this stuff as well." Of his own reputation Steele said: "My track record as a professional is second to no one." Steele acknowledged his memos were works in progress—and was genuinely worried about the implications of the allegations. "The story has to come out," he told Corn.

Corn wrote about the dossier on October 31. It was the first time its existence was made public. At the same time, the *New York Times* published a story saying that the FBI hadn't found any "conclusive or direct link" between Trump and Russian officials.

Steele was at this point anonymous, a ghost. But the ghost's message was rapidly circulating on Capitol Hill and inside Washington's spy agencies, as well as among certain journalists and think-tanks.

Democratic senators now apprised of Steele's work were growing exasperated. The FBI seemed unduly keen to trash Clinton's reputation while sitting on explosive material concerning Trump.

One of those who was aware of the dossier's broad allegations was Senate minority leader Harry Reid. In August Reid had written to Comey and asked for an inquiry into the "connections between the Russian government and Donald Trump's presidential campaign." In October Reid wrote to Comey again. This time he framed his inquiry in scathing terms.

In what was a clear reference to Steele, Reid wrote: "In my communications with you and other top officials in the national security community, it has become clear that you possess explosive information about close ties and coordination between Donald Trump, his top advisors, and the Russian government. . . . The public has a right to know this information."

All of this frantic activity came to naught. Just as Nixon was re-elected during the early stages of Watergate, Trump won the presidential election, to general dismay, at a time when the Russia scandal was small but growing.

Steele had found prima facie evidence of a conspiracy, but by and large the US public knew nothing about it. In November, the dossier began circulating in the top national security echelons of the Obama administration. But it was too late. The Democrats' "election surprise," as it were, had failed. It was a cruel defeat.

In Halifax, on Canada's eastern seaboard, a light drizzle was falling. All sorts of precipitation rolled in from the Atlantic: rain, fog, snow, rain again. From the harbour front the grey sea shaded into a sky of endless white. Georges Island could be seen out in the water, with its lighthouse and eighteenth-century citadel.

It was here in Nova Scotia that millions of passengers from Europe once disembarked in search of a better life in the new world. Cruise ships still pulled up in front of pier 21. There was a railway station, an immigration museum, and a boxy rose-coloured hotel next to a park. The hotel was historic—the Queen had stayed there—and had been through several owners. It was now the Westin Nova Scotian.

It was in Halifax that November that a group of international experts gathered. Their objective: to make sense of the world, in the aftermath of Trump's stunning victory. Most were appalled by this. The three-day event was organized by the Halifax International Security Forum. There were sessions on post-Brexit Britain, the "Middle East mess," ISIS, and relations with Russia.

One of the delegates was Sir Andrew Wood. Wood was the UK's ambassador to Russia from 1995 to 2000. He was taking part in a Ukraine panel. Its theme was the challenges facing the country after Putin's cloaked invasion. (Canada has strong ties with Ukraine: some 1.3 million citizens are of Ukrainian descent.) Another participant was Senator John McCain.

Wood was a friend of Steele's and an Orbis associate. Before the election, Steele had gone to Wood and shown him the dossier. He wanted the ambassador's advice. What should he do, or not do, with it? Of the dossier, Wood told me later: "I took it seriously."

From London, Wood observed Russian affairs with a cool and critical eye. He wrote articles for Chatham House, the foreign affairs think-tank, where he was a fellow in the Russia and Eurasia programme. He spoke at conferences and seminars.

On the margins of the Halifax conference Wood briefed McCain about Steele's dossier—its contents, if true, had profound and obvious implications for the incoming Trump administration, for the Republican Party, and for US democracy.

McCain decided the implications were sufficiently alarming

to dispatch a former senior US official to meet with Steele and find out more.

The emissary was another delegate in Halifax, David Kramer, who had hosted Wood's Ukraine discussion. Kramer was a senior director at the McCain Institute for International Leadership. He had previously worked for the Bush administration in 2008–2009 as assistant secretary of state for democracy, human rights, and labor. He later led Freedom House, the Washington-based pro-democracy think-tank.

The dossier's eventual journey to the Oval Office would take this unlikely route: Moscow to London to Halifax to DC.

Kramer was sufficiently troubled to get on a transatlantic flight to London. Steele agreed to meet him at Heathrow Airport. The date was November 28. The rendezvous involved some old-fashioned spycraft. Kramer didn't know what Steele looked like: at this point there were no public photos of him. He was told to watch out for a man with a copy of the *Financial Times*. After picking up Kramer, Steele drove him to his home in Farnham, Surrey, in London's suburban commuter belt. They talked through the dossier: how Steele compiled it, what it said.

Less than twenty-four hours later, Kramer returned to Washington. Next, Simpson shared a copy of the dossier confidentially with McCain.

It also went to the British government.

Steele gave a copy of a final memo he had written in December to the top UK government official in charge of national security, a former colleague from his days at SIS. The memo offered fresh details of the hacking operation. An encrypted copy was sent to Fusion, with instructions to pass it to McCain and Kramer.

McCain believed it was impossible to verify Steele's claims without a proper investigation. He made a call and arranged a meeting with Comey. Their encounter on December 8 lasted five minutes. The venue, according to one source, was the FBI's headquarters, the J. Edgar Hoover Building in Washington. Not much was said. McCain gave Comey the dossier. According to the same source, Comey didn't let on to McCain that the agency had already begun an investigation into Trump's associates, which at this point was more than four months old.

McCain's intervention now made some kind of bureaucratic response inevitable. This was no longer just an FBI affair; it required co-ordination across the top levels of US intelligence.

A highly classified two-page summary of Steele's dossier was compiled. It was attached to a longer restricted briefing note on Russian cyber interference in the 2016 election. The United States' most senior intelligence chiefs mulled what to do.

Their next task was an unenviable one. As former CIA director Michael Hayden put it to me, the situation was "off the map in terms of what intelligence is asked to do. I didn't envy them." Of the dossier Hayden said: "My gestalt idea when I saw it was that this looks like our stuff."

A day after Steele met with us in the Shakespeare pub in London, the dossier—or at least its most damning accusation—was on its way to the desk of someone who was still—for a short while longer—the world's most powerful person, President Barack Obama.

It was also going to his successor, the next guy in the Oval Office. Comey had the thankless job of briefing President-elect Trump. Trump, it was clear, would dismiss the dossier as a piece of trash. This strategy was problematic for various reasons and would look increasingly ridiculous in the months ahead.

For example, Trump's team had indeed met with Russians in the run-up to the vote, as Steele's sources had alleged and GCHQ and others had detected.

One of Trump's advisers had even conducted an enthusiastic correspondence with a Russian spy. And given him documents. Not in Moscow but Manhattan.

2

I Think He's an Idiot

2013–2017
New York–Moscow

> You get the documents from him
> and tell him to go fuck himself.
> —VICTOR PODOBNYY,
> April 2013, speaking in New York

When Victor Podobnyy became a spy, he had expected his career to be glamorous. He quickly realized that real espionage didn't involve flying helicopters. It wasn't—as he put it—"like in the Bond movies." He had thought his superiors in Moscow would at least give him a false identity and a passport.

Instead, Podobnyy had been sent to New York under his real name. His official job was attaché to Russia's delegation to the United Nations. In reality, he worked for Russia's foreign intelligence service, the SVR. Yes, he was a spy under diplomatic cover. His actual tasks, though, were pretty mundane: gathering economic intelligence.

It was April 2013. In a conversation secretly recorded by the FBI, Podobnyy moaned about his lot. He was sitting in the SVR's New York office. His interlocutor was Igor Sporyshev, an SVR colleague. Sporyshev was working covertly in the United States, too, disguised as a trade representative.

PODOBNYY: The fact that I'm sitting with a cookie right now at the chief enemy spot. Fuck! Not one point of what I thought then, not even close.

SPORYSHEV: I also thought I would at least go abroad with a different passport.

True, the Russians had reason to complain. In summer 2010 the SVR suffered a devastating blow when ten of its long-term sleeper agents in the United States were exposed, including Anna Chapman. Federal agents had rolled up the SVR's network of "illegals," the term used for spies sent abroad under non-diplomatic cover.

Meanwhile, Podobnyy and Sporyshev were left with the tricky job of collecting secret information. One of their tasks was to liaise with another SVR officer, Evgeny Buryakov, who was working under non-official cover at the branch of a Russian bank in Manhattan, VEB. The bank was, in part, an SVR front. Buryakov didn't have diplomatic immunity so had to report to Moscow via his colleagues.

As FBI wiretaps showed, the techniques for meeting with Buryakov were distinctly old-school. Typically, Sporyshev would ring Buryakov and tell him he had to give him "something"—a ticket, a book, a hat, an umbrella. The two would meet outdoors. This sometimes happened outside Buryakov's bank office on Third Avenue—an inconspicuous brown tower with a 1960s abstract sculpture at street level opposite the foyer. They would exchange documents.

Sporyshev's biggest headache was recruiting Americans as intelligence sources. This was tough. He had approached two young women working in financial consultancy who had recently graduated from a New York university. Sporyshev told Podobnyy he was sceptical anything would come of it. Or, as he put it in chauvinist terms: "In order to be close you need to either fuck them or use other levers to execute my requests."

The Russian spies, however, had one promising lead. This was a guy—an energy consultant based in New York City. Unlike the women, he was eager to help. And, it appeared, keen to make money in Moscow. There was a drawback: the source—whom the FBI called "Male-1"—was something of a dimwit.

PODOBNYY: [Male-1] wrote that he is sorry, he went to Moscow and forgot to check his inbox, but he wants to meet when he gets back. I think he is an idiot and forgot who I am. Plus he writes to me in Russian [to] practise the language. He flies to Moscow more often than I do. He got hooked on Gazprom, thinking that if they have a project, he could rise up. Maybe he can. I don't know, but it's obvious he wants to earn loads of money.
SPORYSHEV: Without a doubt.

Podobnyy explained he intended to string Male-1 along. That meant feeding him "empty promises." Podobnyy would play up his connections to Russia's trade delegation, to Sporyshev, and pretend his SVR colleague might "push contracts" the American's way.

PODOBNYY: This is intelligence method to cheat! How else to work with foreigners? You promise a favour for a favour. You get the documents from him and go tell him to fuck himself. But not to upset you I will take you to a restaurant and give you an expensive gift. You just need to sign for it. That is ideal working method.

These tactics may have been crude. In this instance they worked. Podobnyy approached the consultant at an energy symposium in New York. According to FBI court documents, the two swapped contacts. They emailed for several months. Male-1 co-operated, although he says he did not know the Russian was a spy. He even handed him documents about the energy world.

This was a strange business—Kremlin officers careening around Manhattan, spycraft involving fake umbrellas, and an American intelligence source who spent more time in Moscow than his Russian handlers. Plus espionage professionals who turned out to be suffering from ennui.

The American willing to provide information to Putin's foreign intelligence officers rented a working space at 590 Madison Avenue. The building was linked by a glass atrium to a well-known New York landmark, Trump Tower. The atrium had a pleasant courtyard, with bamboo trees, where you could sit and drink coffee. Next door was a franchise of Niketown.

From the atrium you could take the elevator up to the Trump Tower public garden on the fourth floor, with its sparrows and maple trees. The din from West 57th Street meant the garden wasn't exactly tranquil. Or you could queue up with Japanese and German tourists at the Trump Tower basement restaurant and salad bar. Failing that, there was Starbucks on the first floor.

Male-1 had a name. Few had heard of him. He was Carter Page.

Page is a balding figure in his mid-forties, with buzz-cut hair and the super-lean physique of a cyclist or fitness fanatic. When not on his Cannondale mountain bike, he is typically dressed in a suit and tie. When he is nervous, he grins. One person who met him around this period described the encounter as "excruciating." Page was "awkward" and "uncomfortable" and "broke into a sweat."

Page's résumé was curious, too. He spent five years in the navy and served as a Marine intelligence officer in the western Sahara. During his navy days, he spent lavishly and drove a black Mercedes, according to a friend from his academy class, Richard Guerin.

He was smart enough to get academic qualifications: fellow at the Council on Foreign Relations, master's from Georgetown University, a degree from New York University's business school. And a PhD from the School of Oriental and African Studies at the University of London.

His apparent Russian sympathies were evident from the beginning. In 1998 Page spent three months working for the Eurasia Group, a strategy consulting firm. Its founder, Ian Bremmer, later described Page as his "most wackadoodle alumnus." Page's vehemently pro-Kremlin views meant that "he wasn't a good fit," Bremmer said.

In 2004 Page moved to Moscow, where he became an energy consultant with Merrill Lynch. As Page tells it, it was while working as an investment banker that he struck up a relationship with Gazprom. He advised Gazprom on transactions, including a deal to buy a stake in an oil and gas field near Sakhalin, the desolate island on Russia's Pacific coast. He bought Gazprom shares.

According to *Politico*, few people in Moscow's foreign business community knew of him. Those who did were underwhelmed. "He wasn't great and he wasn't terrible," his former boss, Sergei Aleksashenko, told the magazine, adding that Page was "without any special talents or accomplishments," "in no way exceptional," and "a gray spot."

Three years later, Page returned to New York and to his new office next to Trump Tower. From there he set up a private equity business, Global Energy Capital LLC. His partner was Russian—a former Gazprom manager called Sergei Yatsenko. Did Yatsenko know Podobnyy and Sporyshev? Or indeed other members of Russia's underground espionage community?

In the worsening dispute between Putin and the Obama administration, Page sided with Moscow. He was against US sanctions imposed by Obama on Russia in the wake of Crimea. In a blog post for *Global Policy*, an online journal, he wrote that Putin wasn't to blame for the 2014 Ukraine conflict. The White House's superior "smack-down" approach had "started the crisis in the first place," he wrote.

Page's rampant pro-Moscow views were at odds with the US State Department under Clinton and with almost all American scholars of Russia. After all, it was Putin who had smuggled tanks across the border into eastern Ukraine. Not that Page's opinions counted for much. *Global Policy* had a small circulation. It was edited out of Durham University in the north of England.

His relationship with the journal fizzled out when he wrote an opinion piece lavishly praising a pro-Russian candidate ahead of the US presidential election—Trump.

And then something odd happened.

In March 2016 candidate Trump met with the *Washington Post*'s editorial board. At this point it seemed likely that Trump would clinch the Republican nomination. Foreign affairs came up. Who were the candidate's foreign policy advisers? Trump read off five names. The second was "Carter Page, PhD." Given Trump's obvious lack of experience of world affairs, this was a pivotal job.

One former Eurasia Group colleague said he was stunned when he discovered Page had mysteriously become one of Trump's foreign policy advisers. "I nearly dropped my coffee," he told me. The colleague added: "We had wanted people who could engage in critical analysis of what's going on. This is a guy who has no critical insight into the situation. He wasn't a smart person."

Page's real qualification for the role, it appeared, had little to do with his restless CV. What appeared to recommend him to Trump was his boundless enthusiasm for Putin and his corresponding loathing of Obama and Clinton. Page's view of the world was not unlike the Kremlin's. Boiled down: the United States' attempts to spread democracy had brought chaos and disaster.

Podobnyy and Sporyshev approached their duties with a certain cynicism laced with boredom and a shot of homesickness. Page, by contrast, was the rarest of things: an American who apparently believed that Putin was wise and virtuous and kind.

By this point, the Russian spies had been spirited out of the United States. In 2015 their ring was broken up. As accredited diplomats, they were entitled to fly home. Buryakov was less fortunate. At the time that Page joined Trump's campaign, Buryakov pleaded guilty to acting as an unregistered foreign agent. He got two and a half years in a US jail.

In July 2016 Page went back to Russia, in a trip approved by the Trump campaign. There was keen interest. Page was someone who might give sharper definition to the candidate's views on future US–Russian relations. Moscow sources suggest that certain people in the Russian government arranged Page's visit. "We were told: 'Can you bring this guy over?'" one source said, speaking on condition of anonymity.

One of Russia's top private universities, the New Economics School, invited Page to give a public lecture. This was no ordinary event but the prestigious commencement address to its class of graduating students. The venue was Moscow's World Trade Centre.

Seven years earlier, in July 2009, I had watched President Obama give the end-of-year address at the NES. Obama had come to Moscow for talks with Dmitry Medvedev, Russia's president. Obama also breakfasted with Putin, at this point serving a term as prime minister.

The venue for Obama's lecture was Gostiny Dvor, an eighteenth-century trading arcade, now refurbished, not far from St Basil's Cathedral, the Kremlin, and Red Square. I sat at the back. Obama began with a piece of politesse. "Michelle and I are so pleased to be in Moscow. And as somebody who was born in Hawaii, I'm glad to be here in July instead of January."

It was an accomplished speech. Obama began by praising Russia's contribution to civilization—its great writers who had unravelled "eternal truths"; its scientists, painters, and composers. He paid tribute to the Russian immigrants who enriched America. He quoted Pushkin. He reminded his audience of American and Soviet sacrifices in World War II.

Obama then went on to deliver a subtle rebuke. A year earlier, in 2008, Russian military forces had rolled into neighbouring Georgia. Its president, Mikheil Saakashvili—an ally of President George W. Bush—made an unwise attempt to recapture the rebel province of South Ossetia. For Saakashvili, it was a brutal lesson in neighbourhood geopolitics.

"In 2009, a great power does not show strength by dominating or demonizing other countries," Obama said. "The days when empires could treat sovereign states as pieces on a chessboard are over." Obama rejected the doctrine that Russia has "privileged interests" in former Soviet countries, a key Putin idea. That evening I watched Russian state TV report Obama's speech. It fell to the bottom of the schedule.

By contrast Russia's media hailed Page as a "celebrated American economist." This, despite the fact that Page's lecture was distinctly strange—a content-free ramble verging on the bizarre. Page, it seemed, was criticizing US-led attempts at "regime change" in the former Soviet world. Nobody could be sure. His audience included students and local Trump fans, some of whom were visibly nodding off by the end.

Shaun Walker, the *Guardian*'s Russia correspondent, had attended an event given by Page the previous evening. He described Page's PowerPoint presentation as "really weird." "It looked as if it had been done for a Kazakhstan gas conference," Walker said. "He was talking about the United States' attempts to spread democracy, and how disgraceful they were."

Page was Trump's leading Russia expert. And yet in the question-and-answer session it emerged that Page couldn't really understand or speak Russian. Those seeking answers on Trump's view of sanctions were disappointed. "I'm not here at all talking about my work outside of my academic endeavour," Page said. At the end, Walker said, Page was "spirited off."

Clearly, Page was reluctant to give any clues about a Trump administration's Russia policy or how Trump might succeed in strengthening ties where Obama and George W. Bush had both failed.

So what was he doing in Moscow?

According to the Steele dossier—and vehemently disputed by Page—the real purpose of Page's trip was clandestine. He had come to meet with the Kremlin. And in particular with Igor Sechin. Sechin was a former spy and, more importantly, someone who commanded Putin's absolute confidence. He was in effect Russia's second most powerful official, its de facto deputy leader.

By this point Sechin had been at Putin's side for more than three decades. He had begun his career in the KGB and served as a military translator in Mozambique. In the 1990s he worked with Putin in the mayor's office in St Petersburg. Sechin functioned as Putin's scowling gatekeeper. He carried the boss's briefcase and lurked outside Putin's ground-floor office in St Petersburg's city hall.

His appearance was lugubrious. Sechin had a rubbery face, narrow-set eyes, and a boxer's squishy nose. When Putin was elected president, Sechin became his deputy chief of staff and, from 2004, executive chairman of the Russian state oil firm Rosneft, the country's biggest oil producer. A stint as deputy prime minister was not successful. "He's clever, despite looking like a dummy. But he can't speak or do public politics," Sergei Sokolov, deputy editor of the liberal *Novaya Gazeta* newspaper, said of Sechin.

In private Sechin impressed. Chris Barter—the former CEO of Goldman Sachs Moscow—described him as an "extremely charming and smart guy, on top of his numbers operationally. He is someone who can manage both the economic side of the equation and the political agenda at the same time. He has significant power and independence from Putin," Barter said.

It was clear that Sechin had Russia's entire security services at his disposal. He would be willing to personally reward anyone who advanced the objectives of the Russian state, Barter added.

In 2014 Page had written a sycophantic piece that lauded Sechin for his "great accomplishments." In a blog for *Global Policy*, Page wrote that Sechin had done more to advance US–Russian relations than anybody in decades. Sechin was a wronged Russian statesman, in Page's view, unfairly punished and sanctioned by the Obama White House.

This was the backdrop to Page's Moscow trip.

Eleven days after Page flew back from Russia to New York, Chris Steele filed a memo to Fusion in Washington. Dated July 19, 2016, it was titled: "Russia: Secret Kremlin meetings attended by Trump advisor Carter Page in Moscow."

Steele's information came from anonymous sources. In this case that was someone described as "close" to Sechin. Seemingly, there was a mole deep inside Rosneft—a person who discussed sensitive matters with other Russians. The mole may have been unaware its information was being telegraphed to Steele.

In Moscow, Page had held two secret meetings, Steele wrote. The first was with Sechin. It's unclear where this meeting, if it happened, took place. The second was with Igor Diveykin, a senior official from Putin's presidential administration and its internal political department.

Based on his own Moscow experience, Barter said that meetings with Sechin came about at short notice. Typically, Sechin's chief of staff would call up and offer a meeting forty minutes later. "It was always off the cuff, last minute. It was, boom: 'Can you come now?'" Barter said. He personally met with Sechin six times, he added.

Sometimes these meetings took place in the White House, the Russian seat of government. On other occasions they were in Rosneft's tower HQ, overlooking the Moskva River. Of the Steele dossier, Barter told me: "Everything is believable."

According to Steele, Sechin raised with Page the Kremlin's desire for the United States to lift sanctions on Russia. This was Moscow's strategic priority. Sechin offered the outlines of a deal. If a future Trump administration dropped "Ukraine-related sanctions," there could be an "associated move" in the area of "bilateral energy co-operation." In other words, lucrative contracts for US energy firms. Page's reaction to this offer was positive, Steele wrote, adding that Page was "generally non-committal in response."

Sechin's motives for a deal were personal and political. US sanctions had hurt the Russian economy and poleaxed Rosneft. A joint project between Rosneft and Exxon to explore the Russian Arctic had been put on hold. Sechin was banned from the United States. And the EU had sanctioned Rosneft. Sechin no longer joined his second wife, Olga, on their private luxury yacht. When she visited Sardinia and Corsica, her favourite places, she did so without him.

It was rumoured that Sechin had a significant personal stake in Rosneft. If it existed, this, too, had suffered. Some observers said that Sechin had enriched himself relatively late, only once he exited government and devoted himself to Rosneft. As senior journalist Sokolov put it: "Igor is anxious to get rid of sanctions."

Moreover, sanctions made the economy worse at a time when domestic problems already weighed heavily. There wasn't enough money for the state to execute its obligations. These included support for Crimea and rebel parts of Ukraine; new north and south gas pipelines to Europe; and the construction of soccer stadiums ahead of Russia's 2018 World Cup. Plus the bridge being built across the Kerch Strait, linking annexed Crimea to the Russian mainland.

What terrified Russia's leadership was the prospect that a depressed economy could lead to hunger and discontent. This might spread among Putin's conservative base and spark into something bigger and less containable. The spectre was mass revolt.

Steele obtained further information from his high-placed source, which said that the Sechin meeting had taken place on either July 7 or 8—the same day as or the day after Page's graduate lecture.

According to an "associate," Sechin was so keen to lift personal and corporate Western sanctions that he offered Page an unusual bribe. This was "the brokerage of up to a 19 per cent (privatised) stake in Rosneft in return." In other words, a chunk of Rosneft was being sold off.

No sums were mentioned. But a privatization on this scale would be the biggest in Russia for years. Any brokerage fee would be substantial, in the region of tens and possibly hundreds of millions of dollars. At this point nobody outside the top of Rosneft knew the privatization plan existed. Page "expressed interest" and confirmed that were Trump to become US president, "then sanctions on Russia would be lifted," Steele wrote.

Sechin's offer was the carrot.

There was also a stick.

The stick was flourished during Page's alleged second meeting, with Diveykin. The official reportedly told Page that the Kremlin had assembled a dossier of compromising material on Clinton. And might possibly give it to Trump's campaign. However, according to Steele, Diveykin also delivered an ominous warning. He hinted—or even "indicated more strongly"—that the Russian leadership had damaging material on Trump, too. Trump "should bear this in mind" in his dealings with Moscow, Diveykin said.

This was blackmail, clear and simple.

Page was the go-between meant to relay this blunt message to Trump. He was part of a chain of cultivation and conspiracy that stretched from Moscow to Fifth Avenue. Allegedly, that is. Over the coming months, Page would vehemently deny any wrongdoing. Or having taken the meetings. He would assert that he was a victim.

Page's problem was that he had an unfortunate habit of seeking out Russian spies—ones in their twenties like Podobnyy and older ones like Sechin. And Russian ambassadors.

Sergey Kislyak was someone who knew America well. He had lived much of his adult life in the United States. In the 1980s, he spent four years in New York at the Soviet mission to the UN, and this was followed by a similar stint at the Soviet embassy in

Washington. When the USSR broke up, Kislyak continued his career with the Russian Federation. At the Ministry of Foreign Affairs in Moscow he was in charge of science and technology.

Kislyak was a likeable individual. One British diplomat who worked opposite him, Sir Brian Donnelly, described him as "amiable, down-to-earth, matter-of-fact and easy to rub along with." Donnelly knew him in the first half of the 1990s, when the United States, the United Kingdom, and Russia were working on a nuclear non-proliferation treaty. Kislyak was unlike older Soviet envoys, who tended to be brusque, prickly, and opinionated, Donnelly said.

"I always found him constructive, co-operative, and reliable. He was the first Russian diplomat that I came across who seemed comfortable working in the post-Soviet, post-communist world," Donnelly told me. "He was comfortable working in English, which he spoke well with an accent."

Kislyak returned to the United States in 2008, after serving as ambassador to Belgium and NATO, and as a deputy minister of foreign affairs. By this point in late middle age he was a large figure with snow white hair, his frame filling out his jackets.

One senior Obama official who dealt with him "quite a bit" described him to me as a "tough interlocutor" and an unremitting exponent of Kremlin politics. He was "a pain in the arse" but, the former official said, "a professional diplomat" who didn't deserve his later "vilification." He was knowledgeable about US affairs, smart, and demanding of his subordinates. Andrei Kovalev, a former Russian and Soviet diplomat who worked on the same non-proliferation brief and knew Kislyak from Brussels, said he was—by repute— "very creative."

Was he also a spy? The answer was, probably not. At the same time Kislyak would likely have been fully cognizant of the Kremlin's efforts to help Trump in 2016, and he would have been aware of the KGB's activities in the United States in the 1980s, from a generation earlier. As James Clapper put it, Kislyak oversaw "a very aggressive intelligence operation." Moscow had more US-based spies than any other country. "To suggest that he is somehow separate or oblivious to that is a bit much," he added.

Clapper's remarks were prescient: Kislyak came from a celebrated KGB family. His father, Ivan Petrovich Kislyak, was a highly regarded KGB officer who finished his career as a major general.

The Kislyaks were Ukrainian. Ivan Petrovich was born in the village of Terny, in the Poltava region of Soviet central Ukraine. He came from humble origins. Ivan's father worked in the local sugar factory. The family lived in a modest wooden house on *Sovietskaya ulitsa* (Soviet Street).

In the 1940s, Ivan Petrovich took part in operations against Ukrainian nationalists fighting the Red Army. After the war, he joined the MGB, the forerunner to the KGB. In 1949 he was assigned to the personal bodyguard of Lavrenti Beria, Stalin's brutal and depraved security chief. Sergey Kislyak was born in Moscow a year later.

According to ex-KGB sources, Kislyak Senior gained a reputation inside the service for extraordinary good fortune. He was moved to other duties two years before Beria was arrested in the summer of 1953, secretly tried, and shot. The KGB sent Kislyak to western and southern Europe: to Greece, Portugal, France, and Spain. His codename was Maisky. He specialized in secret operations: sniffing out, on Moscow's instructions, a new generation of agents from inside the Greek communist party, for example. (They had to possess "charm" and be "totally reliable ideologically," Kislyak said, according to the KGB's foreign archive.)

Kislyak's career was subterranean. But in many respects it anticipated his son Sergey's later, more public role in influencing and shaping US politics. Between 1972 and 1977, Ivan Petrovich served as the KGB's station chief in Paris. He presided over a large number of secret agents—including a cipher clerk working deep inside the French foreign ministry. He coordinated "active measures" to ramp up US–French tensions. His KGB residency claimed to have directed the editorial pages of *Le Monde*.

Did Kislyak Sr work for the KGB in America? Maybe. In August 1982, Kislyak went back to Terny to attend a school reunion, taking Sergey—his diplomat son—with him. Local historian and resident Anatoly Lesnoy met both Kislyaks there. Ivan refused to take part in the reunion photo—"pictures were forbidden," he said—but a blurry snap of him exists. Lesnoy told me that Ivan spoke perfect English, as well as Ukrainian and Russian. He had flown in together with his son from New York. "He was a very pleasant person. We are proud of him," Lesnoy said of the older Kislyak. The Kislyaks' house was demolished in the early 1990s, he added. A fir tree in the garden is the only thing left.

Ivan Petrovich Kislyak was a loyal servant of Moscow. So, it seemed, was Sergey Kislyak, who in 2016 attended several Republican campaign events. Privately, however, it appeared he had doubts about his government's brazen strategy.

According to the Steele dossier, Kislyak was part of a cautious Kremlin faction that warned of "the potential negative impact on Russia" from the operation to aid Trump. Those of a similar conservative mind included Yuri Ushakov, Kislyak's predecessor in Washington and a presidential adviser, and the Ministry of Foreign Affairs, the dossier said.

Whatever Kislyak's private misgivings, he carried out his duties energetically. When Trump gave a foreign policy speech in April 2016 in Washington, Kislyak sat in the front row. He met the candidate.

The ambassador also attended the Republican Party convention in Cleveland, which happened soon after Page came back from Moscow. Senior Trump aides who talked with Kislyak there instantly forgot the encounter, as if they had stumbled into a magical fog. One of them was Page. Page's account of their meeting was a tortured exercise in denial—first it didn't happen, then the talks were "confidential," then there was little more than a handshake.

Page's multiple interactions with senior Russians were a matter of growing concern to US intelligence. In the coming months, the FBI seemed to grow suspicious that Page might be a Russian agent. That summer the bureau decided it was going to bug Page's phone calls. This was no easy matter. To do this lawfully, federal agents had to obtain a warrant. Any application of this kind was voluminous—as Director Comey put it, these were often thicker than his wrists.

The application included Page's earlier testimony to the FBI. In June 2013 counter-intelligence agent Gregory Monaghan interviewed Page in connection with the Podobnyy–SVR spy ring. Page said he'd done nothing wrong. Since then, Page had held further meetings with Russian operatives that had not been publicly disclosed, the application said.

The FBI presented its evidence before a secret tribunal—the Foreign Intelligence Surveillance, or FISA, court, which handles sensitive national security cases. The bureau argued that there were strong grounds to believe that Page was acting as a Russian agent. The judge agreed. From this point on, the FBI was able to access Page's electronic communications. An initial ninety-day warrant was later renewed.

Meanwhile, Page's career as a Trump adviser was entering its terminal phase. His speech in Moscow had provoked comment, much of it adverse. The campaign's ties with Russia were becoming a source of controversy. According to the *Washington Post*, quoting a campaign manager, Page wrote policy memos and attended three dinners in Washington for Trump's foreign advisory team. He sat in on meetings with Trump. Apparently, his attempts to meet Trump personally failed.

In the classified briefing to congressional leaders in late August Page's name figured prominently. The CIA and FBI were sifting through a mound of intercept material featuring Page, much of it "Russians talking to Russians," according to one former National Security Council member. When Senate minority leader Harry Reid wrote to Comey in early autumn, he cited "disturbing" contacts between a Trump adviser and "high-ranking sanctioned individuals." That was Page. And Sechin.

These embarrassing details surfaced in a report by *Yahoo! News*. Within hours, the Trump campaign had disavowed Page—casting him out as a nobody who had exaggerated his links to Trump. Page exited the campaign in late September. It was an inglorious end, and his troubles were just beginning.

*

Steele's Rosneft source was right. In early December—less than a month after Trump won the White House—Rosneft announced it was selling 19.5 percent of its stock. This was one of the biggest privatizations since the 1990s and, on the face of it, a vote of confidence in the Russian economy.

This, at least, is how Putin presented the sale on December 7, during a televised meeting with Sechin. The president hailed the privatization as a sign of international confidence in Russia, despite US and EU sanctions, and the year's biggest acquisition in the oil and gas sector. Certainly the money raised—€10.2 billion—would help Russia's budget.

There was an enigma, though. It wasn't clear who had actually bought the stake. Rosneft said the buyers were Qatar and the Swiss oil trading firm Glencore. They had purchased 50/50, it said. In fact, Glencore had pumped only €300 million into the deal. The Qataris had put in more—€2.5 billion. An Italian bank, Intesa Sanpaolo, had provided another €5.2 billion. According to Reuters, the source of funding for almost a quarter of the purchase price was unknown.

So who was behind it? The state bank VTB had underwritten the purchase. Shortly before the privatization it had sold bonds to Russia's central bank. It appeared that state money from the Russian budget was driving the deal.

The sale had also been structured in such a way as to make answering the question of ownership tricky. One of the partners in the deal was a firm in the Cayman Islands. The beneficiary wasn't named. Almost certainly, the "owner" wouldn't be an individual. Probably the Cayman firm would lead to another offshore entity, and another, in an infinite chain.

Steele's mole had known about the plan months before Rosneft's management board was informed. The board only discovered the deal on December 7, hours after Sechin had already recorded his TV meeting with Putin revealing it. Even the Russian cabinet had been kept in the dark. "Sechin did it all on his own—the government did not take part in this," one source told Reuters.

In the weeks to come, US and other Western intelligence agencies would examine this deal closely. Where did the money go? Russian journalists were sceptical that it had ended up with Trump; it was more probable, they reasoned, that it would have travelled to Putin and Sechin. There was no proof of this, and neither the Kremlin nor other parties would offer comment.

A day after the Rosneft deal was unveiled, Page flew back to Moscow. During his previous July visit he'd been feted. Since then, however, Page had become a liability to the Trump campaign—and therefore to Russia, too. This time Page was an unperson, a toxic figure, at least officially. Dmitry Peskov, Putin's press spokesman, said government leaders had no plans to meet with him.

Page's own explanation for his visit was vague. He had come to see "business leaders and thought leaders," he told *RIA Novosti*, the Russian state news agency. He would be in Moscow for six days, he said.

In the months to come, Page would vehemently deny the allegations against him. He portrayed himself as a "peace-seeker." He even expressed sympathy for Podobnyy, the spy—whom he described as a "junior Russian diplomat." In an email to the *Guardian*, Page complained that Obama had persecuted Podobnyy, Sporyshev, and him "in accordance with Cold War traditions."

He wrote: "The time has come to break out of this Cold War mentality and start focusing on real threats, rather than obsolete and imagined bogeymen in Russia."

Page's loyalty to the SVR was breathtaking. Podobnyy wasn't an "imagined bogeyman" but a career operative working against the interests of the United States. And, moreover, one who had bad-mouthed Page behind his back.

Whatever Page's motives were for helping Russian intelligence—greed, naivety, stupidity—his woes were about to get worse.

The secret dossier in which he played a starring role was secret no more. Someone was going to publish it.

3

Publish and Be Damned

January 2017
BuzzFeed offices, New York

I know the press only too well. Almost all editors hide
away in spider-dens . . . plotting how they can put over
their lies, and advance their own positions and fill their
greedy pocketbooks by calumniating Statesmen.

—SINCLAIR LEWIS, *It Can't Happen Here*

By early 2017 the allegations concerning Donald Trump and
Russia were the worst-kept secret in politics and the media.
Practically every senior editor and columnist was aware of
the claims, if not the colourful detail. The *Guardian*'s Julian
Borger, the *New York Times*, *Politico*, and others had seen cop-
ies of the dossier. I knew it existed but hadn't yet read it.

The dossier had been passed around in the same manner as samizdat, the Soviet term for works—Pasternak,
Solzhenitsyn—forbidden by the Kremlin authorities and read
at home in the dead of night. Once finished, these typed
manuscripts were passed on in secret.

Steele wasn't leaking his own research. But Glenn

Simpson—convinced of the need to find an audience and mindful that an FBI probe might take years—was behind this campaign of unattributable briefing.

For months, reporters on the national security beat and Moscow correspondents had been working feverishly to substantiate the allegations. There were emails, clandestine editorial meetings, encrypted Signal phone calls, scrambled messages sent using PGP, or pretty good privacy. There were trips to Prague, the alleged possible location, or near-location, of a rendezvous between Trump's lawyer, Michael Cohen, and Russian operatives. And to Moscow.

In October an email written by a person in the Clinton camp reached my inbox. It set out some of the unproven allegations against Trump, including sex with prostitutes in Moscow. The email said the claims came from a source inside the FSB. This was not Steele's work, but some of it echoed the dossier. The email, it struck me, was like an errant copy of a Shakespeare play hastily written down afterwards by an audience member from memory. It was intriguing. But how well would it stand up?

Of this hectic investigative activity, the US public knew little. There was Corn's article in *Mother Jones* and a piece by Franklin Foer in *Slate*. It concerned an email server between the Russian bank Alfa and the Trump team. Allegedly the server was used for secret communications. Fascinating—if true—but what might it mean? Beyond these tantalizing public scraps, not much was published. The media, and intelligence services in the United States and Europe, plus elected representatives, were nursing a gigantic secret.

The dilemma for editors-in-chief here was clear.

The Steele dossier seemed plausible. But unless its key assertions could be verified—that Trump had actively connived with Russians, in particular over the release of stolen emails—it was difficult to see how it might be published. There was no public interest in promulgating wrong information—you ran the risk of looking like an idiot. Plus there was a possibility of legal action. Probably Putin wouldn't sue. The KGB had other methods. The same couldn't be said for Trump, a serial litigant whose default mode was attack in the courts, to wrestle the other guy to the ground, à la WWE.

What changed the editorial dynamics was McCain's fateful intervention. On the brink of Trump assuming the presidency, it tipped the balance towards publication. If US intelligence agencies believed Steele to be credible, and were themselves seeking to verify his claims, then surely this was—*a story?* The fact that the FBI had sought a FISA court warrant to investigate further was certainly reportable.

CNN broke the first news, ten days before Trump's inauguration. It reported that US intelligence agency chiefs had presented classified documents to Obama and to the incoming president. They included allegations "that Russian operatives claim to have compromising personal and financial information about Mr Trump." CNN sourced its information to "multiple US officials with direct knowledge of the briefings."

The pared-down version of the dossier also went to the Gang of Eight—the top four Republican and Democrat party leaders in the House and Senate, plus the chairman and ranking members of the House and Senate intelligence committees—CNN said. The two-page synopsis was highly sensitive and therefore wasn't included with a classified report on Russian hacking shared more widely within government.

CNN said it couldn't prove the dossier's more lurid claims.

Therefore it wouldn't report them. The agency heads had taken "the extraordinary step" of giving the synopsis to Trump because they wanted him to be aware that the allegations about him were now widely disseminated—at least inside the intelligence community and Congress.

CNN's decision to broadcast the story in general terms was bold. And, surely, the right one. For months, insiders had known about this stuff, while the public were kept ignorant.

The decision would earn the channel much grief. One of the contributors who explained the dossier's origins on TV was Carl Bernstein, the original Watergate reporter, now a distinguished-looking white-haired figure of seventy-three. (His erstwhile collaborator, Bob Woodward, still working at the *Washington Post*, was unimpressed with Steele's work. Woodward called it an affront to Trump and a "garbage document.")

Hours later the online media outfit *BuzzFeed* made one of the biggest calls in US editorial publishing history.

The company was based in New York, in offices on East 18th Street in Manhattan. Nearby was Union Square Park, a pleasant green spot with a Barnes & Noble bookshop and artisanal coffee bars. *BuzzFeed*'s staff were young: twenty- and thirty-year-olds, most of whom had never worked on anything as quaint or historical as an inky print newspaper. Founded in 2006, *BuzzFeed* still did listicles—cute lists of anything from cake pictures to cheap hair products. But in 2011 Ben Smith was appointed editor-in-chief, and *BuzzFeed* expanded into serious journalism. It had a network of foreign correspondents. It broke stories. It ran investigations.

In the wake of CNN's reporting, *BuzzFeed* did what no one else was willing to do: it placed the full dossier online. Ironically enough, Simpson had judiciously briefed details around DC but hadn't given it to Smith. *BuzzFeed* obtained a copy from a different source.

Steele's thirty-five-page report was now available for everybody to read—from Phoenix, Arizona to Russia's Kamchatka Peninsula on the remote Pacific. *BuzzFeed* made a few redactions. Some descriptions where it was possible to identify a source from his or her job title were blacked out. One "company comment" was deleted. But the information that practically everybody in the elite already knew was now pumped into the democratic bloodstream.

In an accompanying article *BuzzFeed* said it had published this unverified document "so that Americans can make up their own minds." The allegations, it said, had "circulated at the highest levels of the US government." It noted the report was unverified and had some errors.

The reaction from the president-elect was thunderous. It was delivered via his usual route, above the heads of the detested liberal media, and direct to the fervent millions who had voted for him.

At 1:19 a.m. on January 11 Trump tweeted:

FAKE NEWS—A TOTAL POLITICAL WITCH HUNT!

The fake news claim would swell and be repeated. Trump would go on to dismiss Steele as a peddler of "phony allegations" and a "failed spy afraid of being sued." The people who commissioned him were "sleazebag political operatives, both Democrats and Republicans. FAKE NEWS! Russia says nothing exists."

As for *BuzzFeed* . . . well, it was a "failing pile of garbage" and "a left-wing blog."

This was an angry fugue that would play throughout Trump's presidency as his relations with much of the media descended into open, embittered conflict. In the meantime, Trump's aides repeated their boss's absolutist assertions that there was no substance to any of it.

Cohen, Trump's lawyer, sounded almost sorrowful. This was an ugly and fantastical plot, he told *Mic*. "It's so ridiculous on so many levels," Cohen said. "Clearly, the person who created this did so from their imagination or did so hoping the liberal media would run with this fake story for whatever rationale they might have."

This pushback must have been expected. Team Trump's position was unequivocal: the dossier was fake, a confection, a hit job, baloney, partisan, an ugly liberal smear. Or—to use the slang of Steele's London—complete bollocks.

Smith, *BuzzFeed*'s boss, said he had no regrets. He pointed to the fact that America's own spy chiefs took the material seriously. Otherwise why bother to brief the president? Smith argued that the dossier was already affecting the way elected politicians behaved, prompting Reid and others to raise serious public questions for the FBI. "Sunlight is a disinfectant," he observed.

There was plenty of material to debate here for a newspaper ethics class and for future historians from the late twenty-first century and beyond. No doubt aspiring journalism students will eternally ponder whether *BuzzFeed* was correct in its decision to relay unverified material or had taken reporting to new and shabby lows.

The identity of the dossier's author was, briefly, a mystery. Rumour had it that he was a former British spy. In London, Nick Hopkins and I wondered if that might be Steele. Hopkins sent Steele a text. There was no answer.

On the evening of January 11, I was on a panel on US–Russian relations and cyber espionage. The venue—the Frontline Club— was where Litvinenko had in 2006 denounced Putin after the murder of Anna Politkovskaya, the critical opposition journalist. (Litvinenko was poisoned three weeks later.) Another Frontline panellist was Nigel Inkster, a former deputy director of SIS.

Halfway through our discussion, the *Wall Street Journal* outed Steele as the author.

Among established media organizations there was resentment at *BuzzFeed*'s decision to publish. Rivals said they had the dossier but had chosen not to reveal it. Columnists bashed *BuzzFeed*. Margaret Sullivan, of the *Washington Post*, wrote that there was never a case for spreading rumour and innuendo. Smith had plunged down "a slippery ethical slope from which there is no return." Ditto John Podhoretz, of the *New York Post*. Podhoretz said that journalists should be sceptical of all sources, especially "intelligence" ones.

This theme was shared by critics from the left, including Glenn Greenwald, the former *Guardian* journalist who collaborated with Edward Snowden and published in 2013 Snowden's revelations of NSA mass surveillance. It was, they said, intelligence sources who had confidently asserted ahead of the benighted 2003 Iraq War that Saddam Hussein had weapons of mass destruction. They had lied. Why believe them now? Trump tweeted to the same effect.

Still, there were interesting admissions that the media had failed in its prime duty: to inform the public. Newspapers had run the easy story—the underwhelming scandal of Hillary's emails!—and ducked the hard one—Trump, Russia, sex, and the murky premise that Russia had sought to tip the scale during a presidential election.

The *New York Times*' public editor, Liz Spayd, recounted how the paper's reporters had spent much of early autumn 2016 trying to chase down the Trump rumours. They were aware the FBI was investigating a covert server channel with Moscow. They met with Steele. They even drafted a story. According to Spayd, senior sources inside the FBI persuaded the *Times* not to publish. After heated internal discussion, and a casting intervention by executive editor Dean Baquet, it didn't do so.

Spayd's conclusion: the paper had been too timid. "I don't believe anyone suppressed information for ignoble reasons. . . . But the idea that you only publish once every piece of information is in and fully vetted is a false construct," she wrote.

There was a paradox at work. On the one hand Trump made it clear that he loathed the mainstream media. Not only were they purveyors of fake news; they were also "enemies of the American people," according to another of his tweets. The enemies included the "failing" *New York Times*, NBC News, ABC, and CNN. On the campaign trail Trump called reporters "dishonest," "disgusting," and "the lowest form of humanity." Reporters were, he suggested, amoebas with legs and arms, "human garbage."

Mark Singer, the author of a riotously amusing Trump profile in *The New Yorker*, wrote that the press deserved some of this: "Much of the Fourth Estate, first by not taking Trump seriously and then by *taking* him seriously, assumed roles as his witless enablers. For months, Trump played them like suckers at a sideshow. The more airtime and ink they gave him, the more he vilified them."

No matter how much invective Trump chucked at the media, "the cameras kept running," Singer observed correctly.

He admitted that he, too, was a sucker. "On the distant sideline (specifically my living room sofa), my shaming secret was that I couldn't look away."

Trump's anti-press tone may have been hysterical but his claims post-election were not without a certain logic. The Democratic Party was weak and beaten. Trump's main adversary—if not that of Americans per se—was the liberal media, and in particular the investigative teams now busy pursuing his connections with Russia. The Fourth Estate now occupied an elevated role in the nation's shambling real-life version of the TV drama *House of Cards*. They were not merely observers but protagonists. They were, from Trump's perspective, villains, plotters, enemies, and wreckers.

On the other hand, the forty-fifth president of the United States had a remarkable and beneficent impact on the news media. Previously, morale had been low or, at best, mixed. The advertising model that supported once-great US titles— the *Baltimore Sun*, the *Philadelphia Inquirer*—was bust. The early part of the twenty-first century had been characterized by newsroom layoffs, a diminution in foreign bureaus, and a decline in print sales.

Now new digital subscribers were piling in. Journalists found themselves reinvigorated by what was undoubtedly the biggest story of their professional lives. "It's the most upbeat newsroom I have seen in my entire career," Marty Baron, the executive editor of the *Washington Post*, told me. The insults, the dehumanizing language, and the fact that the *Post*, together with other major titles, was barred from Trump's campaign rallies, well . . . this made his staff work harder, Baron said.

For the first time in a while, the *Washington Post* was in profit. Trump's election had been a boon: the paper that uncovered the

Watergate scandal was now hiring sixty reporters and eight investigative journalists. The president had a healthy impact on fact-checking. Trump told so many lies that the fact-checking desk had doubled in size, from one to two people. The paper even got itself a jaunty new slogan: "Democracy dies in darkness."

As Baron correctly noted, Trump loved the "enemies of the people." Every morning he pored over his press clippings, delivered to him the old-fashioned way: on paper. His preferred interface with reality was TV—in particular Fox News, which presented Trump back to himself in absurdly flattering terms.

At this point he was the most media-accessible president ever. He gave more than twenty hours of interviews to *Post* reporters, who produced an engrossing biography of the candidate, *Trump Revealed*. (Mitt Romney, by contrast, offered forty-five minutes and declined to be interviewed for a similar candidate profile book.)

From the Oval Office, Trump even rang individual reporters on their cell phones. He called the *Post*'s Robert Costa, a long-time confidant. The identity of the number was blocked, so Costa thought the caller was a nutty reader with a complaint. "Hello, Bob," Trump began. You never quite knew when Trump would ring. Reporters would be away from their desks—in Starbucks, in the corridor, at the kitchen table—when the Great Man wanted to speak.

There were other consequences. The Trump–Russia story was so multifarious and so complex that it made sense to co-operate. It was bigger than any individual scoop.

At the *Guardian* we were pursuing leads from both sides of the Atlantic. Among them, how UK spy agencies had first picked up suspicious interactions between the Russians and the Trump campaign and the role played by Deutsche Bank,

Trump's principal lender. We made an investigative pod—Harding, Hopkins, Borger, and Stephanie Kirchgaessner, a talented former Washington correspondent, now based in Rome. We built up a portfolio of sources.

There was healthy competition still, but reporters on different titles began working together on some stories. There were formal press consortiums and ad hoc conversations between one-time rivals. I talked to the *New York Times*, the *Post*, the *Financial Times* in London, Reuters, *Mother Jones*, the *Daily Beast*, CNN, and others. Such conversations took place in New York, Washington, London, Munich, and Sarajevo. Some happened in glossy conference rooms, others in the corners of pubs over warm ale.

Jill Abramson, the former executive editor of the *New York Times*, argued that the "gravity of the matter" called for a change in the press's behaviour. Trump meant a new era. And new post-tribal thinking.

Abramson wrote: "Reputable news organizations that have committed resources to original reporting on the Russia story should not compete with one another, they should co-operate and pool information."

Trump's Republican colleagues showed little interest in investigating whether the dossier's allegations were true. So it was left to the media to carry out this civic function. CNN's Fareed Zakaria noted that in the era of Trump journalism had a renewed elemental purpose. "Our task is simply to keep alive the spirit of US democracy," he said.

Reporters may have fancied themselves as foot soldiers of the Enlightenment, but they had one other important role.

They would become the recipients of leaks from what would turn out to be the leakiest White House since Nixon's second administration. The more Trump decried leakers and leaking, like a petulant child unable to get his own way, the more his enemies leaked against him.

Steele had intended his work to be read by a small, discerning audience of intelligence pros. People like him, in fact, whom he respected. Now everybody had it. For reporters, the dossier was rocket fuel—enough to blast them off on a renewed investigative mission whose final destination (impeachment? or a scandal that fizzled out through lack of evidence?) was unknown. It wasn't clear how long the journey might last. Months certainly, and years possibly. Here there were plenty of leads and not so many hard facts.

Meanwhile, over in Moscow the language used by the Kremlin echoed that of Trump. It was left to Dmitry Peskov, Putin's press spokesman, to denounce the contents of the report. Peskov played a role in the affair himself. According to Steele, he controlled the "dossier of compromising material on Hillary Clinton" collated by Russia's intelligence services over many years. This, Steele wrote, was done "directly on Putin's orders."

First, Peskov denied the Trump allegations. "This information does not correspond to reality and is no more than fiction," he said. Then he insisted that the Kremlin "does not engage in collecting compromising material." Political motives were behind the release—to halt an improvement in the US–Russian relationship, which was currently "degraded," Peskov said. Adopting Trump's own phrase, Peskov called the dossier "a complete fake." It wasn't "worth the paper it was written on."

Anyone familiar with Russian espionage could only crack a wry smile at Peskov's solemn denials. True, nobody outside the FSB could know if the spy agency did indeed have a Trump video. But there was a rich history of the FSB, and its KGB predecessor, collecting compromising material. And on many occasions filming targets when they engaged in sexual activity, even if this was with a wife or husband.

As I myself knew.

During my time in Russia as a correspondent, the FSB broke into our family apartment as part of a low-level campaign of harassment. Typically, as with the KGB in Steele's day, they left demonstrative clues. The British embassy in Moscow gave us advice. It said US and UK diplomats, plus their Russian embassy support staff, suffered from similar "house intrusions." These psychological games dated from KGB times. Probably they featured in Putin's training manual from the 1970s when he went to spy school. Our apartment was now bugged, British diplomats said.

Returning from a holiday in Berlin, I discovered the FSB had visited us again. During this, their latest break-in, they had left a book by the side of the marital bed. It was in Russian. Its title: "Love, freedom, aloneness."

It was a sex and relationships manual.

Putin's guys had helpfully inserted a bookmark on page 110. I turned the pages curiously. The page offered guidance on orgasms. This was a surreal moment: dark, awful, and ridiculous. The FSB's present was—contemplated after a couple of glasses of vodka—almost hilarious. Was there a technical problem? Or a frequency issue with our lovemaking?

Either way, the FSB's message was clear: *We are watching you*.

Putin was well aware of what his spy service did in the bedroom. Especially when it came to filming targets in the company of what the Russian press calls "girls of easy behaviour."

Back in 1999, Russia's prosecutor general, Yuri Skuratov, fell out with Boris Yeltsin. Skuratov's corruption investigations were going down badly with influential people inside the Kremlin, including the oligarch Boris Berezovsky. (At this point Berezovsky was at the zenith of his powers, a fixer and backroom player who was deputy head of Yeltsin's security council.) A government-controlled TV channel released a video of Skuratov in bed with two prostitutes. The video isn't flattering: it shows a flabby, middle-aged man reclining on a sofa with two blondes. The time stamp shows that it's 2:04 a.m.

The episode ended Skuratov's career. He resigned on health grounds soon afterwards. One senior official played a prominent role in the prosecutor's demise and national humiliation. The official—then head of the FSB—testified that he believed the video to be genuine. This was Putin. Putin came up with a memorable quote that stuck with the Russian public.

The figure in the film was "a person similar [in appearance] to the Prosecutor General," Putin said dryly.

Once Putin became president, the FSB continued to film targets in their intimate moments. Covert surveillance was so widespread that UK diplomats arriving to take up a posting in Moscow were briefed about the dangers of honey traps.

In the past even illustrious officials had succumbed to them. In 1968 Britain's ambassador to the Soviet Union, Sir Geoffrey Harrison, had an affair with a maid working at the embassy. The maid, Galya Ivanova, was a KGB employee, as Sir Geoffrey might have known. The KGB sent him the photos; Harrison told London and was immediately recalled. "I let my defences drop," the ambassador admitted.

The attractive young women used to entice Western

diplomats had a name—"swallows." In Soviet times the KGB's second chief directorate sent them.

In 2009 James Hudson—the UK's deputy consul in Yekaterinburg, the principal city in the Urals—was filmed in a local massage parlour. Like Skuratov, Hudson cut a louche figure on the tape and was wearing a dressing gown. There is a kiss, champagne, explicit bedroom moments with two women. The FSB leaked the video to the tabloid newspaper *Komsomolskaya Pravda*, which published it under the playful headline "The Adventures of Mr Hudson in Russia." Hudson quietly quit Russia and the UK foreign office.

A month later the FSB caught another apparent victim, this time an American. The same news outlet released video that it said showed US diplomat Kyle Hatcher dialling up a prostitute. The production values are distinctly amateurish. There is cheesy saxophone music. Hatcher allegedly asks Inna, Sonya, and Veronica in US-accented Russian: "Will you be free in an hour?" Veronica replies: "In an hour and a half."

The Russian paper claimed Hatcher was a CIA officer. His official job was to liaise with Russia's religious communities, including Christians and Muslims, it said, justifying publication on the grounds that Hatcher was something of a hypocrite. The US ambassador John Beyrle said the footage was fake. Beyrle filed a complaint to the Russian foreign ministry.

The FSB's sex stings hadn't changed much since earlier Cold War times. They were carried out for classic secret service reasons: to entrap, recruit, embarrass, and blackmail.

Its operatives were able to carry out such operations with relative ease. Hidden cameras were a lot smaller than in the KGB's heyday. The picture quality was better, too—good enough to broadcast on state TV, if you wanted.

Mostly, the victims of sex stings were Russians. In April 2016 the Russian opposition leader Mikhail Kasyanov was filmed from a concealed camera sitting on a dressing table. Kasyanov had been Putin's prime minister for four years, until he got fired in 2004. He then joined the opposition. Now he was seen stripping off with an aide from his Republican Party of Russia People's Freedom Party, Natalia Pelevine. The NTV channel—used for a series of hit jobs on Putin's critics—screened the footage taken from inside a private Moscow apartment.

It even used the same stiff phrasing that Putin had employed with Skuratov eighteen years earlier. The voiceover intoned: "A person similar in appearance to Mikhail Kasyanov."

From Moscow, Putin's reaction to the Trump dossier was a masterclass in how to send several messages at once. Why, he asked, would Trump arrive in Russia and immediately take up with the city's prostitutes? Trump was a "grown man" and, moreover, one used to spending time with beautiful women at pageants and competitions all over the world. Trump was, Putin implied, proofed against temptation.

Putin continued: "You know it's hard for me to imagine that he went to a hotel to meet with women with a low level of social responsibility, although without a doubt they [Russian prostitutes] are the best in the world, without a doubt. But I doubt that Trump would have got hooked on that."

At face value, this looked like Putin defending Trump, the soon-to-be leader of a mighty superpower. In fact, Putin was signalling that Russian prostitutes were irresistible ("the best in the world"). There was also a note of equivocation: "I doubt that." And an uncomfortable image in which Trump—the fish—was suckered into taking the bait ("hooked," by hookers, in fact).

With his trademark sardonic humour, Putin may have been delivering a second message, darkly visible beneath the choppy, translucent waters of the first. It said: we've got the tape, Donald! If this was Putin's submerged meaning, the president-elect would surely have noticed it.

Moving from light to dark, Russia's president said prostitution wasn't the fault of the young women who engaged in it. They had few options. They were merely trying to earn an income, he said. The real prostitutes were those who had ordered up "hoaxes" against Trump. They were "worse than prostitutes." They had "no moral limitations," Putin added. He meant Steele. And Western spies generally.

It was an effective little speech. One felt sorry for the visiting president of Moldova, Igor Dodon, who had flown in to Moscow for talks with Putin. They had emerged for a joint press conference. Dodon had newly won his country's election on a pro-Russian platform, and here he was, overshadowed by surreal international events. He tapped the side of his lectern nervously. He stared at his microphone. He rearranged his pen.

Putin and Trump were united in their repudiation of Steele's work. They were using the same phrases, the same angry rhetoric, the same *nyet*.

In his tweets the president-elect cited the fact that Russia had dismissed the dossier:

> Russia just said the unverified report paid for by political opponents is A COMPLETE AND TOTAL FABRICATION, UTTER NONSENSE. Very unfair!

And:

> Russia has never tried to use leverage over me. I HAVE NOTHING TO DO WITH RUSSIA—NO DEALS, NO LOANS, NO NOTHING!

And:

> Intelligence agencies should never have allowed this fake news to "leak" into the public. One last shot at me. Are we living in Nazi Germany?

Trump's strategy of flat denial was problematic for two reasons. One, favourably quoting Putin merely reinforced the idea that the two leaders were working in tandem. Two, the Kremlin's track record in telling the truth about anything was extremely poor. Putin lied about big things (undercover Russian troops in Crimea in 2014; the Kremlin plot to murder Litvinenko) and small things. Putin was a "specialist in lying," according to the opposition leader Boris Nemtsov, murdered in Moscow in 2015; his habit of deceit was "pathological."

Western politicians told lies sometimes, too, of course. But deceit and falsification had a long history in Russia, stretching back to tsarist times and the Potemkin villages erected for Catherine the Great. In literature surreal mendacity was rife, notably in Gogol's *The Government Inspector* and *Dead Souls*. And according to Lenin, the truth was subordinate to the class struggle.

For Putin, lying was an operational KGB tactic. Russia's twenty-first-century postmodern media strategy borrowed something from Lenin's relativist ideas. The actual truth was unimportant. What was important was the Kremlin's "sovereign" version of it. This was energetically disseminated inside Russia and increasingly abroad via Russia Today (later, RT) and other state news platforms.

Behind the scenes the FBI was establishing that much of the Steele dossier was true. At several key moments it was uncannily accurate. It laid out a dynamic relationship between the Trump campaign and the Russians—with politically helpful material offered by Moscow, and something given in return. There was, Steele wrote, a "well-developed conspiracy of cooperation."

What exactly might the Americans offer?

One key area of US–Russian tension was Ukraine. According to Steele's sources, the Trump team agreed to sideline Russia's intervention in Ukraine during the campaign. Instead, and in order to "deflect attention," Trump would raise US–NATO defence commitments in the Baltics and Eastern Europe. This would help Putin, "who needed to cauterise the subject."

In return for Kremlin assistance, Trump would soften the GOP's stance on Ukraine and turn his fire on the Baltic states of Latvia, Lithuania, and Estonia. These NATO countries on Russia's doorstep had fraught relations with Moscow. They also had a significant minority ethnic Russian population. These people got much of their information from Russian state TV. The Baltic nations were therefore uniquely vulnerable: to external aggression and to subversion within.

Trump's apparent task was to change the subject—away from Putin's illegal land grabs and military incursions, towards the undeniable fact that few European states were meeting their minimum NATO spending commitments, pegged at 2 percent of GDP. The policy reflected Trump's own isolationist agenda. It also served the Kremlin's interests.

Steele was right. On July 18, Republican Party leaders and delegates arrived in Cleveland, Ohio. Their official task: to nominate Trump as the party's presidential candidate. Those who attended included Mike Pence, the Indiana governor and Trump's new running mate; former senator and presidential candidate Bob Dole; and former New York mayor Rudy Giuliani. Plus campaign chief Paul Manafort, Carter Page, and Corey Lewandowski, Trump's previous campaign manager, now covering the convention as a CNN pundit. And Kislyak.

The week before Trump's coronation, delegates met to agree on a new national security platform. One of the delegates was Diana Denman, a Texan platform committee member who had supported Ted Cruz. Denman was a veteran party stalwart and avid Reaganite. She proposed a platform amendment that previously would have caused little controversy.

It said a future Republican administration should maintain or increase sanctions on Russia, boost aid to Ukraine's pro-Western government, and hand "lethal defensive weapons" to the embattled Ukrainian army. "Today, the post-Cold War ideal of a 'Europe whole and free' is being severely tested by Russia's ongoing military aggression in Ukraine," Denman wrote, adding that Ukrainians were deserving of "our admiration and support."

After this, something peculiar happened.

Members of Trump's team working with Trump-supporting

delegates got the amendment rewritten. A Trump campaign official, J. D. Gordon, told Denman he had to "clear" her language "with New York." According to *USA Today*, Gordon spoke with Kislyak on the margins of the convention. New York made alterations. Out was lethal hardware for Ukraine. In was something vaguer, meaningless even: "appropriate assistance."

Denman told the *Washington Post* she had tried to salvage her original language, telling Trump staffers: "What's your problem with a country that wants to remain free?" Her efforts were in vain. The new watered-down statement was adopted as policy. Denman argued that this meant an abandonment of the Reaganite idea of peace through strength—supporting struggling democracies around the world, especially those facing down Russian or (as Reagan did in the 1980s) Soviet aggression.

It was unclear who was responsible for the alteration. It was one of a few significant changes to the party's platform. Trump later claimed he knew nothing about it. There had been further clues that spoke of collusion. Trump had earlier described NATO as "obsolete" and "disproportionately too expensive (and unfair) for the US." Now Trump—or those around him—was sending encouraging signals to Moscow.

The next week Trump made his notorious appeal to Putin at a press conference in Florida: "Russia, if you're listening, I hope you're able to find the thirty thousand [Clinton] emails that are missing." A day later he returned to the theme of flaky Europeans stiffing the United States. He told a rally in Scranton, Pennsylvania: "I want to keep NATO, but I want them to pay." Trump also floated the possibility that the United States might legally recognize Russia's occupation of Crimea.

This was too much for Carl Bildt, Sweden's former foreign minister. He summed up the mood of Europe's horrified foreign policy establishment. Watching Trump's speech in Scranton, Bildt tweeted: "I never thought a serious candidate for US President could be a serious threat against the security of the West. But that's where we are."

In real time, via speeches and tweets, Trump was refashioning US foreign policy and blatantly undermining NATO, the bedrock of US post-war relations with Europe, and an organization Putin had reviled since his days as a junior KGB spy. In this context, Trump's blatant hacking appeal to Russia made sense.

In the weeks following *BuzzFeed*'s publication, Steele vanished. He no longer visited his office in Victoria. He disappeared from his home in Surrey, where he lived with his second wife, children, and stepchildren, now staked out by the paparazzi. Tabloid newspapers in Britain speculated that he had "fled," fearing for his life. The *Daily Mail* reported that Steele may have gone abroad. Or was holed up in an "MI6 safe-house." They quoted neighbours saying he'd left in a hurry and had asked them to look after his three cats.

In fact, Steele hadn't fled anywhere. "He's fine. He's lying low," one person close to Steele told me that January. He wasn't on the run from a Kremlin hit squad, the friend added, and was merely trying to avoid the press photographers camped out on his drive. With no new images, picture editors improvised. There found a blurry shot of Steele taken from a 2015 Cambridge Union debate event. It was indeed Steele, wearing black tie.

Clearly this public clamour was unwelcome. In the community of spies and former spies people were not supposed to see what you were doing. Becoming the story—the trigger for a global political scandal—was acutely embarrassing. "If there is one professional standard for people from the intelligence world, it's that you shouldn't be seen. Nothing should be visible," the friend said. Steele hadn't wanted his dossier to be published. *BuzzFeed* were "tossers," his friend added.

There was a UK political dimension, too. In the wake of Brexit, some considered it imperative that Prime Minister Theresa May strike up a good relationship with Trump in the hope that this might lead to an early UK–US trade deal. As the Steele dossier went online, Downing Street was seeking to arrange a Trump–May meeting soon after the inauguration. It was even ready to offer Trump a full state visit, complete with red carpet and dinner with the Queen at Buckingham Palace.

It was understandable, then, that May stressed that her government had nothing to do with Steele. "It's absolutely clear that the individual who produced this dossier has not worked for the UK government for years," May said.

Within Steele's old service there was disquiet at May's approach. Some believed that Trump was a temporary aberration. By sucking up to him, the government risked damaging its key intelligence-sharing partnership, they felt. One former officer told me the Trump administration was an "existential threat" to Western intelligence.

Meanwhile, Conservative pro-Brexit newspapers were eager to rubbish Steele and his track record. The former spy was a "confirmed socialist"; his claims were "unsubstantiated" and "far-fetched." London's *Financial Times* offered a more sophisticated view. It said that the Steele affair demonstrated one of the laws of the crepuscular world of private business intelligence. "It might be called the Frankenstein principle: once you dig up information, it can gain a life of its own," the *Financial Times* said.

Whitehall was evidently terrified that the Trump administration would blame it for the dossier—and think British intelligence was behind it, pulling the strings. The Russian embassy in London saw it that way. For the FSB, there was no distinction between the CIA, MI6, and Steele: they were a single hostile entity. The dossier, in the embassy's view, was a useful way of driving a wedge between London and the nascent administration in Washington.

In a tweet adorned with enigmatic black question marks, it said:

Christopher Steele story: MI6 officers are never ex: briefing both ways against Russia and US President.

Steele, meanwhile, believed there was little point in talking to journalists. Inevitably they would want to ask him about three things: his sources, his clients, and his methods. He couldn't discuss any of these. There were also legal worries. Steele wasn't responsible for the dossier's publication—that was *BuzzFeed*—but Orbis might now face litigation from third parties.

Already, a Russian venture capitalist, Aleksej Gubarev, was taking legal action. Gubarev was the owner of a global computer technology company, XBT, and a Dallas-based subsidiary, Webzilla. He vehemently denied any involvement in the hacking operation, as set out in Steele's December memo.

Despite these challenges, Steele was in good spirits, according to friends. He wasn't downcast. The lurid and inaccurate reporting didn't greatly bother him. One said: "He doesn't have to rebuild his credibility. There's plenty of stuff in the public domain which is negative. His relationship with the people he's bothered about is still okay. He cares about a very small number of people. He doesn't care about public opinion."

This group included Steele's clients and his professional peers—intelligence officers on both sides of the Atlantic, including those in the FBI now pursuing Steele's Trump–Russia threads. Orbis's email box filled up with messages. Most were supportive. Well-to-do friends found somewhere for him to live. Steele made only one concession to his fugitive status, as claimed by the tabloids: he grew a beard.

Steele understood perfectly how the FSB operated. He therefore knew that he probably wasn't in any imminent physical danger. Russia's secret services didn't generally kill foreign spies. They might harass, disrupt, and entrap them; bug and surveil them; send "swallows" to seduce them; expel them from the country, as in Cold War times, or humiliate them on state television. But not murder. Murder was reserved for Russians. For those deemed traitors.

The people at risk were Steele's anonymous sources. Whoever they were, they were now in great danger.

4

Hack

2016–2017
FSB headquarters, Lubyanka Square, Moscow

We do not do that at the national level.
Besides, does it really matter who hacked
Mrs Clinton's election campaign team database?
—VLADIMIR PUTIN, September 2016

The conference room had a funereal feel about it. Heavy brown curtains, beige walls, and at the front a sombre stage. There was a podium and a large screen. And an emblem: the two-headed eagle of the Russian Federation, gold against a vivid scarlet background framed by a sword and a shield. Written on the silver shield were three words in Cyrillic: Federalnaya Sluzhba Bezopasnosti. This was the FSB.

The FSB's mission—to protect the state and smite its enemies—hadn't changed much since the days of Lenin and the Bolshevik revolution, nearly a century earlier. Lenin's friend Felix Dzerzhinsky had run the original counter-revolutionary secret police division, the Cheka. When Putin became FSB chief in 1998, he kept a statuette of Dzerzhinsky on his desk. At least this is what the oligarch Berezovsky—once Putin's friend and later his bitter émigré opponent—claimed.

The auditorium was part of the Lubyanka in the centre of Moscow. The neoclassical building had been the home of the KGB, and of Stalin's NKVD before that. Outside was artificial Chekist grandeur; inside it was dismal and boring, one visitor said. During communist times the spy HQ peered over a statue of "Iron Felix" Dzerzhinsky, the secret policeman's secret policeman. The Lubyanka overlooked Dzerzhinsky Square.

Dzerzhinsky had masterminded one of the greatest espionage operations ever. His agents persuaded wealthy white Russians to donate to an anti-Bolshevik "trust," ostensibly set up to resist communism. Its apparent goal: to bring back the monarchy. In fact, the Cheka ran the organization. Dzerzhinsky got exiles to finance their own downfall. "It was an absolutely brilliant operation. A work of complete genius," one admiring person with US intelligence connections told me.

In 1991, Dzerzhinsky's statue was toppled and dragged away from its plinth. Periodically, a debate erupted in newspapers as to whether the statue might be brought back. After all, Chekists—current and former career intelligence officers like Putin—were Russia's undisputed masters. In Soviet times, the KGB was subordinate to the party and the Politburo. Now Russia's secret services were subordinate to nobody. Nikolai Patrushev—who succeeded Putin as FSB chief—summed up this change in a speech to his subordinates. The FSB, Patrushev said, had become "our new nobility."

In December 2016, FSB officers gathered in the Lubyanka's auditorium. They sat in comfortable red chairs. One of them was a figure in his thirties or early forties, still boyish looking and with thinning black hair. His name was Colonel Sergei Mikhailov. Mikhailov was the deputy head of the FSB's Information Security Centre, the main cyber unit of the service, known in Russian by the initials TsIB. A senior spy working on the electronic front line.

What happened next was astonishing. At least according to a version put out by the FSB.

Someone went up to Mikhailov and placed a bag over his head. He was led away, out of the Soviet chamber and through a brown wooden door. He disappeared.

Mikhailov had been arrested. The dramatic manner of Mikhailov's detention before senior colleagues and fellow spies had a chilling meaning. It was evident to all who witnessed it. Namely, that any further traitors might expect the same fate.

There were no cameras to record the event: reporters were rarely allowed inside the Lubyanka. (When they were permitted entry for Putin's annual address to his old service, they had to give up all electronics.) But FSB officers leaked the account to Tsargrad, Moscow's Russian Orthodox television channel, founded by Konstantin Malofeev, a conservative businessman and prominent Putin supporter.

Other FSB sources confirmed the story to *Novaya Gazeta*, the liberal paper read by Moscow's anti-government intelligentsia. The message—this is what befalls traitors—was deliberately spread in all directions.

Mikhailov's arrest, on December 4 or 5, 2016, wasn't a one-off. His deputy, Major Dmitry Dokuchaev—a former criminal hacker hired by the FSB—was reportedly detained at the same time. So was a third suspect, Ruslan Stoyanov. Stoyanov was an executive at Kaspersky Lab, Russia's leading cyber security firm. He had previously worked at Russia's interior ministry, in Department K, its cyber crime unit. Those who knew Stoyanov described him as a patriot, stocky and with a goatee, whose previous company, Indrik, was named after a bull-like beast from Russian folklore. Stoyanov was arrested in the airport on his way to China. An unnamed fourth defendant was also seized.

These arrests of two senior Russian intelligence officers, together with civilians, looked like the Kremlin covering its tracks. They took place after the Obama administration had accused Putin in October 2016 of hacking in the run-up to the US election. Mikhailov was detained days before we met Steele in the pub. By this point Steele's dossier had been widely spread among journalists and in Washington. Almost certainly, the Kremlin had got it, too.

Any foreign government confronted with an assessment like that would try and work out who was behind it. For American agencies, the questions might be: who are the sources, do they have access to this kind of information, and what's their track record? For the FSB, the questions were: who are the traitors and how should we punish them? Its counter-intelligence people would examine the information revealed and try and match it to known officers.

According to Tsargrad, the FSB was already busy. It was carrying out *zachistka*—a military term that denoted cleaning an area of enemy forces. Interfax, the Moscow news agency, gave the charges. It said Mikhailov and Dokuchaev were accused of "betraying their oath and working with the CIA." They had—it was claimed—passed secret information to US intelligence. If convicted, they'd get twenty years in jail. Their trial, everything about it, was a state secret.

It wasn't clear how these arrests related to Russia's intrusion operation and the 2015–2016 hacking of Democratic Party emails. Stoyanov had good contacts with the security services—and the West, including US, German, UK, and Dutch law enforcement. Mikhailov's department specialized in cyber espionage. Did Mikhailov give details of this operation to Washington, either directly or via intermediaries? Was he in touch with Steele? Or, as was most likely, was he merely an accidental victim of a turf war inside Russian intelligence?

There was a further dimension to these apparent purges. It involved Russia's most notorious band of criminal hackers. The group was called Shaltai-Boltai, or Humpty Dumpty. For three years it ran a spectacularly successful guerrilla publishing operation, blending hacking, leaking, and old-fashioned blackmail: pay us or you're screwed! Unlike WikiLeaks—a one-man band run by the high-profile Julian Assange—the Shaltai-Boltai leakers preferred to stay invisible.

To begin with, the group's mission was semi-idealistic. From late 2013 it leaked official correspondence, including emails, that revealed Moscow's role in kick-starting unrest in eastern Ukraine. Its victims included Russia's prime minister, Dmitry Medvedev, whose Twitter feed was hijacked. As one of the hackers, Alexander, told the *Guardian*: "I thought it would be good to troll the Kremlin, and to try to change something in the country."

The group's founder, Vladimir Anikeev, however, had bigger ambitions. Instead of leaking material online for free, why not sell it to anybody who might pay? Anikeev had previously worked for an agency in St Petersburg that specialized in "black PR." Shaltai-Boltai began targeting the personal electronic secrets of influential people—Kremlin insiders, Russian deputies, and rich businessmen. Shaltai-Boltai posted a sample of the hacked material online.

The victim could pay and the compromising material would vanish. If they didn't, everything would come out. Alternatively, someone else could buy the leaked emails. According to Alexander, Anikeev was no master hacker himself. He subcontracted via web forums to other hackers, who obtained passwords to the email accounts of senior Russian officials. This was a lucrative underground enterprise—turning over "$1–2m" in three years. Payment was via bitcoin. No questions asked.

Shaltai-Boltai, then, would offer stuff to the highest bidder. In summer 2014, the *Guardian*'s Shaun Walker met one of its representatives in a European capital. The encounter took place at a little-used boat club on the outskirts of the city. The man—in his forties, floral shirt, tubby—was either cautious or paranoid, depending on one's perspective. He sailed a boat into the middle of the river and spoke only when he had turned on loud music in the cabin to prevent anyone from listening in. He used a burner—a throwaway cell phone.

The representative identified himself as Shaltai. He told Walker Shaltai-Boltai had a stunning archive. It included records of every meal Putin had eaten, as well as thousands of emails sent by the president's inner circle. Reading these internal documents, he said, gave him a rare insight into how Russia was actually run. Putin was a man "without human emotions." And a genuine patriot who believed that his rule was in Russia's best interests, Shaltai said.

"I think he has been in power too long," Shaltai told Walker. "He has grown detached. He really is like a tsar. Below him are people fighting amongst themselves, but they are too scared to disagree with him. He does not have friends in the normal sense. There may be people he likes, but he is extremely paranoid."

Afterwards, Shaltai invited Walker to go drinking with him back on land and to meet some women, an offer the journalist declined. It seemed evident Shaltai-Boltai would sell to anyone. Might that anyone include representatives of British or American intelligence?

According to one version, Mikhailov, the FSB chief, made contact with Shaltai-Boltai in early 2016. He offered the hackers a deal: the group could carry on its activities on the condition the FSB had a right of veto over future publications. And use Shaltai-Boltai as an outlet for FSB leaks. A second version said Mikhailov set up the group. A third that he was its *krysha*, or roof—the patron or protecting power inside Russian state bureaucracy.

Whichever version was correct, it was clear the wall between state assets and criminal hackers was paper-thin. Russia's foreign intelligence agency, the SVR, also used hackers for delicate foreign operations, according to Western cyber experts.

By the second decade of the twenty-first century the cyber world looked like the high seas of long ago. The hackers who sailed on it might be likened to privateers. Sometimes they acted for the "state," sometimes against it.

There were no clear rules or treaties; the Internet was an unregulated pre-sovereign space where it was comparatively easy to carry out raids and then escape afterwards while covering your tracks. Employing outside parties helped with deniability. Modern states have not yet decided what laws should regulate cyberspace, so anything goes. According to Steele, Russian intelligence frequently co-opted hackers. It gave them little choice but to co-operate. The FSB "uses coercion and blackmail to recruit [the] most capable cyber operatives in Russia into its state-sponsored programmes," Steele wrote in his July 2016 memo, his second to Fusion.

Steele's dossier summarized what was known about Russian cyber operations, both official and criminal ones. Moscow had an "extensive" programme of state-sponsored cyber operations, he wrote. The Kremlin had had limited success against major foreign targets: G7 governments, big corporations, banks. It got better results with "second-tier ones." These included private Western banks and smaller states, such as Latvia.

According to Steele, the FSB was the "lead organization within the Russian state apparatus for cyber operations." It had four main targets: Western governments; foreign corporations, especially banks; the domestic elite; and "political opponents both at home and abroad." Its successes typically came through "IT back doors." That meant, for example, exploiting the devices of visiting Americans and Russian émigrés when they went to Moscow.

Steele said his sources were "a number of Russian figures with a detailed knowledge of national cyber crime, both state-sponsored and otherwise." One of them was described as "an FSB cyber operative."

With or without Mikhailov's help, it was clear that by autumn 2016 Shaltai-Boltai had overreached itself. Its newest victim was deputy prime minister Arkady Dvorkovich. Dvorkovich refused to pay. The hackers had been living like outlaws, hanging out in Thailand, and generally operating from outside Russia. In May Anikeev was persuaded to return to Moscow to meet with an FSB official. In November he came back again and was arrested.

The group's Twitter feed—complete with Alice in Wonderland wallpaper and a yellow-and-green-striped Humpty Dumpty—went dark in December. Tsargrad said that the hackers were a front organization for the CIA.

Russia's foremost cyber expert, Andrei Soldatov, disagrees. He believes the leaks about Shaltai-Boltai indicate "a hastily made cover-up" to distract from Russia's role in hacking the US election. Mikhailov and Stoyanov might have known the informal actors who carried out the DNC hack, Soldatov said. If they had passed information to the Americans on this, that would explain the treason charge. Soldatov is sceptical that the FSB dragged Mikhailov off with a bag on his head.

Meanwhile, Mikhailov, Stoyanov, and Dokuchaev were being held at Lefortovo, the FSB's pre-trial detention and interrogation centre. Lefortovo was a place I knew. In 2007 the FSB ordered me there after the *Guardian* published an interview with Berezovsky. The oligarch had claimed from London—without offering evidence—that he was "plotting a revolution against Putin." The story displeased the Kremlin. The FSB investigated. I was summoned as a witness.

Lefortovo was a dispiriting place. I entered via the front door and found myself in a barren reception room, devoid of chairs. The officer on duty could see me through a silvered mirror; I couldn't see him. I handed over my passport and phone. A hairy hand took it. We—my lawyer, Gari Mirzoyan, and I—went down a long corridor and past a cage-like lift that descended to Lefortovo's K-shaped prison below. Litvinenko had once been kept there. On the walls I noticed old-fashioned KGB cameras recording our movements. If anything had changed since Soviet times, I was at a loss to identify it. The corridors were soundless. A worn red-green carpet led to a series of box-like offices.

The interview with Major Andrei Kuzmin—a young, blond-haired FSB officer—was perfunctory. He asked a few questions about the Berezovsky interview, tossing me a colour photo-copy of the *Guardian* front page.

On the table in front of me was a bottle of fizzy water and glasses. The glasses were engraved with four sets of initials: Cheka, OGPU, KGB, FSB. These were the various incarnations of the Kremlin's secret police. After fifty-five minutes Kuzmin announced that our interview was over. I signed a witness statement. I was happy to leave.

Mikhailov, Stoyanov, and Dokuchaev were in a gloomy place indeed. They were fortunate in one respect.

They were alive.

The car parked near Kitai-Gorod was a company vehicle, a Lexus 460—a sleek, black, official-looking saloon. It was 11:50 a.m. The area was in Moscow's historic centre. The Kremlin and its cathedral square were nearby; head south and you reached the embankment and the Moskva River, grey at this late time of year and encrusted with thick plates of ice.

Round the corner was the old palace where Nikita Romanovich, a nobleman, had lived in the sixteenth century. In 1547 Romanov's sister, Anastasia, married Ivan the Terrible. After her death in 1560, Ivan began his reign of terror. He suspected Nikita and other aristocrats may have poisoned her and were forming a parallel and subversive group. His answer was a new secret police force—the *oprichniki*. Its mission was to terrorize the tsar's enemies.

The vehicle had halted in Kitaigorodsky Proyezd—a street devoid of pedestrians and home to government buildings and an unfinished office block. It was three weeks after Mikhailov's arrest, Monday, December 26. At number 9 there is a military academy named after Peter the Great. Guards turn back any errant drivers who try to enter the courtyard.

Sitting in the back seat of the Lexus was a man. He wasn't moving; in fact, he was dead. The man's name was Oleg Erovinkin. He was sixty-one years old. According to Russian press reports, Erovinkin's driver rang the emergency services. When the doctors arrived, they established there was nothing they could do. Soon after, unidentified officers turned up and removed Erovinkin's body to the FSB's morgue.

Erovinkin was someone who understood the state's private affairs. In the late Soviet Union he attended the KGB's Higher School, named after Dzerzhinsky. He graduated in 1980 and spent well over a decade working in intelligence. Then under Yeltsin he got a new and sensitive post with the presidential administration. He became the man in charge of official secrets. His job was to keep them safe.

Erovinkin was close to Sechin. When Sechin became deputy prime minister in May 2008, Erovinkin joined him in the government as chief of staff. And when Sechin left government in 2012 to head Rosneft, Erovinkin went with him. He ran Sechin's secretariat, later moving to other duties. According to the Russian news channel RBK, Erovinkin was responsible for secret documents, their transmission and reception. He was the link man between Rosneft and the Kremlin. It was a trusted position. He prepared the boss's annual declarations about income and property, sending them to the government via secret post.

Rosneft was keen to stress that there was nothing suspicious about Erovinkin's sudden death. "According to provisional information, he died of a heart attack," a company spokesman said. The FSB was carrying out tests. After all, Erovinkin was an FSB general, so this was standard practice. The street where he was found has no shops and cafés; my attempts to make inquiries there got nowhere.

None of this damped down the obvious speculation: that Erovinkin had been murdered. There were two apparent scenarios. One, that Erovinkin was Steele's source deep inside Rosneft—someone sufficiently trusted and senior to have known of the alleged brokerage offer to Carter Page. Two, that he wasn't Steele's mystery insider but had nonetheless been deemed culpable for the embarrassing loss of secret information. Someone had blabbed. British spies had been able to penetrate the company. Erovinkin had paid the price.

Steele was adamant that Erovinkin wasn't his source and "not one of ours."

As a person close to Steele put it to me: "Sometimes people just die."

The person admitted, however, that in the wake of the dossier the Kremlin did appear to be wiping out some kind of American or Western espionage network.

"If there are operations being rolled up, they are CIA operations, not his [Steele's]," the person said. "For the Russians there is no separation between Chris, CIA, and SIS."

It certainly looked that way. In the period before Steele's report was published, and in the weeks afterwards, other Russian government insiders dropped dead. There was no obvious pattern: the deaths took place in Europe, Moscow, the United States, South Asia. On the day of the US election, November 8, a Russian national called Sergei Krivov was found dead in the Russian consulate in New York. Initial reports said he fell from the roof. Consular officials later claimed a heart attack.

According to *BuzzFeed*, Krivov was a consular duty commander. That meant it was his job to stop US intelligence from penetrating the building. He would have had access to the consulate's crypto card—the secret code-breaker used to encrypt and decrypt messages to and from Moscow Centre. It was his job to handle secret cables. Like Erovinkin, might he have failed, and could this channel have been compromised?

Other Russian diplomats met mysterious ends. They included Petr Polshikov, chief adviser to the Russian foreign ministry's Latin American section (shot dead in December in his Moscow apartment), and Andrey Malanin, the Russian consul in Athens, Greece (found dead in January at home). Also, Alexander Kadakin, Russia's ambassador to India (heart attack in Delhi; Kadakin, at least, was ill).

The most high-profile sudden death was that of Vitaly Churkin, Russia's long-time representative to the UN. Churkin's death at the relatively young age of sixty-four was ascribed to a heart attack. The New York City police said there had been no foul play. Whatever Churkin knew about Trump—they had first met in 1986—was no more.

Three days after Erovinkin's death, at a country mansion a ninety-minute drive from Washington, there were signs of frantic activity. Russian operatives were packing up boxes, ripping out communications networks, driving at speed past TV crews waiting at the boundary of the property. They looked like people who were not coming back.

Pioneer Point in Maryland was a pleasant waterfront estate.

Bought by Moscow in the 1970s, it belonged to the Russian government. At weekends Russian diplomats would drop by. There are tennis courts, a swimming pool, and a garden. Close your eyes and you might just imagine you were back in greater Moscow, with its summer dachas, resin-scented pine forests, and cool swimming lakes.

The idyll had ended. The Obama administration announced it was shutting the property, together with another Russian-owned compound, Norwich House, on Long Island in New York. The Georgian-style Maryland mansion wasn't only a diplomatic retreat, US officials said. It was used for spying.

Three weeks previously Obama had directed the intelligence community to conduct a thorough review of what had happened during the election. That morning the White House had published some conclusions. They came in the form of a thirteen-page document written largely for information technology professionals and entitled "GRIZZLY STEPPE— Russian Malicious Cyber Activity."

Hostile Russian cyber espionage groups were given "bear" cover terms. The ones in this case were nicknamed Fancy Bear and Cozy Bear. Fancy Bear was GRU; Cozy Bear FSB. There were plenty of others, from previous attacks. They included Venomous Bear, Voodoo Bear, Energetic Bear, Berserk Bear, and Team Bear. Hence Grizzly Steppe, a continuation of this ursine theme.

The report by the Department for Homeland Security and FBI was damning. Citing "technical indicators," it said that two separate Russian espionage groups had successfully hacked into a US political party. It wasn't named but was understood to be the Democrats. The first group, Cozy Bear, known as Advanced Persistent Threat or APT29, broke into the party's systems in December 2015. The other, Fancy Bear, or APT28, entered the same systems in spring 2016.

According to the report, the groups were made up of seasoned operatives. They had previously targeted government organizations, think-tanks, universities, and corporations around the world. Their operation to hack the Democratic Party involved "targeted spear-phishing campaigns." These included web links to a "malicious dropper" and "shortened URLs." The Russian cyber attackers hid their tracks. Or, as the report put it, "obfuscated their source infrastructure and host domains."

For those who struggled with the technical detail there was a helpful graphic. It showed a faceless hacker in a hoodie against a red background. The hoodie-hackers used tunnels and implants—shown by skull-and-crossbones icons—to break into computers or "targeted systems." They were then able to "silently exfiltrate data."

The report may have been dry reading, but it left no doubt as to the operation's remarkable success. Cozy Bear sent emails containing a malicious link to over a thousand recipients. There were "multiple US government victims." The group "successfully compromised a political party." In spring 2016 Fancy Bear compromised the Democrats again, this time persuading victims to change their passwords. The hackers were able to steal information from "multiple senior party members."

"The US government assesses that information was leaked to the press and publicly disclosed," the report said.

It was this leaking that made Russia's DNC hack different. As General Mike Hayden, the former NSA and CIA director said, stealing your opponent's emails was simply "honourable international espionage." Everybody did that, including the

United States, the United Kingdom, France, Germany, and other Western nations. "It's accepted international practice. If I could have broken into Russian servers, I would have done it," he said.

What made the hack different was what happened afterwards, Hayden suggested—the fact that Russia "weaponized this data" and "shoved it into US space." An army of Russian trolls tweeted the information and made it trend. The result was a covert influence campaign designed to sow confusion and mess with the heads of US voters, he said, many of them already sceptical about Clinton.

Hayden believed that Trump was still the legitimate US president since it was impossible to know if the Russian meddling set out in the report—"putting their finger on the scale"—had influenced the result. Nonetheless, he evaluated it as "the most successful covert influence campaign in history. It took a mature Western democracy. It turned it on its head," the general said.

Obama's response to all this was sweeping. In a statement issued from Hawaii, where he was on vacation with his family, the president said he was unveiling tough new sanctions on Moscow. They included the expulsion of thirty-five Russian diplomats. Those expelled, US officials indicated, were spies. The Kremlin's official espionage network was being summarily rolled up. It was unclear to what extent these individual diplomats had plotted the hacking.

Additionally, Obama retaliated against the two agencies allegedly behind Fancy Bear and Cozy Bear: the GRU and FSB, respectively. In an executive order the president sanctioned nine entities and individuals from the two Russian spy agencies. They included the GRU's top generals: its chief, Igor

Korobov, and deputies Sergey Gizunov, Igor Kostyukov, and Vladimir Alexseyev.

Obama further sanctioned three companies said to have given "material support" to the GRU's offensive cyber operations. They were the St Petersburg-based Special Technology Center; an outfit called Zorsecurity; and the blandly titled Autonomous Noncommercial Organization "Professional Association of Designers of Data Processing Systems." Allegedly it provided the hackers with special training.

The measures reflected Obama's profound exasperation with Putin, at the end of eight tough years. During his first term—and with Hillary Clinton as his secretary of state—the president had tried to "reset" ties with Moscow. The policy had failed. It was predicated on the idea that Dmitry Medvedev— at the time Russia's stand-in president—was a more liberal and malleable figure than the hawkish Putin. In fact, Putin continued to dominate Russian politics from Moscow's own White House and from his temporary post as prime minister.

Viewed in the light of 2016, Obama's well-meaning approach looked like folly. The president said all Americans should be "alarmed by Russia's actions," which had been conducted to damage Clinton and help Trump.

But if this were the case, why had the Obama administration not gone public with the evidence earlier? Before the election, in fact? There had been a report in October, but it had not revealed the full extent of the problem, and by December it was too late.

According to former Obama officials, the administration had a vigorous internal debate about Russia's cyber attack. Some officials subsequently expressed deep regret that more had not been revealed. The administration had chosen not to publicize previously unsuccessful hacks, attributed to Russia, against the White House, the NSA, and the Joint Chiefs of Staff. If they had publicized more earlier, the argument went, this might have deterred Russia's all-out attack on the DNC.

The US intelligence community did raise the alarm. On August 4, John Brennan, the CIA chief, rang the head of the FSB, Alexander Bortnikov, in Moscow. Brennan warned Bortnikov that Russia's meddling in the US election had to stop. Bortnikov conceded nothing but said he would pass the message to Putin.

A special report by the *Washington Post* gave further fascinating detail: later that month a courier from the CIA delivered an envelope with severe "eyes-only" restrictions to the White House. Inside was a report. It was to be shown to just a few people: the president and three senior aides.

Intelligence from deep inside the Kremlin said that Putin had personally directed the cyber operation against the United States. The objective was to defeat—or at least damage—Clinton and to help elect Trump. The material was so sensitive it was kept out of the president's Daily Brief. Brennan set up a secret team of Russia analysts and officers, some from the NSA and the FBI, based at CIA headquarters.

Obama confronted Putin a month later at a meeting of world leaders in Hangzhou, China. According to the *Post*, he told the Russian leader that "we knew what he was doing and [he] better stop or else." Putin demanded proof. And accused the United States of interfering in Russia's internal affairs.

Obama's decision to say little publicly could be explained. First, he—together with the rest of his party, as well as pundits and almost all senior Republicans—had assumed that Clinton would win.

Second, unmasking the scale of Russia's hacking operation to aid Trump would have prompted outraged claims of bias and electoral meddling from the Republican candidate, who was busy embracing the hacked material.

One former senior Obama administration official told me that the intelligence indicating Russian interference got bigger. In the beginning it didn't amount to much, but by the time Trump won the election it was overwhelming. The official said that the GRU hacking team was much less polished than the FSB team and left "lots of clues." The evidence included "Russians talking to Russians" about hacking the election and other measures. The official saw the Steele dossier in November. And alerted people across government.

The Obama administration published a further report on January 6. It sought to answer a fundamental question.

Formulated by Soldatov it went like this: the Kremlin had previously been fearful of the power of the Internet and understood little about the nature of the global network. Putin didn't even use email. So how had Russia found a way to deploy the web against the United States, the country that invented the web and was still its innovative powerhouse?

The three leading intelligence agencies, the CIA, the FBI, and the NSA, co-authored this report. It came in several versions. One was highly classified. The intelligence agency chiefs, plus the Office of the Director of National Intelligence, briefed Trump on its contents during a two-hour session at Trump Tower. A second version—unclassified and with the same conclusions—was made public shortly afterwards.

The report was a detailed assessment of what had happened in 2015–2016. It said:

We assess Russian President Vladimir Putin ordered an influence campaign in 2016 aimed at the US presidential election. Russia's goals were to undermine public faith in the US democratic process, denigrate Secretary Clinton, and harm her electability and potential presidency. We further assess Putin and the Russian Government developed a clear preference for President-elect Trump. All three agencies agree with this judgment. CIA and FBI have high confidence in this judgment; NSA has moderate confidence.

The report said the operation represented the "most recent expression of Moscow's longstanding desire to undermine the US-led liberal democratic order." Putin's influence effort was "unprecedented," "the boldest yet" in the United States. There was a "significant escalation in directness, level of activity, and scope of effort."

At the same time the operation to hack the United States flowed directly from tactics employed during the Cold War. Back then the Soviet Union used agents, intelligence officers, forgeries, and "press placements" to disparage candidates who opposed the Kremlin. After communism's collapse, Russian spies didn't try to alter events. Instead, they concentrated on collecting the inside line to help Russian leaders make sense of administration plans.

According to the agencies, Moscow's approach evolved over the course of the election. As with its operation to win the 2018 World Cup, the Kremlin needed plausible deniability. So it made extensive use of cut-outs. They included a hacker called Guccifer 2.0—who was in contact with Trump's long-time associate Roger Stone—plus the platform DCleaks.com, registered in April.

Then there was WikiLeaks, a platform that Trump openly praised in the months before the election. "We assess with high confidence that the GRU relayed material it acquired from the DNC and senior Democratic officials to WikiLeaks," the report said, adding: "Moscow most likely chose WikiLeaks because of its self-proclaimed reputation for authenticity."

Julian Assange, WikiLeaks' editor in chief, disputes this and says the leaks didn't come from a "state party." The agencies don't believe him. The report suggests that WikiLeaks had become, in effect, a sub-branch of Russian intelligence and its in-house publishing wing. In September WikiLeaks moved its hosting to Moscow.

There were further intriguing details. Russian hackers penetrated local and state US electoral boards, the report said, but made no effort to alter voting tallies. According to the Department of Homeland Security, they targeted twenty-one states. The hackers scanned systems. Their efforts were compared to burglars who shook and rattled doors, trying to break in. (Later the story partly unravelled when the department admitted voting systems hadn't always been targeted. In Wisconsin and California, the hackers hit a network belonging to other state agencies, it said.)

The hackers also collected material on some "Republican-affiliated targets." None of the Republican stuff was ever leaked.

The report speculated as to why Putin had ordered the operation. Russia's president, it said, had a long list of grudges. They included anti-Kremlin protests in 2011–2012, which Putin blamed on Clinton; the exposure of Russia's state-sponsored sports doping programme; and the Panama Papers. I had been involved in the last project and was one of a consortium of journalists who had discovered the offshore fortune of Sergei Roldugin, one of Putin's oldest friends.

The January 6 document argued that Putin had a clear preference for international partners in the mould of Italy's Silvio Berlusconi or Germany's Gerhard Schröder. Both were "Western political leaders whose business interests made them more disposed to deal with Russia."

Trump was definitely in that category.

Overall the CIA–FBI–NSA report was persuasive: Moscow had indeed sought to tilt the election in Trump's favour, even if the result—a Trump victory—had caught the Kremlin by surprise. It omitted one big truth. Namely, that the operation was so successful because it exploited pre-existing fault lines in American society.

From June 2015, Russian operatives purchased a series of advertisements on Facebook. The Russians were sitting in St Petersburg, but they pretended to be American activists. Their fake Facebook accounts promoted anti-immigrant views. One slogan pasted over a US flag said: "We're full, go home." Another depicted a cartoon of Trump holding a mini-Mexican, with the headline: "You have to go back, pal!" There were "divisive social and political messages," as Facebook put it, on race, guns, and LGBT rights.

Facebook would eventually admit that Russia had employed 470 "inauthentic accounts and pages" as part of its influence campaign. It worked. One page, Secure Borders, got 133,000 followers before it was closed down. The page dubbed immigrants "freeloaders" and "scum." Moscow spent $100,000 on more than three thousand ads, Facebook said. The numbers could be higher, Mark Zuckerberg, its CEO, acknowledged later.

According to the *New York Times*, Russian intelligence also made extensive use of bots. These spread anti-Hillary messages on Twitter.

The bots in conjunction with the leaked emails and the Facebook ads fuelled an anger that Trump voters already felt towards Clinton. As General Hayden, the former NSA director, put it, the divisions in US society ran deep. Trump modelled himself on Andrew Jackson, the United States' seventh president, whose portrait he hung in the Oval Office. Jackson was an outsider and a white nationalist who viewed the United States as a nation, a *Volk*, a *narod*, Hayden said, citing the German and Russian equivalents.

Those who supported Clinton took another view. For them, the United States was an Enlightenment idea, rather than a chunk of land that belonged exclusively to one ethnic group. It was best expressed by Alexander Hamilton, President Woodrow Wilson, and the dictum "We, the People." The Hamiltonian approach was fact-based, humble in the face of complexity, and respectful of evidence, Hayden said. None of which applied to Trump's incoming administration.

Meanwhile, the US State Department said the expulsion of Russians wasn't only because of hacking. This was also retaliation for the "pattern of harassment" meted out to American diplomats in Moscow over the previous four years. There had been, it said, a "significant increase" in aggressive activity in 2015–2016.

This harassment carried out by the FSB was pervasive and unpleasant. It included the home intrusions my family had experienced in Moscow from 2007 to 2011 and that Steele and his wife got earlier. US diplomats found themselves routinely followed and hounded by police. In June 2016 a policeman wrestled a US diplomat to the ground as he tried to get inside the US embassy. Moscow said the diplomat was a CIA spy; state TV channels broadcast personal details of diplomats that, Washington said, put them at risk.

The expelled Russian diplomats had seventy-two hours to pack their bags. Moscow sent a plane to collect them. The reaction from the Kremlin was predictably scathing, with Sergei Lavrov, the foreign minister, indicating that Russia would respond in kind. Writing on Facebook, ministry spokeswoman Maria Zakharova described Obama and his team as a "group of foreign policy losers, angry and ignorant." The Russian embassy in London tweeted a picture. It was a duck with the word "lame" on it. The row was "Cold War déjà vu," it said.

The Russian government was equally dismissive of the hacking report—a baseless, unsubstantiated, rather amateurish, and emotional document, according to Peskov. President-elect Trump agreed. Earlier he had dismissed claims of Russian meddling as overblown, absurd, and a ridiculous ploy by "Dems" to distract from their humiliating election failure.

Who the hell knew who was responsible? It could have been Russia or China, he had said in a debate, or even an overweight four-hundred-pound guy sitting on a bed in New Jersey. Trump now modulated his position. He said that he would meet with the intelligence community to be briefed on the "facts of the situation" but suggested "it's time for our country to move onto bigger and better things."

It seemed inevitable that Putin would kick out thirty-five American diplomats from Moscow and the US consulate in

St Petersburg. In earlier crises the Kremlin had delivered a symmetric response. In 2007 the UK's then Labour government expelled four Russian diplomats in protest at Putin's refusal to extradite Andrei Lugovoi, one of Litvinenko's two polonium killers. Russia expelled four British envoys. This, by Kremlin standards, counted as restraint.

Lavrov announced that Russia was shuttering the US embassy's dacha in Serebryany Bor, Moscow's Silver Forest. The island was a bucolic territory of pines and sandy beaches protruding into the Moskva River. It was one of our favourite spots during our time in Moscow, reached by taxi, tram, or clanking trolley-bus, and home to many expatriates and their families. There were log cabin cafés selling ice tea and kebabs. In summer you swam or sunbathed; in winter you could skate on the river, take your kids on ice slides, and—on Orthodox Epiphany—plunge beneath the freezing water with the Russian faithful.

Across from the island is Troitse-Lykovo. The village with its twinkling silver-domed baroque church was the home of Alexander Solzhenitsyn, who revealed the Soviet gulag system and in later life gave Putin broad approval.

The US embassy dacha wasn't much. It had a pool table, a dartboard, and a picnic area. One visitor likened it to a scout hut. Still, it offered a weekend refuge for Americans keen to escape from Moscow's remorseless urban grind.

The Kremlin's answer, when it came, was a surprise. After sixteen years in power Putin had mastered the art of wrong-footing his enemies and keeping everyone guessing. This was one such moment. In a statement Moscow said that it wouldn't expel any US diplomats: "We will not drop to this level of irresponsible diplomacy." Instead, Putin's administration would "take further steps to help resurrect Russian–American relations."

The president-elect was enthralled. His reaction was obsequious. He tweeted:

Great move on delay (by V. Putin)—I always knew he was very smart!

Clearly, Putin had calculated that a Trump White House would be more sympathetic to Moscow than a Clinton one. But was that it? The Obama White House was taken aback by Putin's uncharacteristic restraint. And suspicious that there may have been some kind of backroom accord with the incoming Trump team. According to the *New York Times*, US intelligence agencies began looking for information, clues.

In the period between Obama's announcement on sanctions and Putin's clement response, General Michael Flynn spoke to Kislyak, Moscow's Washington ambassador. Flynn was about to become Trump's national security adviser. There were five phone calls. The conversations, Flynn initially insisted, didn't touch on US sanctions against Russia or the possibility that the new administration might lift them.

Flynn said he had merely wished the ambassador a Happy New Year.

5

General Misha

2013–2017
Moscow–Cambridge–London

Suvorov: "What sort of fish are swimming there?"
Boss: "There's only one kind there—piranhas."
—VIKTOR SUVOROV, *Aquarium:*
The Career and Defection of a Soviet Military Spy

The Aquarium was a nickname given to a Moscow building. It belonged to the most secretive organization in Russia— the GRU. Or, to give it its full title, the Main Intelligence Directorate of the General Staff of the Armed Forces of the Russian Federation. Of the three Russian spy agencies involved in espionage, the GRU was the biggest and the most powerful.

Its job was to collect military intelligence. This was done through various methods—eavesdropping, military satellites, and traditional spycraft. The GRU is believed to have a larger network of agents abroad than the SVR, its foreign intelligence counterpart. Very little is known about its organizational structure. Since there's no press office, there isn't anybody to ask. Its activities are a state secret.

Inside the Aquarium's cavernous entrance is a large yellow and blue map of the world, with Russia at its centre. A symbol of a winged bat is engraved on the granite and marble floor. This represents the Spetsnaz, the troops of "special purpose." These are the GRU's own brigade of elite special forces, deployed in Afghanistan and Chechnya and in Russia's recent military actions, such as in Syria.

Senior generals have offices looking on to a cosy inner courtyard. There is a fountain; in winter and summer you can sit, drink coffee, and chat. Other officers live with their families in a surrounding colony of grey tower blocks that screen the building from outside. Retired officers are housed there also. There is a basement pool, a gym, and a helicopter pad on the roof. Putin landed there in 2006, when he opened the new Aquarium complex.

In 2013 the Aquarium got an unusual visitor. The visitor who arrived at the GRU's HQ was a career soldier. He had spent thirty-three years working in military intelligence. He had served in Afghanistan, Iraq, and Central America. Now he was the director of a mighty spy agency. Nothing odd about that, apart from the fact that the visitor was from the United States and had grown up in Middletown, Rhode Island, one of nine children from a poor Irish Catholic family.

His name was Michael T. Flynn. Flynn claimed to be the first American to be allowed inside the Kremlin's most secret espionage facility. It was a rare honour. At this point he was the head of the Defense Intelligence Agency (DIA) and the Senior Military Intelligence Officer in the Department of Defense.

He was also a self-styled maverick, "an atypical square peg in a round hole," as he put it.

Obama had appointed Flynn in April 2012. By the time of his Moscow visit Flynn was disillusioned with the Obama administration. It had, he felt, succumbed to enfeebling political correctness. It failed to appreciate that the United States was losing in a world war, a war being waged by radical Islamists and "evil people." The White House didn't even recognize its principal enemy—the Islamic Republic of Iran.

The GRU staff officers who witnessed Flynn's arrival must have experienced a moment of cognitive wonder. For decades, they had worked to undermine what the KGB referred to as the *glavny protivnik*—the main adversary, the chief enemy—the United States. The pause in the Cold War hadn't changed this. Most of them had never seen an American spy. Now here was one made flesh, an object of intense professional interest.

Flynn had come to Moscow to deliver a lecture on leadership. "I was able to brief their entire staff. I talked a lot about the way the world's unfolding," he told the *Washington Post*. The GRU talk was "fully approved," he said, adding: "It was a great trip." As Flynn saw it, Moscow and Washington had a mutual interest in defeating ISIS and terrorism across the Middle East. They could work together.

What was less clear is why the GRU invited Flynn. Viktor Suvorov—a former GRU major who defected to the West—described Flynn's visit to me as "very strange." Suvorov was a friend of Litvinenko's. I got to know him after Litvinenko's death. Suvorov had lived in the United Kingdom since 1978, after defecting from the Soviet mission in Geneva, where he was a "third secretary" under diplomatic cover.

His real name was Vladimir Rezun. As Suvorov, a pseudonym,

Rezun had written a thrilling novel, *Aquarium*, closely based on his GRU career, and books on the Soviet army and Soviet military espionage. The novel opens with a chilling scene: of a man, still alive and bound to a stretcher with metal wire, being fed into the Aquarium's crematorium. The man had betrayed the motherland. When the GRU recruited Rezun–Suvorov, they showed him a black-and-white film of the man's final moments.

The GRU was different from the KGB, Suvorov said, adding that the two organizations were often at each other's throats. The GRU was lower profile, "always in the shadows," burning its own secret papers, a thin transparent smoke rising from its chimney. Suvorov said that when he heard news of Flynn's Aquarium drop-in, he was stunned. "Oh my God, I had to eat my tie," he said.

Suvorov added: "There's something fishy going on. Can you imagine a top Russian adviser being invited inside MI6 or to lecture at the CIA: 'We don't know about leadership. Please tell us'?" The GRU was checking Flynn out, Suvorov said. "Maybe the Russians have some kind of material on him, or have him under control," he speculated.

Flynn's host was GRU's director, Igor Sergun. More than two years later Sergun was to die in mysterious circumstances in Lebanon, apparently while on a secret mission. While in Moscow Flynn met with Ambassador Kislyak, the first of many encounters. It was Kislyak who had invited him to Russia in the first place and co-ordinated his trip, Flynn said.

Was this merely a friendly overture to a senior US general? Or—as Suvorov believes—was there something more calculating going on? The Steele dossier suggests that Kislyak's wooing of Flynn was deliberate, and part of a strategic US-facing operation. One of its aspects was to identify "sympathetic US actors." And, among other things, to bring them over to Moscow.

In February 2014 Flynn gave another lecture—this time in England. His host was the Cambridge intelligence seminar. This was a forum where scholars from Cambridge University, former spies, and the odd journalist got together to discuss espionage matters, past and present.

Several of the Russians who spoke there had subsequently died in mysterious ways. In January 2003 Boris Berezovsky—later found hanged in his ex-wife's home—had been a guest. A young Cambridge student, Vladimir Kara-Murza, collected Berezovsky from London, together with Berezovsky's friend, Litvinenko.

Berezovsky was the speaker. Standing at one end of a long table, Litvinenko talked briefly in Russian about Putin, with Kara-Murza translating. In 2006 Litvinenko was poisoned. After graduating Kara-Murza went home to Russia and joined the democratic opposition. There he was himself poisoned, not once but twice. A team of Moscow doctors saved his life. (Tests suggested Kara-Murza suffered binary poisoning—from two unknown toxins introduced separately.)

The person who invited Flynn to Cambridge was Professor Christopher Andrew, now an emeritus fellow and the official historian of MI5. Andrew convenes the seminar with Sir Richard Dearlove, the former head of Britain's secret intelligence service, MI6. Dearlove was Steele's former boss.

The venue for Flynn's (and Berezovsky's) talk was Corpus Christi College. Dating back to the fourteenth century, the college is a place of tranquil charm: a front quad done in Perpendicular Gothic style; a silver collection that survived the

English Civil War; and a painting that hangs next to the senior common room, attributed (wrongly?) to Poussin. Portraits of former college masters look out on a lofty dining hall.

Cambridge had numerous links with the world of spying. One of Corpus's sixteenth-century undergraduates was Christopher Marlowe, the poet and playwright, who went on secret missions for the Elizabethan government and was stabbed to death in a pub in London in 1593, possibly during a brawl over the "reckoning," or bill.

But it was the twentieth century when Cambridge became synonymous with spying and defined Cold War politics. In the 1930s the Soviets recruited a group of communist-leaning students and one tutor—the Magnificent Five. Three of them—Kim Philby, Guy Burgess, and Donald Maclean—defected to Moscow. At the moment when he vanished from Beirut, Philby was writing for the *Observer*, the future sister paper of my employer, the *Guardian*.

There was traffic in the other direction, too. In 1974 Corpus's master, Sir Duncan Wilson, took in the Soviet cellist Mstislav Rostropovich when he fled the USSR. A decade later the KGB spy and British double agent Oleg Gordievsky escaped Russia. Andrew became Gordievsky's friend; they wrote books together. During Christmas 1989 the pair sat on Andrew's sofa and watched the collapse of the Soviet bloc on TV. Six years after that Andrew collaborated with another defector and former KGB archivist, Vasili Mitrokhin. SIS exfiltrated Mitrokhin from Russia. He brought with him six large cases of top-secret material, an exhaustive record of the KGB's worldwide operations.

Flynn's Cambridge lecture was an obvious draw, in a term card that featured a talk on George Blake, another British KGB spy who fled to Moscow. The audience included academics, students, and retired intelligence professionals. Flynn brought his own Defense Intelligence Agency entourage. Afterwards there was a dinner at Pembroke College, where Dearlove had been master.

Writing in the *Sunday Times* in 2017, Andrew recalled the evening. He said that Flynn got into conversation with a talented Russian-British postgraduate. The woman, born in Moscow, showed Flynn some of her recent discoveries in the Russian archives. Flynn was so struck with her that he invited her to accompany him on a forthcoming visit to Moscow, as his official interpreter.

The trip didn't come off: soon afterwards Putin annexed Crimea. According to Andrew, Flynn and the postgraduate student subsequently conducted an "unclassified correspondence" via email. Their discussions were on Soviet history. The woman had written her dissertation on the Cheka. She was researching the role played by GRU spies in infiltrating the fledgling US nuclear programme for a future book.

The woman, Svetlana Lokhova, is understood to dispute some aspects of Andrew's account. There is no suggestion she is linked to Russian intelligence. Flynn would normally have been expected to report any meeting with a foreign national to the DIA. He didn't.

In his emails, Flynn signed off in an unusual way for a US spy. He called himself "General Misha."

Misha was the Russian equivalent of Michael.

Flynn's tenure as DIA chief was controversial. Within the agency, and inside the Obama administration, there were growing concerns about his erratic behaviour. One source, citing DIA sources, spoke of Flynn's obsession with Iran and his incapacity for "linear thought." He had a tendency to "jump around. People thought Flynn was crazy," the source said.

Other colleagues noted Flynn's preference for conspiracy theories. This proclivity developed into what became known as "Flynn facts"—alternative explanations for actual events with little basis in reality. At times it seemed he was deliberately sabotaging White House policy.

Another person who worked with him told me Flynn had always enjoyed "keepers" during his military career. One was General Stanley McChrystal, chief of Joint Special Operations Command. It was at JSOC that Flynn revolutionized the way military intelligence was collected in the field in Iraq and Afghanistan. Real-time data from captured mobile phones, scraps of papers, anything, was fed back to analysts and used as the basis of immediate raids. McChrystal kept in check Flynn's more obnoxious tendencies, the person said.

When Flynn became DIA boss, he no longer had a mentor or supervisor, I was told. He was on his own. His qualities—impetuosity, self-absorption, a conviction he was always right—became a liability. "Flynn frankly was raised above his level of competence," I was told.

Then there was the general's chaotic management style. According to a leaked email written by former secretary of state Colin Powell, Flynn was "abusive with staff" and "didn't listen." In a presentation Flynn even advised female DIA employees how to dress, telling them to avoid the "Plain Jane" look: "Make-up helps women look attractive."

In August 2014 Flynn exited government and the army. He went a year early. Clapper, the director of national intelligence, told him his time was up. Flynn blamed his dismissal bitterly on Obama and said he'd been fired because the president didn't like his uncompromising warnings about ISIS. Two months later the DIA wrote Flynn a letter. It set out the ethics restrictions that would apply to him in retirement. If he earned money from a foreign power, he had to declare it.

Flynn's next moves were typical for an ex-general. He joined a speakers' agency, went on the lecture circuit, and became a TV pundit. He set up a consulting firm, the Flynn Intel Group. And he wrote a book—a rambling, darkly alarming neoconservative manifesto, co-written with the right-wing scholar Michael Ledeen. Its title borrowed from Homer's *Iliad*: *The Field of Fight: How We Can Win the Global War Against Radical Islam and Its Allies.*

The book gives vent to Flynn's frustration with Obama—one of the "two worst presidents ever elected." (The other one was Jimmy Carter.) Flynn offers one idea. It's a single morbid obsession: that the West is losing the international fight against evil Islamists. What the United States needed was a new leader, an un-Obama, someone tough-minded, patriotic, and decisive.

There are interesting passages where Flynn recalls his late parents—his father, Charlie, who spent twenty years in the military, fighting in World War II and Korea; and his "brilliant, courageous" mother, Helen. Flynn recalls how as a teenager he got arrested for "unlawful activity."

"I was one of those nasty tough kids, hell-bent on breaking rules and hardwired just enough not to care about the consequences," he writes, a "sort of irreverent rascal." The army saved him, he adds. As an officer he continued to identify with those who defied the system—with "the misfits, rebels, and troublemakers" from Apple's famous slogan.

Much of Flynn's book, though, is the literary equivalent of an angry man ranting in a bar. Flynn criticizes Obama's Russia policy—too soft! He writes that the two countries might work together to beat radical Islam.

Flynn's anti-establishment views and mono-mindedness about the Muslim world meant that he had much in common with Trump. In August 2015—a few weeks after Trump announced his candidacy—the two men reportedly met for the first time in New York. The ninety-minute meeting went well. Flynn began to function as an informal foreign policy adviser.

Meanwhile, Flynn hadn't fallen off Moscow's radar. Rather the reverse. In December 2015 he returned to Russia. The Kremlin invited him to a special event: a tenth-anniversary gala to celebrate the launch of the television channel RT.

The Kremlin's favourite personalities were there. Julian Assange—stuck in the Ecuadorian embassy in London—appeared by satellite. RT anchor Sophie Shevardnadze interviewed Flynn on stage, in front of around a hundred guests. There were a few Putin-friendly questions. Flynn sat against a backdrop of the channel's green logo.

There was one other well-known American in town: Green Party candidate Jill Stein. At the gala dinner Flynn and Stein were seated at the top table.

The organizers found a special place for Flynn. Right next to him was Vladimir Putin.

Also present were Peskov, Putin's press spokesman; Sergei Ivanov, the president's chief of staff; and Ivanov's number two, Alexander Gromov. Plus RT's editor in chief, Margarita Simonyan, and an assortment of oligarchs and Russian celebrities. A few Europeans had flown in: the German politician Willy Wimmer and Bosnian film director Emir Kusturica.

(Kusturica was a big fan of RT. If he were Russian he would vote for Putin, he told the channel.)

Why had the Russians invited Flynn? The answer to this one was easy, said Mike McFaul, the former US ambassador to Moscow. It was because of Flynn's proximity to candidate Trump.

Speaking to the *Washington Post*'s Dana Priest, Flynn said he had nothing to do with the seating arrangement. He hadn't asked to sit next to Putin. Flynn said they were introduced but didn't chat. He did learn that Russia's president had a dim view of Obama and that Putin had "no respect for the United States' leadership."

Flynn's exchanges with Priest over RT are revealing. He seems oblivious to the fact that it's a propaganda channel.

PRIEST: Have you appeared on RT regularly?

FLYNN: I appear on Al Jazeera, Sky News Arabia, RT. I don't get paid a dime. I have no media contracts . . . [I am interviewed] on CNN, Fox . . .

PRIEST: Why would you go on RT, they're state run?

FLYNN: Well, what's CNN?

PRIEST: Well, it's not run by the state. You're rolling your eyes.

FLYNN: Well, what's MSNBC. I mean, come on . . . what's Al Jazeera? What's Sky News Arabia? I have been asked by multiple organizations to be a [paid] contributor but I don't want to be.

PRIEST: Because you don't want to be hamstrung?

FLYNN: That's right. I want to be able to speak freely about what I believe.

Flynn declined to say how much he was earning from RT. The answer, it later transpired, was $33,750. The money was compensation from a foreign government. Flynn should have requested permission in advance from the Department of Defense to accept this cash, but once again he didn't. He made two further fee-paying speeches in Washington on behalf of Russian interests.

By spring 2016 Flynn was a vocal supporter of Trump and foreign policy adviser to his campaign. On Twitter he became increasingly strident in his criticism of Clinton—a crooked, dishonest, terrible woman. He spread conspiracy theories cooked up by others—Obama was a money-laundering "jihadi"—and tweeted "fear of Muslims is RATIONAL." There was talk that Flynn might be nominated as Trump's vice president.

This didn't happen, but Flynn was rewarded with a prime slot at the RNC's Cleveland convention. His speech was a piece of hubris that would haunt Flynn in the months to come—an invitation, practically, to the gods to strike him down for his folly, self-ignorance, and foolish pride.

The mood inside the hall was frenzied. "We do not need a reckless president who believes she is above the law," Flynn told delegates. They broke into chants of: "Lock . . . her . . . up!"

Flynn looked stern, nodded, and said:

"Lock her up, that's right!" Clinton's use of a private email server meant she was a threat to the "nation's security," Flynn told the crowd, to further cries of "Lock her up!"

He went on:

"Damn right, exactly right, there's nothing wrong with

that. . . . And you know why we're saying that? We're saying that because if I, a guy who knows this business, if I did a tenth, a tenth, of what she did, I would be in jail today.

"So, crooked Hillary Clinton, leave this race now!"

Even by the standards of the 2016 contest, this was a defining low—an inglorious and squalid attack from a man who, unbeknown to Republican supporters and the American voters, was actually on Moscow's payroll. The Kremlin was the only party that knew the detail. It followed events in Cleveland closely; Kislyak was there.

In the aftermath of Cleveland, Steele sent two memos to Fusion GPS. These were based on conversations with what he called "well-placed and established Kremlin sources."

The two sources spoke of "divisions and backlash" in Moscow and set out a row between Ivanov and Peskov, both of whom had sat at Flynn's RT gala table. Ivanov was widely seen as the most powerful member of Putin's inner circle after Sechin. The memo claimed Ivanov was "angry at the recent turn of events"—the hacking and release of DNC emails, blamed on Russia. He believed the Kremlin team led by Peskov had overreached itself, "gone too far." The "only sensible course of action now for the Russian leadership was to 'sit tight and deny everything,'" Ivanov reportedly said.

Medvedev, the prime minister, shared Ivanov's apparent disquiet. Medvedev wanted good relations with whoever was in power in the United States, "not least so as to be able to travel there in future, either officially or privately." There was speculation inside the Kremlin that Trump might be forced to withdraw from the presidential race, "ostensibly on grounds of his psychological state and unsuitability for high office."

Steele's second memo—dated August 10—gives further

detail. It cites Ivanov, "speaking in confidence to a close colleague in early August." Ivanov, a former KGB officer, defence minister, and first deputy prime minister, was now upbeat. He felt that even if Clinton won, she would be "bogged down" in healing America's divisions and less able to focus on "foreign policy which would damage Russia's interests." According to Ivanov, Putin was "generally satisfied with the progress of the anti-Clinton operation to date."

The memo said:

> This had involved the Kremlin supporting various US political figures, including funding indirectly their recent visits to Moscow. S/he named a delegation from Lyndon LAROUCHE; presidential candidate Jill STEIN of the Green Party; TRUMP foreign policy adviser Carter PAGE; and former DIA director Michael Flynn, in this regard and as successful in terms of perceived outcomes.

The Kremlin, then, was happy with its Flynn investment. The money was well spent.

Two days after the memo Putin unexpectedly fired Ivanov from his presidential team. The Russian press said nothing about the probable cause: a row over the wisdom of hacking America. State TV showed footage of Putin accepting Ivanov's resignation "at his own wishes." Ivanov smiled. He was trying his best to accept this fate with dignity. Still, Ivanov looked pained.

By late summer Flynn had become Trump's fervent advocate. He was a staple in TV studios and on talk shows. He was also receiving classified intelligence. On August 17 he joined Trump at Trump Tower for a secret briefing given separately to both candidates. US officials told NBC News that Flynn repeatedly interrupted the briefers, prompting New Jersey Governor Chris Christie to tell him to calm down. Not true, said Flynn.

At the same time, Flynn was earning money for his lobbying activities, this time from the Turkish government. In July President Erdoğan survived a coup attempt. Amid mass arrests and sackings, Erdoğan blamed the uprising on supporters of Fethullah Gülen, an exiled cleric living in Pennsylvania. In Cleveland, Flynn welcomed the attempted coup, stating that Erdoğan was "close to President Obama."

In the two months before the US election, Flynn began calling for Gülen's extradition. He even described the preacher as Turkey's Osama bin Laden. What changed? The answer: Flynn's consulting company signed a new and lucrative contract. Officially, it was with a Dutch company, Inovo BV. In reality, the firm was linked to the Turkish government. The contract was for $600,000.

There were suspicions—unproven ones—that Russia may have arranged this. Putin and Erdoğan fell out bitterly in November 2015 after Turkey shot down a Russian jet on its border with Syria. By summer, however, they had made up, amid what critics called the Putinization of Turkey. The Flynn contract was agreed the same day that Putin and Erdoğan held talks in St Petersburg.

Once more, Flynn failed to register as a foreign agent. The day after polling day Erdoğan rang Trump to offer congratulations.

From inside the outgoing administration, and the US

intelligence community generally, there were fears that Flynn was now heading for a senior security post. The concerns stemmed from the general's behaviour. Flynn's multiple contacts with Russia, his acceptance of cash from murky foreign sources, his inappropriate conduct, his deceit—all raised doubts about his suitability for high office.

Obama said as much during his meeting with Trump in the Oval Office, the day after Trump's stunning election victory. According to three former officials, speaking to NBC, Obama told Trump explicitly: don't hire this guy. Trump ignored Obama's warning. Three days later he announced that Flynn would be his new national security adviser. This was a staff job of great power. It meant Flynn would spend more time with Trump than any other member of his national security team.

During the transition period, Flynn continued to interact with Kislyak. In early December he met the ambassador in Trump Tower together with Jared Kushner. There were no photos: seemingly the envoy crept in via a back entrance.

When Russia's ambassador to Turkey was shot dead—a gunman executed him at an Ankara art gallery—Flynn called Kislyak again to offer condolences. This was mid-December. On Christmas Day he texted the envoy with holiday greetings. Another phone call took place on December 28. The talk was of a Trump–Putin phone call and of forthcoming peace talks on Syria, to be hosted by Moscow in Kazakhstan.

The following day Flynn rang Kislyak numerous times, according to former White House officials. It was twenty-four hours since Obama ejected Russian diplomats in protest at the Kremlin's hacking. These calls were to prove fateful. They would lead to Flynn's downfall shortly afterwards—and to the question first asked during the Watergate hearings in 1973 by Republican senator Howard Baker:

What did the president know and when did he know it?

Flynn entered the US Army in the early 1980s. He might have been expected to join the infantry. Instead, he became part of a new and emerging field. He trained as an intelligence officer specializing in signals intelligence and electronic warfare. His mission was to eavesdrop on the enemy.

Flynn was deployed to Panama, Honduras, and other parts of Central America, where the Reagan administration was fighting proxy wars against what it viewed as Soviet-backed insurgents. Flynn—a platoon leader with the 313th Military Intelligence Battalion—took part in the US invasion of the Caribbean island of Grenada. It was 1983.

In *The Field of Fight*, Flynn recalls how he was sent in to defeat a rebel far-left militia that had just deposed and exe-cuted the prime minister, Maurice Bishop, plus various Cubans on the island. Flynn swiftly moved with his team and took over the phone company in downtown St George's. There, they got to work:

"We tapped the telecommunications network on the island and started listening for Cuban communications for those try-ing to escape," he wrote.

Later he went back to the US-controlled airfield. It was "a superb location offering a line of sight into the city, and along the southern and western part of [Grenada].

"We could, in essence, electronically 'see' and 'hear' any communications," Flynn explained.

Flynn, then, knew everything about the United States'

ability to bug conversations—it was his professional speciality. In the subsequent three decades these powers had increased. As former head of the DIA, he must have known that Russian envoys in New York and DC would be routinely monitored. All of which made his behaviour that December and January truly bizarre.

On January 12—two days after the Steele dossier came out—the journalist and writer David Ignatius published a column in the *Washington Post*. It compared the dark drama in Washington over Trump–Russia to the ghosts and other strange goings-on haunting Elsinore in Shakespeare's *Hamlet*. "After this past week of salacious leaks about foreign espionage plots and indignant denials, people must be wondering if something is rotten in the state of our democracy," Ignatius noted. (In his telling, Obama played the role of prince of Denmark—dithering while "dastardly deeds" like Russian hacking unfolded before his eyes.)

Ignatius examined the troubling questions. And then, almost as an afterthought, quoted a "senior US government official," who told him Flynn had spoken to Kislyak on December 29, the day after Obama threw out the thirty-five diplomats. This was followed by Putin's curious response— no Americans would be expelled from Moscow. The columnist wondered if Flynn had breached the Logan Act, which bars American citizens from correspondence meant to influence foreign governments involved in "disputes" with the United States.

Flynn, it appeared, had cut an informal deal in his chats with Kislyak. There was no public proof, of course. But a logical explanation of events would suggest that the general had given a few hints. He had conveyed a message that a future Trump administration would drop sanctions imposed by Obama against Russia. Or, at a minimum, reduce them.

Trump transition officials dismissed this interpretation. One told the *Post* that "sanctions were not discussed whatsoever." Sean Spicer, Trump's press spokesman, echoed this. Two days later Flynn spoke to Vice President-elect Mike Pence and told him the same thing—there'd been no discussions of sanctions. Pence and Reince Priebus, Trump's incoming chief of staff, gave the same message on Sunday morning TV shows. "None of that came up," Priebus declared.

Flynn, it would soon emerge, was lying.

Certainly, he was lying to Pence. And possibly to the FBI, who interviewed him at the White House on January 24. Reportedly he spoke to investigators without an attorney present. Lying to federal agents would have been unwise. That was a crime.

Inside the Department of Justice, Flynn's public comments were a cause for alarm. Evidently, a classified transcript of the Flynn–Kislyak conversation was circulating inside government.

Sally Yates, Obama's acting attorney general, still in office for the time being, realized that the situation was spinning out of control. Flynn was lying to Pence. Pence was misleading the American people. What's more the Russians were aware of this discrepancy. That left Flynn—the new national security adviser—open to blackmail.

Two days after Flynn's FBI interview Yates called up Don McGahn, the White House's counsel. She told him she "had a very sensitive matter she needed to discuss with him." It couldn't be done by phone. That afternoon, according to her testimony to the Senate's judiciary subcommittee, Yates visited McGahn at his White House office. The conversation was held in a Sensitive Compartmented Information Facility, or SCIF—a place where secret material can be examined.

She explained the situation—that Flynn's "underlying conduct" had "created a compromise" that Moscow might exploit. Yates said Pence was entitled to know that the information he was conveying "wasn't true." McGahn asked about Flynn's FBI interview, saying: "How did he do?" Yates was non-committal. She hadn't seen the FD-302 form, the official summary of Flynn's FBI statement. She had been given a readout.

The next morning, Friday, January 27, McGahn called Yates and asked her to come back to the White House. There was some discussion as to whether Flynn might now face criminal statutes. McGahn's view of the situation was weirdly lackadaisical. According to Yates, he asked her: "Why does it matter to the Department of Justice if one White House official lies to another White House official?"

Yates replied: "It was a whole lot more than that. . . . To state the obvious, you don't want to have your national security adviser compromised by the Russians."

Yates had assumed that the Trump administration would do something. The White House's priority, it appeared, was different: to find out what the FBI had on Flynn. McGahn said he wanted to look at the underlying evidence. Yates said her officials would work over the weekend to make that possible.

This was the moment for President Trump to show leadership—and to fire Flynn. Flynn's conduct and pattern of deceit had laid the United States open to Russian string-pulling, or worse. The lies were piling up. Instead, Trump responded by firing Yates. He sacked her after she told Justice Department attorneys not to defend his new executive order banning travellers arriving in the United States from seven Muslim-majority countries.

Did McGahn pass on Yates's warning and tell Trump? Why was the White House's response a stupefying nothing? The answers were not clear. Yates never discovered what happened.

For the next eighteen days Flynn remained in post. The Democratic senator Sheldon Whitehouse made an analogy with Watergate—and the missing 18½ minutes of tape recorded from Nixon's Oval Office. (The section was from a 1973 conversation between Nixon and his chief of staff, Bob Haldeman. It was never found.)

On January 28 Putin rang Trump and congratulated him. Flynn sat in on the Oval Office call. The two leaders spoke for an hour. The press summary of their conversation was a single paragraph. A week later Flynn told the *Washington Post* that he "categorically denied discussing sanctions" with Kislyak.

Flynn's apparent strategy was to tough things out and hope that his multiple problems might somehow go away. The strategy died a day later when the *New York Times*, citing current and former American officials, revealed that sanctions had in fact been discussed during the late-December call. The general's spokesman then admitted that Flynn "could not be certain that the topic hadn't come up." Trump, meanwhile, did his best to pretend the scandal wasn't happening. Asked by reporters on Air Force One if Flynn had misled him, he replied: "I don't know about that."

There was one final surreal scene when Trump, Flynn, and the Japanese prime minister, Shinzo Abe, huddled together on the patio of Mar-a-Lago, the president's Florida resort. They discussed how to respond to North Korea's latest missile test. As other diners and—one imagines—foreign spies posing as well-heeled guests looked on, the leaders peered at their mobile phones.

On February 13 Trump reluctantly fired Flynn. As usual, the president blamed the press rather than the person who had dissembled and cheated, possibly committing federal crimes along the way. Flynn was a "wonderful man." What had befallen him was "really a sad thing," Trump said. "I think he's been treated very, very unfairly by the media—as I call it, the fake news media, in many cases."

Flynn had lasted twenty-four days. It was the shortest tenure ever of a national security adviser. He had the rare distinction of being fired twice. In his letter of resignation, Flynn admitted he had "inadvertently" briefed Pence with incomplete information. The general said he had been "extremely honoured" to have served Trump, Pence, and their superb team. They would, he wrote, "go down in history as one of the greatest presidencies in US history."

Flynn was right about history: it won't forget Trump in a hurry. But Flynn's almost messianic tone was at odds with what was actually happening: a series of pratfalls, errors, and crass self-inflicted wounds from a presidency scarcely out of its cradle. Flynn's implosion was one example. What might explain the national security adviser's kamikaze-like behaviour?

One scenario was that in his dealings with the Russians, Flynn was engaged in a piece of reckless freelancing and the White House knew nothing about it.

There was a second, more troubling scenario. In it Flynn wasn't acting on his own at all. Rather, he was following instructions from Trump, or people close to him. These instructions were to send a message to the Russians via Kislyak that the Trump administration was minded to scrap sanctions. Flynn's subtext: give us time and we will deliver.

If true, this meant that Trump himself might soon be sucked into the FBI's investigation. Any conversations he had with Flynn would be key. The disgraced general was now in a position of unusual power. Should he chose to co-operate with federal agents—a big if—he could pull Trump into the abyss.

In the coming months Trump would continue to defend Flynn, and even send him encouraging messages. "This level of fealty is puzzling," Charles M. Blow wrote in May in the *New York Times.* "It seems to me there is something else at play here, something as yet unknown."

Blow added: "Trump's attachment to Flynn strikes me less as an act of fidelity and more as an exercise in fear. What does Flynn know that Trump doesn't want the world to know?"

Three days after Flynn exited the White House I got into a taxi at a London train station. I learned my destination at the last minute. It was a Thursday and the half-term school holidays. On the pavements were families with children; the city's mood was bright; the first snowdrops were appearing beneath tall plane trees. As we trundled south, along Hyde Park, a spring sun broke through misty clouds.

I leafed through a copy of the free newspaper *Metro.* On the front page was a photo of Donald Trump and the headline: "The Spies Who Bug Me—Angry Trump at War with Own Security Services over Russia Leaks." Trump, I read, was furious at the way his intelligence chiefs were briefing journalists. His latest tweet:

The real scandal here is that classified information is being ille-
gally given out by "intelligence" like candy. Very un-American.

The taxi rounded a Gothic Revival monument with a golden figure at its centre. This was Prince Albert, Queen Victoria's beloved German husband. We arrived at the Royal Albert Hall. I paid the cab and walked around the concert venue to the café at the back. After ten minutes, Steele arrived—the same person I'd met in December but now with a grey-white beard. He looked, he later told friends, a bit like Saddam Hussein. We found a couple of bar stools at the rear of the café, out of sight. I got out my Faraday bag, a black sack that cuts out radio signals and prevents eavesdropping. We put our mobile phones inside.

The purpose of the meeting was to discuss how Steele might return to normal life. For more than a month he had been living away from home—seeing his wife, children, and stepchildren only fleetingly. Despite this, he was bearing up. Steele had followed events in Washington closely and had listened to the denials by Trump's associates that they had had anything to do with Russia.

"They are all lying," he said simply.

The best answers to the story of collusion were to be found in Moscow, Steele felt, where there had been a major cover-up. Finding information from inside Russia was tricky, I pointed out. The Kremlin was evasive and opaque. My own investigation into Litvinenko's murder came to a halt of sorts in February 2011 with the authorities and the FSB deporting me from the country, in the first case of its kind since the Cold War.

In the United States the FBI was making progress, we agreed, getting some evidence.

Of the wider conspiracy, Steele said: "It's massive. Absolutely massive."

The immediate question was Steele's return to professional life and to his office in Victoria. At his home in Surrey he had installed new security gates. The paparazzi still dropped by, though. The solution was for Steele to appear again in public. He didn't have to say a huge amount, I explained—but might make a brief statement for the cameras. This could be arranged. After that the press would leave him in peace.

Steele left the café first. I departed soon after. It had been a fitting place to meet. The steps leading up to the rear of the Albert Hall had featured in the classic 1965 British espionage film *The Ipcress File*, starring Michael Caine as Harry Palmer. (Palmer, a British spy, fights with Housemartin, the bald chief of staff of the traitor Eric Grantby. Palmer throws Housemartin down the steps. But Housemartin escapes and drives off.)

I returned to the *Guardian* office on a red double-decker bus. I sat upstairs. I finished the paper. The front-page *Metro* story turned to page 5. It quoted Trump as defending Flynn, calling him a "wonderful man." It mentioned another Trump associate now being sucked into the investigation.

This person had masterminded Trump's campaign for president. He had even closer connections to Moscow than General Misha.

6

He Does Bastards

2004–2017
Ukraine

An evil genius.

—ALEX KOVZHUN, on Trump's campaign
manager Paul Manafort, summer 2016

It was mid-morning. In an attractive town square, bathed in autumnal sun and lined with fir trees, a crowd was waiting. A tall figure bounded onto a stage. His supporters cheered and started waving their flags. There were balloons and campaign slogans. The candidate looked like a modern Western politician. He was wearing a suit. There was a note of informality: his top button was undone. He had vigorous hair. Had he, I wondered, blow-dried it?

The town wasn't in Texas or the Rust Belt states of Michigan, Wisconsin, or Iowa. Instead, we were in Eastern Europe—more specifically, Ukraine, in a place called Ostroh. Arriving by helicopter, I had spotted a medieval castle and a gold-domed monastery twinkling below. The candidate, meanwhile, wasn't Trump. He was Ukraine's prime minister and a man seeking re-election. His name was Viktor Yanukovych.

It was September 2007 and a week before polling day. The crowd broke into chants of "Ya-nu-ko-vych, Ya-nu-ko-vych." Earlier, in Ukraine's capital, Kiev, I had met supporters of Yanukovych's arch rival, Yulia Tymoshenko. Typically, they were the better educated and middle class: attractive students wearing tight-fitting orange T-shirts. Generally, they spoke English.

Yanukovych's supporters, by contrast, were distinctly unglamorous. They were provincial, Russophone. Most were Soviet-born old ladies wearing headscarves. They were holding blue flags. This was the colour of Yanukovych's Ukrainian parliamentary bloc, the Party of Regions. A few waved Orthodox icons.

After months of political turmoil, Ukrainians were about to vote. The country's pro-Western president, Viktor Yushchenko, had called an early election because of a stand-off with Yanukovych, the prime minister since August 2006. Yushchenko had previously fallen out with Tymoshenko, an ally whom he sacked as prime minister.

In 2004 Yanukovych was the villain of the country's Orange Revolution. Backed by Moscow, he had tried to steal the presidential election using intimidation and fraud. During the 2004 campaign Yushchenko narrowly survived an assassination attempt. He was poisoned with dioxin; his face erupted in blisters. Nothing was proven but suspicion fell on Moscow. Yushchenko won a rerun vote.

Since then, Ukraine's Orange actors had fallen out and—largely unnoticed by the West—Yanukovych had made an unexpected comeback. His Party of Regions was ahead in the polls, at 32.9 percent. Yushchenko called an election that May after Yanukovych lured away several of the president's deputies to join the Party of Regions.

The previous evening I had met the man responsible for Yanukovych's unlikely electoral return.

He was not Russian, but American. His name was Paul Manafort.

Manafort, originally from Connecticut, was a veteran political consultant. His grandfather James had emigrated to the United States from Sicily in 1919. His father had once been mayor of the city of New Britain and leader of the Italian American community there.

And just as Henry Higgins in Shaw's *Pygmalion* had transformed Eliza Doolittle from Cockney flower girl to fine lady, so Manafort had transformed Yanukovych from an oafish Soviet-hewn loser to a plausible Western democrat. Yanukovych had grown up in eastern Ukraine's industrial Donbas region. He spoke Russian. Manafort had, with some success, got him to learn Ukrainian, the country's official language and the one used in its west.

I had flown to Ukraine to report for the *Guardian*. I was staying in the Hotel Dnipro in downtown Kiev, at the bottom of Khreschatyk Street, lined with attractive chestnut trees. Yanukovych's new Western advisers had promised me an interview with the candidate. That evening I was invited to meet some of his team. They included Kostyantin Gryshchenko—Yanukovych's future foreign minister—and Manafort, whose name was unfamiliar to me. Political observers in Kiev told me he was the person who had brought voter-friendly hand gestures to Yanukovych's campaign and got him to loosen his top button. I wrote the name in my reporter's notebook for the first time, spelling it "Maniford."

Our meeting took place in the Cabinet of Ministers. This was a short uphill walk from my hotel along a cobbled street that led to the Rada, Ukraine's parliament. Close up, Manafort looked every inch the Washington lobbyist. He was wearing an expensively cut suit and tie, conservative and in dark colours. He was a tall, bulky figure, with lustrous chestnut brown hair. It struck me that he looked not unlike Yanukovych, the politician whom he was advising. Or was it the other way round?

In 2004 political technologists from Russia had masterminded Yanukovych's disastrous campaign. Exit polls had put Viktor Yushchenko in front but the results gave Yanukovych victory. This, it transpired, came about after Yanukovych's team hacked into Ukraine's central election commission from a nearby cinema in . . . Moscow Street. (The team added 1.1 million votes to Yanukovych's tally.) Tens of thousands of people protested, turning Kiev's central Maidan Square into a tent city. Yanukovych's defeat in the subsequent rerun poll was, for Putin, a rare humiliation.

Manafort had an interesting story to tell. According to his version, Yanukovych was a wronged individual, and someone whom the West had almost wilfully misunderstood. This was true especially of its partisan media. Since 2004, Yanukovych had "grown" and "learned a lot" from his time out of power. One symbol of this change was sitting in front of me: Yanukovych had brought in American consultants.

"The other side is not the other side," Manafort said to me. "People are still looking at the political system in this country through the prism of 2004. That's not at all the situation here." He continued: "I can understand this misunderstanding going into the last election. But there's no excuse anymore for people not giving the right impression."

Manafort, I realized, was delivering a rebuke. The media had cast Yanukovych in the role of pantomime pro-Russian baddie. In fact, he said, the prime minister had made "more overtures to the West than to Russia." Ukraine's culture, history, and geography—not to mention its parlous economic situation—meant that Moscow couldn't be ignored. But: "He has done more things with the West." There were "consultations" with the United States, he said.

Other advisers echoed this theme. "He's very changed. He's become a democrat," Serhiy Lyovochkin, the head of Yanukovych's private office, assured me. The candidate was now studying English. He had even started playing tennis with the US ambassador!

According to Manafort, Yanukovych hadn't conspired against democracy in 2004. He was merely the "candidate of a system that was tied to Russia." When Yanukovych came back to the political stage as prime minister in 2006, "he was his own man." He wasn't against America. He had brought stability back to Ukraine. He was a strong leader. He had a plan.

Manafort added: "He's still his own man. There is no Russian influence in this campaign. The perception that he is the candidate of Russia against the interests of the West is bad reporting."

I never got my exclusive with Yanukovych. I was allowed to ask him a single question in Ostroh, while kneeling in a semi-circle with a gaggle of fellow press members and TV crews. I asked him about his foreign policy priorities. Yanukovych said that under his leadership Ukraine would be "a reliable bridge between Europe and Russia."

Still, Manafort's lecture was fascinating. It was made all the more remarkable by the fact that the person delivering it was a former senior adviser to the Republican Party. He had worked in 1976 on the US presidential campaign of Gerald Ford. After that with Ronald Reagan, George W. Bush, and Bob Dole. That, surely, must count for something?

I kept my notes from my Manafort interview and put them in a cupboard. After I got kicked out of Moscow they travelled with me to London. Over the next few years it turned out that Manafort's version of history was more than wrong. It went beyond spin or political PR.

Everything he told me was a lie.

Ukraine was a long way from Washington, DC—nearly eight thousand kilometres, in fact. What was a veteran Republican fixer doing in this murky post-Soviet corner, dominated as it was by oligarchs and others whose sources of wealth were never very transparent? The answer, it appeared, was money. Lots of it.

Manafort began working for Oleg Deripaska, a billionaire Russian oligarch who made his fortune in the aluminium industry during the 1990s. Deripaska's alleged ties to the mafia meant that for some years he was unable to get an American visa. Deripaska denies these allegations. Like all super-rich Russians Deripaska understood Putin's requirements perfectly: when called upon, you did what the president commanded. (Mikhail Khodorkovsky, once Russia's richest man, who spent a decade in jail, illustrated the fate of any who demurred.)

According to the Associated Press, Manafort signed a $10 million annual contract with Deripaska. In return, the

American proposed a wide-ranging political plan to undermine Putin's opponents in Europe and the United States and in former Soviet republics. Manafort's pitch covered politics, business dealings, and news coverage. He would influence them positively in Moscow's favour.

In a 2005 memo Manafort told Deripaska: "We are now of the belief that this model can greatly benefit the Putin government if employed at the correct levels with the appropriate commitment to success." It would offer "a great service that can re-focus, both internally and externally," the Kremlin's policies. The plan was not made public.

How much work Manafort performed under the terms of his contract is unknown. Next, Deripaska recommended the Republican lobbyist to fellow oligarch Rinat Akhmetov, Ukraine's richest man. Akhmetov was the main financial backer of the Party of Regions. He was considering listing his holding company, System Capital Management, on the London Stock Exchange and was in need of PR advice.

At Akhmetov's request, Manafort visited Ukraine in December 2004, between the second and third rounds of presidential voting. Manafort's view—correct, as it turned out—was that Yanukovych's campaign was doomed.

In summer 2005 the two men met for the first time in the Czech spa town of Karlovy Vary. It was a place known for its ties to the Russian mafia, in a country long used by Soviet and Russian intelligence as a base of operations. The meeting in western Bohemia went well. That autumn the Party of Regions hired Manafort and his team—including long-term aide Rick Gates—as advisers.

The Americans kept a low profile. They rented an anonymous Kiev office at number 4 Sophia Street. It was opposite the stop for the 16 and 18 trolley buses and the premises of Golden Telecom. Typically its white blinds were drawn. When Mustafa Nayyem called round—he was Ukraine's leading investigative reporter—he was politely told to leave.

Gradually, though, word got around. In a confidential 2006 cable to the State Department in Washington, subsequently leaked, US diplomats in Kiev reported that the Party of Regions had undergone a transformation. The party—"long a haven for Donetsk-based mobsters and oligarchs—is in the midst of an 'extreme makeover,'" they observed.

The party had enlisted "help and advice from veteran K Street political tacticians," the State Department was told, referring to DC's lobbying district. Manafort's firm—Davis, Manafort & Freedman—was busy "nipping and tucking." Its goal was to rid the party of its clumsy gangster image and to change it, in the minds of Ukrainians and others, into a "legitimate political force."

I didn't meet Manafort again. But I returned to Ukraine regularly. In 2009 I watched Yanukovych speak at the Yalta European Forum. This was a conference for bigwigs and international grandees held every year at the Livadia Palace, the seaside spot on the Crimean coast where Churchill, Roosevelt, and Stalin divided up post-war Europe at the 1945 Yalta conference.

Yanukovych was still an uninspiring politician. His speech was unmemorable. Maybe that was the point. His Manafort training was holding up well, though. In my notebook I wrote: "Calm. Statesman-like. Quiet." Yanukovych hadn't become prime minister again. (His Party of Regions topped the 2007 parliamentary poll, but Tymoshenko got the job after a coalition deal.) Instead, he was aiming higher: to win the 2010 presidential election.

By the close of 2009 Yanukovych was tantalizingly close to that ambition. Yushchenko's poll ratings were miserable. Manafort confirmed to the US embassy—with whom he was on friendly terms—that his client had "a double digit lead." The novelist Andrey Kurkov told me in Kiev that people were tired of what he called Yushchenko's "semi-romantic Ukrainian nationalism." They were also weary of Tymoshenko, whose campaigning passion felt familiar.

Yanukovych's aides had honed their critique of Tymoshenko. She was widely expected to face Yanukovych in a presidential run-off vote. They argued that it was she, not Yanukovych, who was Putin's choice as leader, and a danger to the country's fragile democracy. Tymoshenko's key objective was to rein in Ukraine's powerful oligarchs. She could do this only with Putin's help. The same oligarchs—Akhmetov and now gas tycoon Dmytro Firtash—were Yanukovych's primary backers.

The election went as predicted. I was in Kiev in January 2010 to witness Yushchenko's elimination. I came back in February for the final run-off between Yulia and Viktor. On election night most journalists went to Tymoshenko's election party, held in the swanky surroundings of Kiev's Hyatt Hotel. I found the usual young English-speaking crowd. There were canapés, wine, beautiful people.

It was the Party of Regions, however, that had reason to celebrate. It gathered at the InterContinental Hotel, just across Saint Sophia Square from the Hyatt and next to Ukraine's foreign ministry. The hotel had served as Manafort's operations

HQ. The downstairs ballroom was full. Many of Yanukovych's supporters looked like mafia bosses on a day out. They were enormous, with thick bouncer-like necks stuffed into dinner jackets. There were fewer women than at Yulia's bash.

Throughout the campaign Yanukovych had spoken in Ukrainian. This was down to Manafort. There was a sinister aspect to this, too, however. The Party of Regions had used the Russian language and its political status as an electoral weapon—a campaign tool to galvanize support in the traditional Russophone areas of eastern Ukraine. The same tactics alienated many in the west of the country—and in turn fuelled support for radical Ukrainian nationalism.

Yanukovych wasn't a bad pupil. (He still made verbal gaffes, though, describing Anton Chekhov as a "Ukrainian poet.") By the end, his Ukrainian was more than decent. Yanukovych appeared in the early hours of the morning. I didn't spot Manafort among those partying, but for sure this was his victory. A one-time crook, jailed twice during the Soviet period for hooliganism, and written off as a dummy, had just become president of a European state of 45 million people.

Yanukovych made his short statement to the media. He spoke in Russian. It was a sign of things to come.

Soon after, on a cold February morning, Yanukovych was inaugurated as president. The well-known reporter Serhiy Leshchenko watched the event, as men and women wearing tailcoats and evening gowns hurried towards Kiev's Lenin monument.

"There was a little bit of a commotion at the entrance," Leshchenko wrote in the *Guardian*. "Rinat Akhmetov, the richest Ukrainian man and the right arm of Yanukovych, was trying to make way for an inconspicuous American. It was only me and a few of my colleagues who recognized the mysterious stranger's face: it was Paul Manafort."

Within a few months it became clear that Yanukovych was hell-bent on reversing the modest democratic gains of the Orange Revolution. His goal was simple: to destroy the opposition. This meant destroying Tymoshenko and the independence of Ukraine's institutions.

Yanukovych moved quickly to consolidate all instruments of power: the courts, parliament, the prosecutor's office. Plus the media and TV. The claim that Yanukovych was a reformed character was unfounded. In power, he was behaving—as Manafort must have known he would—as a classic bully and thug. Underneath the aggressive behaviour there seemed a person shot through with insecurity and cowardice.

Judges charged Tymoshenko with corruption. The allegations dated back to the 1990s, when Tymoshenko was known as the gas princess, and to recent deals with Russia. Nobody was above the law, the Party of Regions said. True or not, this looked like a case of selective justice. The same allegations of embezzlement could be made against practically all of Ukraine's politicians, including Yanukovych.

By 2011 Tymoshenko was in jail. The West called repeatedly for her release. Yanukovych shrugged this off. On the foreign policy front, he renewed the lease on Russia's Black Sea naval fleet, stationed in Crimea. In return, Putin gave him a discount on Ukraine's gas bill. Negotiations continued over an association agreement with the European Union.

Then in November 2013, Yanukovych announced he was dropping the EU plan and accepting a $15 billion loan from Moscow. The decision meant that Ukraine had given up on closer integration with the West. Instead, it would remain part of Russian political and economic space—with key decisions over the country's future and foreign policy taken, in effect, by the Kremlin. Yanukovych would be Putin's provincial viceroy. The loan was a bribe.

For some Ukrainians this vision of the future was unappealing. It came on top of four years of misrule during which the president had robbed the state. In particular Yanukovych had enriched his family members and cronies. His son Oleksandr, a dentist, accumulated a fortune estimated at hundreds of millions of dollars.

Nayyem, the reporter, never actually met Manafort, though he told me he did once glimpse him in the lobby of the InterContinental Hotel. That November Nayyem posted a question on Facebook. It asked: Was anyone planning to go to the Maidan? Within an hour his post had more than a thousand "likes." "That night four hundred people showed up. They stayed until 6 a.m. Most of them were my friends from Facebook. It was the so-called creative class," he told me.

Nayyem's Maidan protest went through several iterations. For weeks it was peaceful. Then the government used brutal force. This was counterproductive: the demonstrations grew. Ukraine's official opposition leaders—Vitali Klitschko, Arseniy Yatsenyuk, Oleh Tyahnybok—came along but were habitually booed and referred to by protesters as "those three clowns." By February 2014 the mood in Kiev was febrile. Prominent anti-government activists were disappearing; some turned up dead, others alive but showing signs of torture. Paid pro-Yanukovych thugs—*titushki*—roamed the streets, beating and killing. Crowds of protesters built barricades. The riot police fired tear gas.

The revolution had many aspects. It was not unlike the post-crash Occupy movements that had filled the streets of

New York, London, and Madrid. It was also strikingly retro—with protesters donning home-made shields and helmets, and using medieval-style catapults to chuck stones at the cops. Additionally, it was the anti-Soviet revolution that failed to happen when Ukraine exited the USSR in 1991. A lot of Lenin statues were toppled.

In the final hours of the regime, government snipers killed dozens. Video footage shows them firing on unarmed protesters trying to advance across open ground. Twenty police also died.

Yanukovych was at his palace on the outskirts of Kiev. He was in no physical danger, but he chose to flee the country. He took $32 billion with him (having stolen an estimated $100 billion in four years), leaving by helicopter and escaping to Russia. Other members of his government ran away, too, stuffing money and jewels in their luggage like comedy gangsters.

Putin's response was to seize Crimea and declare that the uprising in Ukraine was a "fascist coup." He pledged to defend the ethnic Russians whom Manafort had previously targeted as election fodder. Soon after Putin started a war in eastern Ukraine—albeit a covert one, done with undercover troops and clandestine agents. The conflict that gripped Ukraine in 2014 wasn't, as Moscow claimed, a civil war. In reality it was a Frankenstein-like conflict, artificially created by the Russian government and given life by the external brute shock of military force and invasion. The GRU—the outfit that would go on to hack the DNC—played a key role.

The real coup took place in Crimea, where, a week after Yanukovych's flight, masked gunmen—actually Russian special forces troops—seized the parliament building in Simferopol, Crimea's regional capital. Meanwhile, in the eastern cities of

Donetsk and Luhansk, pro-Russian groups began storming government buildings.

The Kremlin rapidly escalated this dispute in the east by providing hardware to anti-Kiev rebels. It included tanks, artillery pieces, and anti-aircraft systems. That spring, summer, and autumn Russian soldiers—sometimes repackaged as "volunteers'—did much of the fighting. When it appeared that the rebels were on the brink of defeat, Moscow used its regular units to smash Ukrainian forces.

Without Russia there wouldn't have been a war in 2014. There would undoubtedly have been tension between the central government in Kiev and its predominantly Russian eastern regions—a political dispute about autonomy, devolved power, the multiple failures of the Ukrainian state, and the status of the Russian language. But Ukraine wouldn't have fallen apart. Fewer people would have died.

Boiled down, Yanukovych had sold himself out to a foreign power. He had committed treason. He had also stolen very large sums of money.

How much of this was down to Manafort? Might he be blamed for the Ukraine disaster? And to what extent was Yanukovych's kleptocratic family presidency a model for Donald Trump?

For sure, the fault lines in Ukraine—between Catholic west and Orthodox east, between those looking to Europe and those nostalgic for the lost Soviet universe—existed before Manafort arrived on the scene. The charge against Manafort is that he cynically exploited these divisions for short-term electoral gain, without caring much about the consequences. These were, in the end, catastrophic.

Before signing on with Trump in spring 2016, Manafort spent over a decade working in Ukraine. Yanukovych hired him to run four election campaigns: the presidential one and three parliamentary polls. After Yanukovych left, Manafort continued to work for the defeated Party of Regions. He helped reshape it. This was at the behest of Lyovochkin, Yanukovych's former chief of staff. Manafort renamed it the Opposition Bloc. He visited Kiev up until late 2015.

According to Nayyem, among Trump's entourage it is Manafort who has the closest ties with Russia. Nayyem acknowledged Manafort's gifts as a political technician and said: "Manafort tried to civilize Yanukovych. He told him: 'You are so ugly. I will present you to the West.'"

Nayyem described the American as "deeply cynical." "He didn't think about the history or about the people of Ukraine. He treated Ukraine as if he was playing a computer game, dividing the country into three parts, making these clashes."

Other critics noted that Manafort specialized in "bastards." His previous client roster included Philippine dictator Ferdinand Marcos, Angola's Jonas Savimbi, and Zaire's Mobutu Sese Seko. "He's an evil genius," Alex Kovzhun—former image-maker to Tymoshenko—said of Manafort. "He doesn't work statesmen. He works dictators and all-round bad guys."

Manafort sold the unsellable product, Kovzhun told me, adding: "If you have a dead horse and you need to sell it, you call him."

Manafort's speciality, according to Kovzhun, is running expensive campaigns and targeting the "big unwashed." "It's the same element who voted for Putin, supported Brexit, back Erdoğan, and who like Trump. Manafort works the lowest common denominator. I find him repulsive and his message ugly. He leaves destruction in his wake."

There were parallels between Manafort's campaign for Yanukovych and his work for Trump in 2016, Kovzhun said, adding that he recognized the same "moves": "He gets his clients to do corny stuff with bland political slogans and uncreative Soviet-style imagery. With Yanukovych it was: 'I'll Hear Everyone!' With Trump it's 'Make America Great Again!'"

Some of those who worked closely with Manafort in Kiev make a countercase. They say that Yanukovych "listened to what Paul said" between 2007 and 2010 but then failed to heed his advice. This wasn't Paul's fault, they say. Oleg Voloshin—a former aide to foreign minister Kostyantyn Gryshchenko—described Manafort as extremely intelligent, with an impressive knowledge of law, history, and public affairs.

In strategy meetings Manafort would typically sit and listen, Voloshin said. "He didn't speak Russian. He had an interpreter with him. At the end he would speak for fifteen minutes." The American's advice was always non-ideological. Manafort would calmly explain that "these people won't vote for you, don't bother with them," and then suggest "promote this message, promote that message."

According to Voloshin, Manafort was an advocate for US interests. So much so that the joke inside the Party of Regions was that he actually worked for the CIA. He promoted American oil companies, like Exxon and Chevron. He supported Ukraine's association with NATO and with the EU. He warned Yanukovych not to lock up Tymoshenko.

"If it weren't for Paul, Ukraine would have gone under Russia much earlier," Voloshin told me. "He was the one dragging Yanukovych to the West. In the end the Russians had to make threats against Yanukovych about his personal safety. Yanukovych is very stubborn. But when he breaks, he breaks totally."

Ultimately, Voloshin claimed, Manafort's engagement with Ukraine was about the challenge rather than the money. I wasn't persuaded by this: Manafort would later admit to earning over $17 million from the Party of Regions in just two years, between 2012 and 2014. The tougher the client the greater the success, Voloshin said. Manafort was a person capable of doing miracles:

"In 2004 Yanukovych was dead. He was seen as a Russian puppet. It was Paul who resurrected him."

Manafort's relationship with Trump went back a long way. In 1980 Manafort founded a lobbying company. One of his partners was Roger Stone, Trump's long-time political mentor and campaign adviser.

As the *Washington Post* reported, Stone played a small but notable role in the original Watergate scandal and would go on to feature prominently in the Trump–Russia story. In 1972 he donated money to Nixon's Republican rival in the primary race, Pete McCloskey—not in his own name but as the Young Socialist Alliance. Stone then tipped off the press that McCloskey was taking money from alleged communists.

In 1980 Stone met Trump while looking for contributions to Reagan's election campaign. Trump then became an early client of Manafort's company, Black, Manafort, Stone, and Kelly. Trump sought advice from Stone. He hired Manafort, an attorney, to look after gambling and real estate issues. In the intervening years, Manafort did much of his work outside

DC—in central and east Africa, the Philippines, Russia, and Ukraine. It was this outsider backstory that endeared Manafort to Trump when the lobbyist came looking for a job.

According to the *New York Times*, Manafort contacted Trump in late February 2016. At this point Trump was the front-runner in the Republican race, having won New Hampshire and South Carolina. However, he also faced strong resistance from the Republican establishment ahead of a possibly contested convention in Cleveland, Ohio. Victory was by no means guaranteed.

Manafort's pitch—delivered via a mutual friend, Thomas Barrack Jr—was a masterclass in self-promotion. He pointed to the fact that he had managed presidential campaigns around the world, while stressing that since 2005 he'd kept away from Washington. "I will not bring Washington baggage," he said. Barrack recommended Manafort to Trump's daughter Ivanka and her husband, Jared, describing him as a "killer" and "the most experienced and lethal of managers."

Trump was favourably impressed. This feeling grew when the two men met. The *New York Times* reported that Manafort began by saying that he lived on an upper floor of Trump Tower. (Soon after he started working for Deripaska, in 2006, he bought an apartment there for $3.6 million.) Manafort cited his successful track record with oligarchs and other international figures. Trump told aides that he liked Manafort's manner and tanned appearance—noting that for a man in his mid-sixties the lobbyist had a rich head of chestnut hair. There was a final clinching factor: Manafort said he would work for nothing.

A month later, on March 29, Trump unveiled his new convention manager, stating that Manafort was "volunteering" his insight and expertise. The candidate called Manafort a "great asset" and said that he would ensure it was Republican voters and not the "Washington political establishment" that got to pick the nominee. Manafort said he was "honoured" to serve "Mr Trump's campaign." He added: "I am confident that he [Trump] will be the next president of the United States."

Manafort quickly settled into his new post. His colleague, Rick Gates—whom I met in Kiev in 2007—became his deputy. As with Manafort's remarks to me about Yanukovych, the strategy was to try to persuade sceptics that Trump wasn't the man he seemed. Unlike the brash reality-TV showman who trash-talked his rivals, the real Trump was measured, rational, and statesmanlike.

"The part he's been playing is now evolving into the part you've been expecting," Manafort told the *Washington Post* in April.

The problem was that Trump seemed unaware of his impending metamorphosis. Instead, during a TV debate he got into a row over the size of his penis, telling Marco Rubio—his Republican rival—that there wasn't "a problem."

By May Manafort had become Trump's campaign manager and strategist-in-chief—Corey Lewandowski retained the role officially but was effectively sidelined. This harmonious state of affairs lasted until July, when WikiLeaks released the first tranche of Kremlin-hacked DNC emails. With Russian meddling becoming the top story, it was inevitable that Manafort's Moscow–Kiev links would come under scrutiny. Investigative journalists began sniffing around.

It was Manafort, according to the *Post*, who persuaded Trump to pick the Indiana governor, Mike Pence, as his running mate. Trump's inclination had been to go for an outsider, a troublemaker like himself—a Flynn, or Chris Christie, or Newt Gingrich, the former Speaker of the House. Pence, by contrast, was an insider who might attract the support of mainstream Republicans who were uneasy with Trump. Ivanka and Jared reportedly supported Manafort's choice.

Manafort's six months as Trump's campaign lieutenant ended abruptly in mid-August, days after the *New York Times* published a front-page story. It read: "Secret Ledger in Ukraine Lists Cash for Donald Trump's Campaign Chief." The ledger had been found in a third-floor room inside the Party of Regions HQ in Kiev. In February 2014 anti-government protesters had ransacked the building.

One of those who examined the ledger was Leshchenko, the journalist, who was now a newly elected member of Ukraine's post-Yanukovych parliament. It included several hundred pages of entries. There were names and dates, written by hand in blue ink. One of the names was Manafort's. It appeared twenty-two times. Between 2007 and 2012 Manafort had allegedly received $12.7 million in cash. Apparently these were secret payments from a political slush fund.

It was unclear whence this shadow money had come. Party of Regions officials told the *New York Times* that the room had once contained two safes, stuffed with $100 bills. Seemingly, some had gone on legitimate election business like exit polls. Other tranches of cash—$2.2 million, in one case—were funnelled to US lobbyists via a Yanukovych linked non-profit organization.

Manafort denied any connection to this cash. The black ledger was a fake, he said. To claim otherwise was unfounded, silly, and nonsensical. Trump repudiated the story, too. He dismissed the *New York Times* as a "garbage paper."

In a statement Manafort said: "I have never received a single 'off-the-books cash payment' as falsely 'reported' by the *New York Times*, nor have I ever done work for the governments of Ukraine and Russia. Further, all the political payments directed to me were for my entire political team: campaign staff (local and international), polling and research, election integrity and television advertising."

"Ukrainians are concerned about the theft of public money. We want the chain of corruption to end. That's why many are troubled that Manafort's name has emerged in this investigation," Leshchenko wrote that August.

Soon after the *New York Times* story broke, Manafort quit. His departure came amid rumours that Trump had cooled on him. The Ukraine story had become a "distraction," the candidate's son, Donald Trump Jr, said to Fox News. Manafort's replacement was Stephen Bannon, chairman of Breitbart.

This was the official story of Manafort and Trump. But the Steele dossier suggests that Manafort's role went well beyond shaping the candidate's campaign message. According to one of Steele's early memos, Manafort was at the centre of the alleged "extensive conspiracy" between Trump's campaign team and Moscow.

In late July Steele's Source E reported that this "conspiracy of co-operation" was "well-developed." On one side was the Russian leadership. On the other, Trump and his top aides.

Of the conspiracy Steele wrote:

This was managed on the TRUMP side by the Republican candidate's campaign manager, Paul MANAFORT, who

Christopher Steele, former British intelligence officer. Steele worked for MI6 in London, Moscow, and Paris before leaving the service and founding his own corporate intelligence firm, Orbis, in 2009. This photo was taken as he returned to work in March 2017 after a period of lying low. *Courtesy of AP Images*

The young spy. Steele spent three years in Moscow between April 1990 and April 1993. He had a front-row seat on history. Steele was on duty during the KGB-led coup of August 1991. He walked into town and watched from fifty yards away as Boris Yeltsin climbed onto a tank and denounced the plotters. *Courtesy of Anatoly Andronov*

Steele was based at the British embassy in Moscow. He travelled across newly accessible parts of the Soviet Union and became the first foreigner to visit Stalin's secret bunker away from the front. This photo, taken in early 1991, shows him with newspaper editors in the Tatar city of Kazan. *Courtesy of Anatoly Andronov*

COMPANY INTELLIGENCE REPORT 2016/080

US PRESIDENTIAL ELECTION: REPUBLICAN CANDIDATE DONALD TRUMP'S ACTIVITIES IN RUSSIA AND COMPROMISING RELATIONSHIP WITH THE KREMLIN

Summary

- Russian regime has been cultivating, supporting and assisting TRUMP for at least 5 years. Aim, endorsed by PUTIN, has been to encourage splits and divisions in western alliance

- So far TRUMP has declined various sweetener real estate business deals offered him in Russia in order to further the Kremlin's cultivation of him. However he and his inner circle have accepted a regular flow of intelligence from the Kremlin, including on his Democratic and other political rivals

- Former top Russian intelligence officer claims FSB has compromised TRUMP through his activities in Moscow sufficiently to be able to blackmail him. According to several knowledgeable sources, his conduct in Moscow has included perverted sexual acts which have been arranged/monitored by the FSB

- A dossier of compromising material on Hillary CLINTON has been collated by the Russian Intelligence Services over many years and mainly comprises bugged conversations she had on various visits to Russia and intercepted phone calls rather than any embarrassing conduct. The dossier is controlled by Kremlin spokesman, PESKOV, directly on PUTIN's orders. However it has not as yet been distributed abroad, including to TRUMP. Russian intentions for its deployment still unclear

Detail

1. Speaking to a trusted compatriot in June 2016 sources A and B, a senior Russian Foreign Ministry figure and a former top level Russian intelligence officer still active inside the Kremlin respectively, the Russian authorities had been cultivating and supporting US Republican presidential candidate, Donald TRUMP for at least 5 years. Source B asserted that the TRUMP operation was both supported and directed by Russian President Vladimir PUTIN. Its aim was to sow discord and

Steele's famous dossier, written in MI6 house style. The dossier runs to thirty-five pages. Steele wrote it between June and December 2016. It was based on information from secret sources and alleges that Trump received intelligence from the Kremlin on rival Hillary Clinton. Moscow had been "cultivating, supporting and assisting TRUMP for at least 5 years." *Courtesy of* BuzzFeed *via DocumentCloud*

In the summer of 1987, Trump travelled to Moscow for the first time with his wife, Ivana. The photo shows them in Leningrad. Trump was a guest of the Soviet government and the state travel agency Intourist—a branch of the KGB. His hotel room next to Red Square would have been bugged. *Courtesy of Maxim Blokhin/TASS*

General Vladimir Kryuchkov, KGB foreign intelligence chief. In 1984 he circulated a secret note to KGB station chiefs abroad, urging them to do more to recruit Americans. They should exploit personal weakness and use "creative" methods, including "material incentives." *Courtesy of TASS/TASS/ Getty Images*

Trump in Moscow again for the 2013 Miss Universe beauty contest. His host was Aras Agalarov (middle, next to his son, Emin), an Azeri-born property tycoon. The pair discussed building a Trump Tower Moscow. The project never happened but was still being secretly discussed in 2015–16 as Trump campaigned for president. *Courtesy of Victor Boyko/Getty Images Entertainment/Getty Images*

Moscow's glitzy Ritz-Carlton, at the bottom of Tverskaya Street. According to the Steele dossier, Trump watched two prostitutes perform a show in his presidential suite. The FSB spy agency recorded everything, it says. Trump denies this. *Courtesy of Alex Shprintsen*

Agalarov's pop-star son, Emin, sang at Miss Universe and became friendly with Trump. Emin is pictured with his British publicist, Rob Goldstone. In June 2016 Goldstone sent an email to Donald Trump Jr offering "incriminating" Russian government material on Hillary. *Courtesy of Aaron Davidson/Getty Images Entertainment/Getty Images*

For months, Donald Trump Jr denied meeting Russians. Actually, he accepted Goldstone's email offer, replying with the words: "I love it." A secret meeting took place in June 2016 at Trump Tower. Details leaked a year later. *Courtesy of John Moore/Getty Images News/Getty Images*

A mid-level Russian lawyer, Natalia Veselnitskaya, flew in from Moscow to meet with Donald Jr in Trump Tower. Also present were Paul Manafort, Jared Kushner, and Rinat Akhmetshin, a lobbyist who worked in Soviet counterintelligence. *Courtesy of Yury Martyanov/AFP/Getty Images*

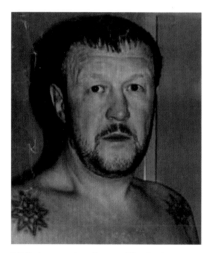

Mafia boss and racketeer, Vyacheslav Ivankov was a legendary figure in the Soviet and Russian underworld. In 1992 he moved to a new theatre of operations: America. The FBI spent three years looking for him. The agency eventually tracked down his hiding place—Trump Tower.

Moscow's ambassador to the United States, Sergey Kislyak, meeting Trump in the Oval Office, in a photo taken by the Russian foreign ministry. Kislyak's father, Ivan, was a top KGB spy who served in European capitals, including Athens and Paris, where he was a *rezident* in the 1970s. *Courtesy of Alexander Shcherbak/ TASS/Getty Images*

During the campaign, Trump repeatedly praised Russia's president, Vladimir Putin. The two finally met at the G20 summit in Hamburg. Later that evening, Trump talked to Putin over dinner without his US interpreter. What they discussed is unknown. *Courtesy of REUTERS/Carlos Barria*

Trump's future national security adviser, Michael Flynn, sitting next to Putin. The 2015 event was a dinner to celebrate the tenth anniversary of RT, the Kremlin's propaganda channel. On a previous Moscow visit, Flynn toured the HQ of the GRU, Russia's military spy agency. *Courtesy of AP Images*

Lawyer, lobbyist, and adviser to dictators, Paul Manafort joined Trump's campaign in the spring of 2016. He was on intimate terms with ex-Soviet oligarchs, including Putin's ally Oleg Deripaska. In July 2017 the FBI raided Manafort's apartment as part of its collusion probe. *Courtesy of AP Images*

Carter Page, Trump's foreign affairs adviser. Page worked in Moscow, where—in the words of one Russian spy—he "got hooked on Gazprom." The dossier alleges that he held secret meetings with Igor Sechin, Putin's de facto deputy, and a Kremlin aide. Page denies this. *Courtesy of REUTERS/ Sergei Karpukhin*

Trump was increasingly vexed by what he called the "Russian thing." In May 2017 he fired the man who had failed to make it go away—FBI chief James Comey. Comey's Senate testimony was a riveting piece of political history. His firing came about after Trump asked for "loyalty," and Comey refused. *Courtesy of Chip Somode-villa/Getty Images News/Getty Images*

Enter the prosecutor. In the wake of Comey's firing, former FBI chief Robert Mueller was appointed special counsel. His remit: to investigate allegations of "coordination" between the Trump campaign and Russia. Mueller's heavy-weight team didn't leak. It appeared to be following the money. *Courtesy of AP Images*

The president's unsackable son-in-law. In December 2016 Jared Kushner met with Kislyak and asked if it would be possible to set up a secret back channel to Moscow. Kushner held another meeting with Sergei Gorkov, a banker-spy, in Trump Tower. *Courtesy of AP Images*

In 2008 oligarch Dmitry Rybolovlev purchased Trump's seaside Florida mansion for $95 million, $50 million more than Trump paid for it in 2004. The Russian never lived there and eventually demolished it. During the campaign, his plane was spotted on the tarmac next to Trump's—a coincidence, Rybolovlev said. *Courtesy of REUTERS/Eric Gaillard*

Putin's scowling gatekeeper and the head of Russia's biggest oil producer, Rosneft. The dossier claims that Igor Sechin offered Page the "brokerage fee" on a privatization deal worth billions, with US sanctions on Moscow dropped in return. Page denies this. *Courtesy of Sasha Mordovets/Getty Images News/Getty Images*

Russian foreign intelligence ran an undercover spy ring in Manhattan. The FBI busted it. Two Moscow spies had diplomatic immunity, but the third, Evgeny Buryakov, didn't. In 2015 Buryakov pleaded guilty to espionage and got thirty months in jail. *Courtesy of AP Images*

was using foreign policy advisor Carter PAGE and others as intermediaries. The two sides had a mutual interest in defeating Democratic presidential candidate Hillary CLINTON, whom President PUTIN apparently both hated and feared.

Source E admitted that the "Russian regime" was behind the release of DNC emails published by WikiLeaks. Crucially, the alleged operation "had been conducted with the full knowledge and support of TRUMP and senior members of the campaign team."

In other words, Steele claims, Manafort knew. Manafort has repeatedly denied that he has done anything wrong.

It's unclear to what extent, if any, Manafort was involved in supplying intelligence to Russia, another of the dossier's allegations. This was the back-channel through which information was fed to the Kremlin on the activities of business oligarchs and their families inside the United States. That Manafort was willing to accept compromising information supplied by Moscow would later become clear. Certainly, Manafort was well placed; he had extensive contacts in this world.

The dossier further claimed that the candidate's team were "relatively relaxed" about adverse publicity concerning Russian interference:

> [This] deflected media and the Democrats' attention away from TRUMP's business dealings in China and other emerging markets. Unlike in Russia, these were substantial and involved the payment of large bribes and kickbacks which, were they to become public, would be potentially very damaging to their campaign.

Manafort appears in subsequent Steele memos. One follows his August resignation and is titled: "The Demise of Trump's Campaign Manager Paul Manafort." On August 15—a day after the *New York Times* broke the ledger story—Yanukovych held a secret meeting with Putin, it said. The venue was near Volgograd in southern Russia, not far from Yanukovych's base-in-exile at Rostov-on-Don.

Western media revelations about Manafort and Ukraine featured prominently on the agenda, the memo said.

YANUKOVYCH had confided in PUTIN that he did authorize and order substantial kick-back payments to MANAFORT as alleged but sought to reassure him that there was no documentary trail left behind which could provide clear evidence of this.

Putin had always held a dim view of Yanukovych. He viewed him as uncouth and something of an idiot. This occasion was no different. The dossier said:

Given YANUKOVYCH's (unimpressive) track record in covering up his own corrupt tracks in the past, PUTIN and others in the Russian leadership were sceptical about the ex-Ukrainian president's reassurances on this relating to MANAFORT. They therefore feared the scandal still had legs, especially as MANAFORT had been commercially active in Ukraine right up to the time (in March 2016) when he joined TRUMP's campaign team. For them it therefore remained a point of potential vulnerability and embarrassment.

There was a further piece of gossip. An unnamed political consultant working on the Trump campaign said it was true the Ukraine revelations had played a part in Manafort's demise. Additionally, several senior players close to Trump had wanted Manafort out. They had sought to loosen Manafort's control "on strategy and policy formulation." Chief among them was Lewandowski, "who hated MANAFORT personally and remained close to TRUMP."

Beyond the dossier there were lingering questions over Manafort's long-time colleagues in Ukraine. Some were rumoured to have links with Russian intelligence.

On the day that Manafort quit Trump's campaign, *Politico* published a long profile of Konstantin Kilimnik. Kilimnik worked with Manafort from 2005. He led Manafort's office in Kiev and helped to advise the new opposition bloc. In 2016 Kilimnik flew to the United States twice to see his old mentor—once in May, two weeks before Manafort became Trump campaign chairman, and again in August. The second meeting took place at the Grand Havana Room, an upmarket New York cigar bar. The two men discussed the forthcoming election, Ukraine, and unpaid bills, Kilimnik told the *Post*.

In addition, Manafort and Kilimnik swapped a large number of private emails. In one, sent two weeks before Trump accepted the nomination, Manafort delivered a message via Kilimnik to Deripaska. It made an offer: Manafort was willing to give the oligarch the inside track on Trump's election campaign. "If he [Deripaska] needs private briefings we can accommodate," Manafort wrote on July 7. Deripaska's close relationship with Putin meant that any such briefing would reach the Kremlin. The two colleagues also discussed money owed to them by various clients. This cash was referred to in euphemistic terms as "black caviar."

The briefings never happened. The emails were "innocuous" and the offer "routine," Manafort's spokesman said.

Still, the exchange raised further questions, not least because Kilimnik's biography had unusual moments. Born in Soviet Ukraine, he attended a Soviet military school, where he learned to speak fluent English and Swedish. According to *Politico*, his first job was as a Russian military interpreter—a post that inevitably brought him into contact with army intelligence and the Aquarium. (In Suvorov's day, the GRU did everything possible to persuade its officers to acquire foreign languages. You got a 10 percent salary bonus for a Western language; 20 percent for an Asian one, he wrote.)

In 1995 Kilimnik joined the International Republican Institute in Moscow. His American colleagues there knew about his past and referred to him as "Kostya, the guy from the GRU." This wasn't a problem since the institute didn't engage in sensitive work. Former officials described Kostya as smart, non-ideological, and interested in money. An IRI alumnus, Phil Griffin, hired him to work with Manafort.

Kilimnik soon became a trusted member of the team—travelling on Manafort's planes, including to Crimea, and serving as his interpreter. Some associates believed he still had links with "Moscow Central." Others that the military intelligence episode happened long ago.

That August I sent Kilimnik an email. Might he talk about his time with Paul? His reply was friendly. Then the *Politico* piece appeared. I emailed again. Was he, by any chance, a spy? Kilimnik was scathing. He replied:

Thank God *Politico* hasn't figured out that I taught Colonel Putin German and judo. And that visit to Dallas in November 1963—phew, how could they have missed it. :))

Then:

Seriously though—nobody gives a shit here about such stuff because it is so insane. It is well understood by everybody that the real goal of this whole campaign is to push Manafort away from Trump and annihilate his chances of winning, which are there as long as Manafort runs his campaign. My guess is Trump understands this well and HRC's strategy has not worked so far.

People who matter here, including the President himself [Petro Poroshenko], understand very well Manafort's role here and do not buy into all the gibberish about the black ledgers etc. Manafort will make billions on this free PR working for the same people he used to work. And probably get a lot of new clients with his newly found fame.

I am just a minor casualty in the US political game, which honestly has nothing to do with Ukraine or its future. If I am the biggest issue this country has—then we are all seriously in trouble. :)) But now I could write spy novels.

Off to collect my paycheck at KGB. :))

K

Kilimnik's tone was one of cheerfully aggrieved mockery. Anyone who suggested he was a Putin agent, he implied, was a tin-hatted conspiracy theorist. The black ledger, the campaign against Manafort, Hillary's smears—all this was media candy floss, spun from nothing in a moment of left-wing American hysteria.

The thing that gave me pause was Kilimnik's use of smiley faces. True, Russians are big emoji fans. But I'd seen something similar before. In 2013 the Russian diplomat in charge of political influence operations in London was called Sergey Nalobin. Nalobin had close links with Russian intelligence. He was the son of a KGB general; his brother had worked for the FSB; Nalobin looked like a career foreign intelligence officer. Maybe even a deputy *rezident*, the KGB term for station chief.

On his Twitter feed Nalobin described himself thus:

A brutal agent of the Putin dictatorship :)

By spring 2017 Manafort was at the centre of various investigations. There was the FBI's probe into links between the Trump campaign and Russia. There were ongoing hearings in the Senate and the House. Additionally, agents from the US Treasury Department were actively scrutinizing Manafort's affairs. The FBI, I was told, visited Ukraine in search of clues.

Manafort's activities in Eastern Europe extended well beyond conventional campaign politics. He had lobbied on behalf of Yanukovych in Washington. According to Nayyem, this was an extensive operation to look after Yanukovych's interests in the United States. It encompassed visas—for the president and his team—and arranging top-level meetings. It included business deals.

According to leaked emails, Manafort and Gates ran an undercover US lobbying operation between 2012 and 2014. Its goal was to attract positive coverage for Yanukovych in the *New York Times*, the *Wall Street Journal*, and so on. At this point European leaders were calling on Ukraine's president to free Tymoshenko. The campaign sought to undermine US sympathy for her.

Gates enlisted two Washington lobbying firms to help— Mercury and the Podesta Group. They received around $2.2 million for their efforts, which Gates personally directed. The money was routed via a Yanukovych-linked "foundation." There was a compelling case that Manafort should have registered at this point as a foreign agent since he was lobbying on behalf of a foreign government. He didn't do so.

Meanwhile, by 2017 Manafort's previous statements regarding the black ledger were coming apart. The Associated Press published financial records that confirmed at least $1.2 million listed in the ledger next to Manafort's name had been received by his consulting firm in the United States. The payments— made in 2007 and 2009—were for $455,249 and $750,000. They were real.

Previously Manafort had dismissed the ledger as a fabrication. Now, in the face of incontrovertible evidence, he was saying something different. He told the AP that the transactions were for "legitimate payments for political consulting work. . . . I invoiced my clients and they paid via wire transfer, which I received through a US bank." His clients had specified the method of payment, he said.

This method was odd. Rather than paying him directly, the "clients" had used an exotic offshore route. It was difficult to trace. The $750,000 had first gone to Central America and to a company registered in Belize, Neocom Systems Ltd. From there it had travelled to Manafort's account at a branch of Wachovia National Bank in Alexandria, Virginia. The other payment went via another Belize shell firm.

Like his oligarchic clients, Manafort was a prolific user of shell companies. The AP reported that another $1 million went from a mysterious firm to a Manafort-linked company. The October 2009 payment was made via the Bank of Cyprus. The next day the cash was split into two chunks of approximately $500,000. It was then disbursed into other accounts with no obvious owner. Cyprus is well known as a centre for money laundering and as a destination for dubious Russian wealth.

There's nothing illegal about using offshore entities and Manafort rejects any charge of wrongdoing. Nonetheless, the pattern of his financial dealings is an eyebrow-raising one—encompassing tax havens, shell firms, and big transactions made in cash. The lobbyist used multiple bank accounts, according to court papers. The US Treasury Department's Financial Crimes Enforcement Network was investigating, sources in Cyprus told AP.

There were further puzzling transactions featuring New York real estate.

Between 2006 and 2013, Manafort bought three properties in New York City—his Trump Tower apartment; a brownstone in Brooklyn; and a place in SoHo. He purchased all three using shell companies, paying the full amount in cash. Next, he re-registered the properties in his name. Then he took out large mortgages against their value. Three days before Trump's inauguration, Manafort borrowed $7 million against his Union Street Brooklyn home, bought four years earlier for $3 million.

Manafort insists that these were ordinary business transactions, done in a transparent manner, and with his identity fully disclosed.

Others, however, allege in court papers that Manafort used real estate transactions to launder money for his Ukrainian and Russian oligarch friends.

In 2011 Tymoshenko sued Manafort in the district court of New York. Her lengthy writ claimed that Manafort "played a key role in [a] conspiracy and racketeering enterprise." The alleged scheme saw money "skimmed off" from natural gas transactions in Ukraine. Part of it was then laundered "through a labyrinth of New York-based shell companies and bank accounts." The cash was "funneled back" to Europe and used to bribe corrupt Ukrainian officials, Tymoshenko alleged.

In particular, she pointed the finger at Dmytro Firtash, Yanukovych's wealthy supporter. Firtash was the public face of RosUkrEnergo, the intermediary company that imported gas from Russia. Tymoshenko's writ alleged that the company was a mechanism for massive corruption. Its real owner, she claimed, was Semion Mogilevich, the Ukrainian-Russian mobster wanted by the FBI, who was believed to be hiding in Moscow.

Firtash did invest money in Manafort's real estate deals. One Manafort scheme was to buy the site of the demolished Drake Hotel in Manhattan and redevelop it at a cost of almost $900 million. Firtash transferred at least $25 million to the project. Tymoshenko alleged that the plan was never serious, with the cash merely sent to the United States for the purposes of money laundering.

Firtash denied this, too. A federal judge threw out Tymoshenko's lawsuit on the grounds that the allegations were outside US jurisdiction.

For Firtash there were more serious problems. In February 2017 the appeals court in Vienna ruled that he should be extradited to the United States to face bribery charges. Manafort's one-time business partner was also wanted in Spain, to answer accusations of money laundering.

Collusion, possible treachery, tax havens, offshore shell companies, and a shifting trail of cash stretching from Eastern Europe via Cyprus to the heart of Manhattan—this was a difficult story that would take some unravelling. One could sympathize with the FBI agents charged with the job of making sense of all this. It was going to take time. Their investigation was unlikely to be quick.

There was one consoling thought: that FBI director, James Comey, was only four years into a ten-year term. This extended period in office was a deliberate feature of the US system. It was designed to place the agency's chief above politics and partisanship. No one would want to meddle with that. What mattered here was the law and the slow, steady, and impartial pursuit of justice, even if the trail led all the way to the White House.

7

Tuesday Night Massacre

Spring–Summer 2017
Washington

A nut job.
—DONALD TRUMP on James Comey,
speaking to Russian foreign minister Sergei Lavrov
and Sergey Kislyak

The scandal that engulfed Washington in the spring of 2017 took place in a remarkably compact area. It had begun at the Democratic National Committee headquarters at 430 South Capitol Street. When I walked by, the signs on the DNC's perimeter fence looked—given everything that had happened—mordantly superfluous. They said: "Beware, you are under video surveillance."

The intruders who had bust into the building were incorporeal. They hadn't jumped the wall or broken a window. Instead, the Russian hackers had entered electronically, like an unstoppable army of ghosts. They had grabbed what they wanted and exited—not that they were inside. The *New York Times* ran a memorable photo from inside the building. It showed a computer server next to an old filing cabinet, broken into in 1972 as part of the Watergate burglary.

I found the DNC office locked up and deserted. It was a Sunday. I sat outside in the spring sunshine and scrawled a few notes. The building looked modernist, with a curvilinear design. There was a Stars and Stripes in one window; on the pavement daffodils. Cars droned on a flyover; in the middle distance a factory belched grey smoke—all was urban normality.

Two blocks away, along a shaded road of handsome brick houses and front gardens decked out with pansies, was another building. The road climbed upwards. This was the Republican National Committee at 310 First Street. Outside pink cherry trees blossomed. If you believed US intelligence, the ghosts had got in here, too. The RNC's emails hadn't been released but sat on a server somewhere in Moscow.

A few hundred yards north was Capitol Hill. Here was the US Congress. By this point Congress was home to an inquisitorial process—or, to be more accurate, processes. They involved the House and Senate intelligence committees, the Senate's judiciary committee, and the House's oversight and government reform committee. Four committees, in all.

Their broad subject was what Twitter had taken to calling #Russiagate or #Kremlingate. These names hadn't quite stuck, but the political scandal was real, and getting bigger.

Another investigation was going on nearby. A diagonal walk from Capitol Hill led to Pennsylvania Avenue and the J. Edgar Hoover building, the headquarters of the FBI. From the outside the building looked impermeable, its secrets safe. Trump, however, had changed that. The concrete 1970s complex—unlovely, lumpish, and softened only by a line of trees—was now one of the most porous places in Washington, a palace of leaks.

Almost next door was DC's former post office and clock tower. In autumn 2016 Trump reopened it as a luxury hotel, just before he became forty-fifth president. It was raining when I got there. I went inside to dry off. A giant US flag hung in a cavernous atrium. There were security guards with earpieces; above the bar TV sets were tuned to Fox and CNN. Families were having lunch. The women and their daughters wore Alice bands; the men wore golfing sweaters.

Trump had had dinner there a few weeks earlier, in late February. One of his guests—added at the last minute—was Nigel Farage. Farage was the grinning architect of Britain's Brexit and the public face of the anti-immigration UK Independence Party. And a Trump cheerleader. Other guests included Ivanka, Jared, and Florida governor Rick Scott. (Back in London, ten days later, Farage dropped in to see Julian Assange at the Ecuadorian embassy.)

Trump's actual office, the White House, was close by. In the surrounding streets—*Mother Jones* in F Street, the *Guardian* in Farragut Square—investigative journalists were hard at work. Some research happened here, some out of office. Later that evening I met someone in the Tabard Inn, an idiosyncratic English country house-style bar and hotel on N Street. Here reporters and bureaucrats got together over pale ale. Information—Washington's currency of choice—flowed in all directions.

In the lead-up to the US election, the intelligence community hadn't taken Trump terribly seriously. They had—according to one source I spoke to—viewed him as quirky and entertaining. There was a widespread assumption that he wouldn't win. Now, with Trump in the Oval Office, there was a new, unsettled mood. "There is a very high level of anxiety inside the tent. It stretches across all agencies. It concerns who Trump is and what he's up to," the source said. "And his entourage."

Previously, the FBI's 35,000-odd employees tended to avoid politics. They packed their sandwiches each day and went to work—field agents, intelligence analysts, support staff. A large majority were Republicans. (Indeed, the FBI's New York field office hated Clinton with a "white hot passion," I was told.) Trump's apparent connections with Moscow meant that politics was now unavoidable.

The situation in which the agents found themselves was confounding and unprecedented.

The question being asked inside the FBI was a troubling one: Was the president of the United States a patriot? Increasingly, the answer was no. "Trump's priority is to take care of his personal interests. These may not align with the interests of the country," the source said, adding: "Russia is a point of great sensitivity."

The source continued: "Most [intelligence community] people haven't seen a president like that. They frequently have ones they disagree with on policy. They don't fundamentally question whether they are patriots."

The man who had to steer the agency through this period of turmoil was James B. Comey, FBI chief since September 2013. Comey was, by inclination, a Republican. He had donated to the presidential campaigns of John McCain in 2008 and Mitt Romney in 2012. Comey was also an accomplished lawyer, a former terrorism prosecutor, and a former deputy attorney general.

It was in this last role that Comey had faced down George W. Bush, in one of the most extraordinary moments of Bush's presidency. Bush and his deputy, Dick Cheney, had sought the Department of Justice's approval for their top-secret programme of domestic surveillance: spying on Americans. They had asked attorney general John Ashcroft to renew it. He had refused. Ashcroft was in the hospital and dangerously ill.

A delegation from the White House went to Ashcroft's hospital bedside to persuade him to change his mind. Comey got there first. Ashcroft held firm. The White House was furious. When Bush reauthorized the programme anyway, Comey wrote a letter of resignation. He quoted what he'd said at his confirmation hearing, when asked what he would do if faced with an "apocalyptic situation." (That meant a course of action Comey believed to be "fundamentally wrong.")

Comey told Bush: "I don't care about politics. I don't care about expediency. I don't care about friendship. I care about doing the right thing."

Next Comey met Bush in the Oval Office and informed him that the then FBI director Bob Mueller was quitting, too. Bush was taken aback. He called in Mueller. Comey and Mueller left the White House together, sitting for a while and chatting in the back seat of their bulletproof vehicle. Bush climbed down. He amended some aspects of the surveillance programme.

This 2004 drama made Comey's reputation. It established him as someone willing to stand up to the executive branch—ready to defy even the president, if necessary. It showed that he could play the Washington game at the highest level. And that his loyalty was to the Justice Department and what he called "this great group behind me," rather than to any individual politician. The episode turned him into a household name.

Comey's method was interesting, too. His daily routines, as *The New Yorker* noted, were those of a clerk. Immediately after his meeting with Bush, Comey switched on his BlackBerry and sent an email of what had happened to six Justice Department colleagues. He left a contemporaneous trail. He understood the importance of creating a record. This made it harder for others to lie in future about contentious past events. It was done, too, one suspects, with an eye to history.

Now Comey was facing another apocalyptic situation. This was, if anything, trickier than the bedside dash of 2004. As a candidate, Trump had praised Comey's decision to reopen the Clinton email investigation. In October 2016 Trump told supporters at a campaign stop in Michigan that it had taken "a lot of guts. . . . I really disagreed with him [Comey]. I was not his fan. I tell you what, what he did, he brought back his reputation," Trump said.

Two days after he took office, Trump saw Comey at a White House law enforcement reception. "Oh, there's James! He's become even more famous than me," Trump said, as Comey advanced sheepishly across the Blue Room towards the president. Trump then attempted a man-hug. And whispered in Comey's ear: "I really look forward to working with you."

It was an awkward encounter: at six foot eight, the FBI director towered over his executive boss. (Comey later revealed that he'd tried to avoid Trump by blending into the curtains.)

In the meantime, the House Intelligence Committee summoned Comey and NSA chief Mike Rogers to give evidence. It was March 20, 2017. The two were star witnesses. Their testimony was keenly awaited. The committee was investigating Russian interference in the 2016 election. Inevitably, though, the hearing would want to examine this: had Trump or his entourage colluded with the Russians?

In his opening remarks, Adam Schiff, the ranking Democrat, summarized what was known and what wasn't. Moscow, he said, had "blatantly interfered in our affairs." It had done so "upon the direct instructions of its autocratic ruler Vladimir Putin." Putin's goal was to help Trump. Schiff said: "We will never know whether the Russian intervention was determinative in such a close election."

He continued:

> We do not yet know whether the Russians had the help of US citizens, including people associated with the Trump campaign. Many of Trump's campaign personnel, including the president himself, have ties to Russia and Russian interests. This is of course no crime. On the other hand, if the Trump campaign or anyone associated with it aided and abetted the Russians, it would not only be a serious crime, it would also represent one of the most shocking betrayals of our democracy in history.

Schiff cited the Steele dossier. He said that Steele "is reportedly held in high regard by US intelligence." There was an awful lot of circumstantial evidence, he said—Page and his trips to Moscow; Manafort and the junking of armed support for Ukraine; Flynn's multiple conversations with Ambassador Kislyak. It was possible, Schiff said, that all these events were unconnected.

It was equally possible that they were "not coincidental." And: "That the Russians used the same techniques to corrupt US persons that they have employed in Europe and elsewhere. We owe it to the country to find out," Schiff said.

Up to this point, there had been no official confirmation of an FBI collusion investigation. Typically, the FBI would say nothing about an ongoing operation, especially if it involved classified and sensitive intelligence.

Now, though, Comey took the unusual step of making a public statement:

> I have been authorized by the Department of Justice to con-firm that the FBI, as part of our counterintelligence mission, is investigating the Russian government's efforts to interfere in the 2016 presidential election and that includes investi-gating the nature of any links between individuals associated with the Trump campaign and the Russian government and whether there was any coordination between the campaign and Russia's efforts.

As with any counter-intelligence investigation, it would include "an assessment of whether any crimes were commit-ted," Comey said.

It had been assumed that this was the case. And yet confir-mation made the FBI's counter-espionage probe an empirical fact, an un-fake event. The news—now flashing on TV screens, and punched out via text alerts—was a stunning rebuke of Trump, who had previously dismissed collusion claims as a ludicrous plot-cum-excuse by bad loser Democrats.

There were fresh details. The investigation, Comey said, began back in late July 2016, after the first DNC leak. It had been going for eight months. This was "a fairly short period of time." The FBI's work was "very complex." There was no timetable for when it might conclude, Comey said.

The FBI director then delivered further unwelcome news

to the White House. Trump had asserted that he was the victim of wiretapping—ordered by President Obama at Trump Tower in Manhattan and conducted by Britain's GCHQ.

This claim had originated in . . . Moscow. A discredited former CIA analyst, Larry Johnson, floated the conspiracy theory on RT. Johnson was a source for Andrew Napolitano, Fox News's legal analyst. Napolitano went on the *Fox & Friends* show, saying that Obama had used the Brits to circumvent US intelligence. From here, the zombie claim reached Trump. Sean Spicer, the president's press secretary, cited the Fox report to back up the president's claim.

The story, of course, was rubbish. It was an example of how a propaganda trope dreamed up by state TV in Moscow entered the global media echo chamber, where pro-Trump media and the alt-right seized on it. The lie then reached its ultimate destination: the president's brain. It had become, by a process of RT–Fox alchemy, an alternative "fact."

GCHQ was appalled. The eavesdropping agency was known for its silence. It normally refused to comment on intelligence matters. On this occasion GCHQ responded with a rare fuck-off. It called Napolitano's claims "nonsense." A spokesperson said of them: "They are utterly ridiculous and should be ignored."

In the hearing, Schiff read aloud one of Trump's tweets on the matter:

Terrible! Just found out that Obama had my "wires tapped" in Trump Tower just before the victory. Nothing found. This is McCarthyism!

Schiff asked Comey if this was true. The FBI director gave a deadpan reply: the bureau had no information that supported those tweets. The Justice Department shared this assessment, he said.

Then:

SCHIFF: Were you engaged in McCarthyism, Director Comey?
COMEY: I try very hard not to engage in any isms of any kind, including—including McCarthyism.

It was a smart reply, and one that brought laughter to the committee room. Trump, however, watching the proceedings on TV, may have seen this as a semi-humiliation. And an act of disloyalty. Sensing the exchange was going well, Schiff read out another Trump tweet:

How low has president Obama gone to tapp [sic] my phones during the very sacred election process. This is Nixon–Watergate. Bad (or sick) guy!

Comey admitted he was a kid during Watergate and had studied it quite a bit at school. Asked if Trump's wild and inaccurate claims damaged relations with British intelligence, the United States' closest partner, Rogers admitted: "I think it clearly frustrates a key ally of ours."

What was at stake here was enormously serious—a break-in not by domestic burglars but by a foreign power using cyber means. The committee was bipartisan. Its leading Republicans, however, seemed less interested in examining collusion. Their focus, at this and other hearings, was on leaks. Who was leaking? How were reporters getting their information? What was the FBI doing about identifying the leakers and chucking them in jail?

This strategy—led here by Republicans Devin Nunes and Trey Gowdy—was diversionary. It looked like an attempt to deflect attention from the president's links with Russia and focus on the process instead. Gowdy was incensed by the sheer number of current and former US officials talking to journalists—nine in one *Washington Post* article!

Back in the 1970s, Nixon and his allies were similarly incensed by leaks emerging in the first stages of the Watergate investigation. The leaker—the FBI's Mark Felt—had disclosed information because he feared that attempts were being made to shut down the FBI's inquiries and to maintain a cover-up. Was this happening again?

Comey and Rogers agreed that leaking was a "serious crime." Both said under oath that they had never leaked restricted stuff. Leaks weren't exactly new, though, Comey pointed out: "I read over the weekend something from George Washington and Abraham Lincoln complaining about them. But I do think in the last six weeks, couple of months, there's been at least— apparently a lot of conversation about classified matters that's ending up in the media."

The two agency chiefs gave an accomplished performance. Comey was fluent, good-natured, likeable. Nothing floored him. His answers amounted to: I am a man of integrity. Comey and Rogers, it seemed, enjoyed a healthy rapport. The FBI director was equally at ease in two worlds—the one of his own hermetic institution and the high-stakes public interrogation taking place before Congress.

It was left to Democrat Joe Heck to offer the big picture. He described the evidence as "terribly disturbing"—"that this was, in part, an inside job from US persons." There were "willing American accomplices or terribly naïve ones, or probably both—who helped the Russians attack our country and our democracy."

Heck asked Comey why we should care if Russia used US persons to destabilize "our democracy."

Comey replied: "Well, like Admiral Rogers, I truly believe we are a shining city on a hill, to quote a great American. And one of the things we radiate to the world is the importance of our wonderful, often messy, but free and fair democratic system and the elections that undergird it."

Trump continued to brood on the FBI's probe. That the matter continued to vex him was evident from his bitter public commentary. In April he told the *Washington Examiner* that the Russia story was a "faux story," a hoax. Trump told Fox the same thing. The story was "phony," he said, put about by his "embarrassed" political foes.

According to *Politico*, quoting two advisers, Trump was deeply frustrated about his inability to shut down the Russia story. He repeatedly demanded of aides why the investigation wouldn't go away. He told them to speak out for him. Trump would even sometimes scream at television clips about the probe, an adviser said.

Phony wasn't how Clinton saw it. In one of her first post-defeat appearances, and speaking in New York, Clinton said she took "absolute personal responsibility" for her failure. Even so there were several factors that had made a difference, she said, including misogyny and "false equivalency" in the news media.

Two things above all had cost her the presidency, she said—the release of John Podesta's hacked correspondence "an hour or two after the Hollywood Access tape was made public" and

Comey's October 28 letter saying he'd reopened the investigation into her private email server. Putin is not "a member of my fan club," she said, calling Russian interference "unprecedented." "There was a lot of funny business going on," she added. This was undoubtedly true.

Meanwhile, Comey was preparing to testify again, this time before the Senate Judiciary Committee. It was May 3 and an annual oversight hearing—and one that would inevitably be dominated by further questions over Russia.

Comey's replies were those of a person enjoying his work. And of someone keen to continue. He began by quoting what John Adams, the country's second president and a founding father, had written to Thomas Jefferson: power always thinks it has a great soul. The way to guard against abuse was accountability—"having people ask hard questions," he told the committee.

"I know you look at me like I'm crazy for saying this about this job. I love this work. I love this job. And I love it because of the mission and the people I get to work with," he said.

The hearing moved along now-familiar lines—with Republicans keen to chase down who was leaking. Comey was relaxed and authoritative. He batted away some questions by saying he couldn't give an answer in an unclassified setting; he affirmed others with "sure." A memorable exchange came when Comey was asked, by Senator Dianne Feinstein and others, why he had publicized his Clinton investigation.

Comey was forthcoming—if not entirely convincing. He claimed he'd faced an invidious choice between keeping silent (and facing accusations of a cover-up) or telling Congress. "It makes me mildly nauseous to think that we might have had some impact on the election. But honestly, it wouldn't change the decision," he said. He insisted he'd treated the Clinton and Trump investigations the same way. He had revealed both only months after they'd begun.

On Trump–Russia, "we follow the evidence wherever it takes us," Comey promised. But what if it led to the president? Comey said he had briefed the chair and ranking members of the committee as to which individuals were currently in the spotlight. "That's as far as we're going to go," he told Democrat Richard Blumenthal.

BLUMENTHAL: So, potentially, the president of the United States could be a target of your ongoing investigation into the Trump campaign's involvement with Russian interference in our election, correct?

COMEY: I just worry—I don't want to answer that—that—that seems to be unfair speculation. We will follow the evidence. We'll try to find as much as we can and we'll follow the evidence wherever it leads.

The Republican chair, Chuck Grassley, tossed in a couple of hostile questions on Steele: Did the FBI interact with him or pay him? Comey said he couldn't answer "in this forum."

Steele watched the hearing on TV from his home in Surrey. He had been back at work for some weeks. By arrangement, the Press Association had photographed and videoed him, now minus the beard, on the front steps of Orbis. Steele had given a quote of Politburo-like blandness: "I'd like to say a warm thank-you to everyone who sent me kind messages and support over the last few weeks." He was now focusing on the "broader interests" of his company, he said.

Comey's newest Senate hearing was a moment of worry for

Steele: What might the director say? "The best-case scenario would have been for Comey to confirm the dossier. The worst for him to say something disobliging," one friend told me. In the end, the outcome was "acceptably neutral," the friend added.

The week beginning Monday, May 8, was the end of spring. Summer was coming. The days were getting lighter, brighter, and warmer. The mood in Washington was febrile. The city was spinning—the pace and sheer destructive tempo of the Trump presidency was exhausting for everyone. It was as if a thundercloud was about to burst.

The FBI's investigation was gathering pace. In Alexandria, Virginia, the US Attorney's Office was busy. The first subpoenas were sent out to associates of Michael Flynn, according to CNN. A grand jury had been convened. A second federal grand jury, I was told, had been secretly assembled in the Southern District of New York in connection with Paul Manafort.

For Comey, it was another busy week. That Thursday he was due to return to Capitol Hill. Another public session was scheduled before the Senate Intelligence Committee. In the meantime, he took a plane to Florida—a secure one, fitted out with communications equipment that gave him instant access to the president. His next stop was California and a diversity forum for FBI agents.

Soon after arriving in Los Angeles, and before he had made his speech to FBI employees, Comey caught sight of a TV screen. There was urgent breaking news. It reported that President Trump had fired the director of the FBI. That was him. Comey assumed this was some kind of prank—an in-house joke arranged by his security detail or others on his personal staff.

It wasn't. The news was real. Comey was out—fired and terminated in brutal fashion. The president might have broken the news in person. Instead, he had chosen to strike while Comey was away from station. The director was unable to clear his desk, say farewell to his staff, or take away personal documents.

Comey stepped into a side room at the bureau's LA office. There he confirmed he had indeed been sacked. At this point the White House hadn't informed him of anything directly. Soon afterwards, Trump's long-time personal bodyguard, Keith Schiller—an ex-cop and now part of White House security—hand-delivered a letter from the president to FBI headquarters. It came in a manila envelope.

The date was Tuesday, May 9. The letter—on White House paper—began "Dear Director Comey." It said Attorney General Jeff Sessions and Deputy Attorney General Rod Rosenstein had recommended his dismissal. Trump had accepted their recommendation, and "you are hereby terminated and removed from office, effective immediately."

The next paragraph was strikingly odd. It began with a subclause. It said: "While I greatly appreciate you informing me, on three separate occasions, that I am not under investigation, I nevertheless concur with the judgment of the Department of Justice that you are not able to effectively lead the Bureau."

It went on: "It is essential that we find new leadership for the FBI that restores public trust and confidence in its vital law enforcement mission. I wish you the best of luck in your future endeavors." Then Trump's hedgehog-like signature.

The letter revealed what was foremost in Trump's mind: Russia. The investigation it referred to was Comey's expanding probe into Kremlin collusion. According to Trump, Comey had exonerated him three times. Or at least that was what the president claimed.

The attached letters from Sessions and Rosenstein, however, said something completely different: that Trump had fired Comey because of his mishandling of the Clinton email affair. Sessions's letter was vague. It said that the FBI chief had strayed from the Justice Department's "rules and principles." Sessions said that as attorney general he was committed to a "high level of . . . integrity."

This last claim was somewhat hilarious. At his January confirmation hearing Sessions was asked if he'd been in contact with anyone from the Russian government during the 2016 campaign. Sessions's answer under oath: no. It later emerged that he had met Kislyak at least twice, in the summer and early autumn of 2016; like Flynn and Page he had been afflicted with sudden memory loss over his dealings with the ambassador. Sessions survived Democratic calls to resign for lying but was forced to recuse himself from all things Russia.

It was left to Rosenstein to explain. His letter said Comey had been wrong to announce in July 2016 that he was closing down the Clinton investigation—in effect, usurping the role of the attorney general. Comey was also wrong to tell the media he was reopening the probe—a "textbook example of what federal prosecutors and agents are taught not to do." Since Comey wouldn't admit his mistakes, he couldn't be expected to fix them, Rosenstein wrote.

Officially, then, Trump fired Comey because he disapproved of the way Clinton had been treated. This explanation was so lacking in credibility as to be entirely, woefully ridiculous. Why had the president waited until May 9 to act? Where had his sudden compassion for Clinton come from? Wasn't it more likely that the president had already decided to fire Comey and had merely asked Sessions to come up with a legal excuse?

According to the *New York Times* and the *Washington Post*, Trump had spent the previous weekend stewing at his New Jersey golf resort. He had watched the Sunday talk shows and concluded that there was "something wrong" with Comey. Trump had believed for a while he had to get rid of the FBI director and was "strongly inclined" to do so after Comey's latest appearance before Congress.

What had especially irked Trump was Comey's statement that he felt "mildly nauseous" at the possibility that his late intervention in the email affair might have cost Clinton the election. Trump seemed tortured by the idea that he wasn't the legitimate president. This insecurity had clearly gnawed at him. Here, as he saw it, was Comey questioning his role in history, diminishing his victory, pandering to his enemies.

Trump reportedly shared his thoughts with a small group of advisers—Pence, McGahn, Kushner, Schiller. They agreed that Comey should be made to walk. Bannon, the chief strategist, argued it might be better to delay and was concerned about backlash. Overall, the White House seemed sincerely to hold the view that Democrats would welcome Comey's humiliation, having complained about him previously.

Trump's decision was reckless and impulsive. The president could, of course, do this: the move was constitutional. It would turn out to be spectacularly self-defeating.

It flowed from a profound suspicion within the administration towards Washington and its federal agencies. As Mike Hayden put it to me, the Trump team had "this incredible distrust, almost contempt," for the outgoing government they were replacing. They believed that the intelligence community served Obama. This was wrong; it didn't. But the perception stuck. The intelligence family was "fairly indifferent to who the president is," Hayden said, adding: "We got off on a very bad foot." And "Trump the human being" made everything worse.

For the president, the optics of Comey's firing would prove disastrous. Those who had been sceptical about claims of collusion were now beginning to wonder if there was perhaps something there after all. The public articulation of why he'd been sacked didn't pass the smell test.

Meanwhile, FBI employees were an unhappy and bewildered lot. Former agent Bobby Chacon called it "a punch in the stomach to agents." It was, he told the *Guardian*, a disrespectful and outrageous act that had besmirched the FBI's reputation. Others predicted it would have a "chilling effect" on the ongoing Russia investigation. One said: "The rule of law has to prevail, not the rule of whim."

The night of May 9, press secretary Sean Spicer and his colleague, Kellyanne Conway, emerged from the West Wing. Spicer gave an interview to Fox in one of the tents erected along the White House driveway. About a dozen reporters lurked nearby, including the *Guardian*'s David Smith. They were puzzled when Spicer disappeared for a few minutes. Eventually he emerged from a pathway lined with bushes. He agreed to take some questions but asked for TV cameras to be turned off.

The *Post* reported this strange event, which ended with Spicer giving an informal press conference in deep gloom. The White House objected to the *Post*'s characterization of Spicer's location. The paper—whose Democracy Dies in Darkness motto had never seemed more appropriate—agreed to make a correction. It said that Spicer hadn't hid *in* the bushes but *among* them. Normally corrections are a matter of mild embarrassment. This one had been done with glee.

According to Spicer's official version, Rosenstein had reached his decision independently, with Trump acting swiftly upon it. There was no cover-up. Conway told reporters: "This has nothing to do with Russia," and said Comey had simply lost the confidence of everybody—his subordinates, Congress, and of course the president. Spicer's deputy, Sarah Huckabee Sanders, said of the Russia story: "Frankly, it's kind of getting absurd. There's nothing there."

Even by the dysfunctional standards of the White House, these events were surreal. As the comedian John Oliver pointed out, what was happening at dazzling speed resembled not so much Watergate 2 as Stupid Watergate. It was a pastiche version of the original 1970s scandal, replayed by clownish dimwits and brainless plotters. Stupid Watergate was happening more quickly than the original version, even if the ending—impeachment?—seemed uncertain.

Those who lived through the Nixon era likened Comey's firing to the Saturday Night Massacre. This was when Nixon called on his senior Justice Department officials to sack Archibald Cox, the special prosecutor investigating the Watergate burglary. Two officials—Attorney General Elliot Richardson and his deputy, William Ruckelshaus—refused. They resigned. The next one down, Solicitor General Robert Bork, agreed to the president's wishes.

This time round there was no pushback. Sessions and Rosenstein caved in to Trump's demands. Since Comey was fired on a Tuesday, the episode became known as the Tuesday Night Massacre. Rosenstein's behaviour, in particular, disappointed many. Philip Allen Lacovara, the senior surviving member of the Watergate special prosecutor's office, asked Rosenstein to explain why he'd been so malleable. The deputy attorney general had put his "generally applauded credibility into a blind trust," Lacovara wrote.

Trump had been in power for a little over one hundred days. During that period his less attractive qualities had been on painful display. One of these was Trump's astonishing lack of loyalty to his own subordinates and team. He was quite prepared to throw his own White House staff under the bus, to trash their reputations and burn their political capital if it suited his temporary need or impulse. Meanwhile, he demanded absolute fealty from them.

With Washington reeling from the Comey affair, Trump gave an interview to NBC News's Lester Holt. This was the moment, surely, for the president to say that he had nothing to do with Comey's dismissal. And that he had merely heeded the advice of the Department of Justice, a slave to protocol.

Instead, he said this:

"What I did is I was going to fire Comey. My decision. It was not . . ."

HOLT: You had made the decision before they came into your office.

TRUMP: I—I was going to fire Comey. I—there's no good time to do it, by the way.

HOLT: Because in your letter, you said . . .

TRUMP: They—they were . . .

HOLT: . . . I—I accepted—accepted their recommendations.

TRUMP: Yeah, well, they also . . .

HOLT: So, you had already made the decision.

TRUMP: Oh, I was going to fire regardless of recommendation.

Then:

"And in fact, when I decided to just do it, I said to myself—I said, 'You know, this Russia thing with Trump and Russia is a made-up story. It's an excuse by the Democrats for having lost an election they should have won.'"

Trump was confirming he'd decided to sack Comey before he reached out to his legal officials. Oh, and "the Russia thing" was foremost in his mind at the time. Trump said he'd asked Comey if he personally was under FBI investigation. The director's answer was no, he wasn't, Trump said.

If the president was now telling the truth about Comey's dismissal, that meant his press team had spent the previous forty-eight hours misleading the American public. Of Comey, Trump said: "He's a showboat, he's a grandstander, the FBI has been in turmoil. You know that, I know that. Everybody knows that."

It was a stunning admission, made more incredible by Trump's next set of White House guests. The day after Comey was out, two Russian visitors made their way to the Oval Office. One had leathery features, a rasping voice (a lot of cigarettes here), and a sarcastic manner, deployed over a period of many years in the service of the Russian state. The other was a slightly jollier-looking figure—a rotund person with a pale face, double chin, and white hair. These were Moscow's two top diplomats: Foreign Minister Sergei Lavrov and Ambassador Sergey Kislyak.

Obama administration officials who had dealt with Kislyak

viewed him with grudging respect. Times, however, had changed. Kislyak was the man whose connections with Trump's team were not just embarrassing but a subject of criminal inquiry. Flynn, Sessions, Carter Page, Kushner—all had met him and all had concealed these meetings afterwards. Now the ambassador was talking to the president.

No American press were allowed in to record the meeting. Lavrov, however, had brought a photographer who worked for the state news agency, Tass. In Soviet times, journalists for Tass were typically KGB or GRU officers. The photographer took equipment into the Oval Office. What, exactly? The photos show Trump warmly shaking Lavrov's hand. Another reveals him patting Lavrov on the shoulder. Trump and Kislyak posed together. The president grins.

Trump seemed happy, relaxed, among friends. His manner here was in contrast to the one he had deployed with traditional US allies—a glum, handshakeless encounter in March with Germany's Angela Merkel, for example.

The conversation with the Russians, leaked to the *New York Times* a few days later, was also comradely. And astonishing. "I just fired the head of the FBI. He was crazy, a real nut job," Trump told Lavrov. "I faced great pressure because of Russia. That's taken off," Trump said, adding: "I'm not under investigation." Trump joked that he was the only person who hadn't met Kislyak. He said the Russia story was fake and added that Americans wanted his government to have a healthy relationship with Moscow.

There were foreign policy discussions. Trump reportedly said that he wasn't personally concerned by the fighting in Ukraine, but asked if the Russians might help solve the conflict there. There was talk of Syria.

It was at this point that Trump revealed details of a highly classified intelligence briefing he had been given. It concerned an Islamic State plot. The intelligence wasn't actually Trump's to share. It had come from Israel, the United States' closest ally in the region. Trump told the Russians the name of the Syrian city from where the information came. Seemingly, the Israelis had a double agent deep inside ISIS. Though there was no confirmation, the agent appeared to have supplied details of an attempt to smuggle explosives onto a plane using laptop computers.

Now the Russians knew about this source. Probably Bashar al-Assad—Syria's president and Russia's close ally—would soon learn of it, too. It was an astonishing breach. One former intelligence officer said that it wasn't sharing the information per se that was significant; it was the relaying of material obtained from a partner. "You don't even reveal the colour of a carpet without consulting the ally first," the officer told me. Another called it "fucking unbelievable." Alarmed White House officials notified the CIA.

Lt. Gen. H. R. McMaster, Flynn's replacement as national security adviser, defended the president's blunder. McMaster said no secrets were given away. Trump, meanwhile, tweeted that as president he had "an absolute right" to share classified material on terrorism with anybody he liked. Russia agreed. The story was the latest manifestation of fake news, the foreign ministry said.

Trump had called for Clinton to be jailed for her use of a private email server. Now he had leaked "code word" information to the Russians, a classification beyond top secret. Since he'd done it, that was okay—or so Trump seemed to be suggesting. Even Republicans were dismayed by the president's lack of discipline.

There were two ways of explaining it. Neither was good. Either the conspiracy sketched out in the Steele dossier was true, or the president was an idiot—or, if not a complete idiot, at least someone unfamiliar with the ways of Washington and therefore unaware of what he was doing. These two explanations were not incompatible, but Paul Ryan, Speaker of the House and a Trump loyalist, chose to go with the second one. In the coming months, Ryan would argue that the president was new to the job, a well-meaning neophyte who couldn't be held accountable for his errant behaviour.

The Lavrov–Kislyak episode had an epilogue. After the meeting, the American media had been expecting to see Trump with his Russian guests. Instead, they found the president sitting next to a well-known ninety-three-year-old man—a shrunken individual, still alert, owlish, and with penetrating brown eyes. This was Dr Henry Kissinger. Kissinger was Nixon's secretary of state. His surprise presence seemed at first like a cosmic joke: one of the central figures from the Watergate era was literally back.

Kissinger was part of the United States' political and cultural fabric. John Ehrlichman—Nixon's counsel and assistant—served a year and a half in prison for his role in the Watergate conspiracy. His novel *The Company* is a fictional account of the period. In it, Kissinger appears as Carl Tessler. Ehrlichman describes Tessler as a "physical anomaly," with a large head, a broadening girth, and "small almost dainty" hands and feet. Tessler/Kissinger was a geopolitician. He had a "brilliant mind." He thought of himself as "a sort of universal Man of the Age in foreign affairs." Tessler kept himself under "rigid self-control," rarely revealing the "hidden man" beneath.

Traditionally, US presidents sought out Kissinger's advice.

Obama had notably failed to do so, something that clearly rankled with the doctor. Kissinger hadn't endorsed Trump. And yet here he was, back at the centre of events, with the world's most powerful man, and meeting the Russians as in Cold War times. Kissinger had described the Watergate scandal as a "domestic passion play." Now he sat next to another scandal-engulfed White House incumbent.

Reporters asked the president why he'd fired Director Comey.

"Because he wasn't doing a good job," Trump said to the cameras.

Kissinger, it appeared, was back in the Oval Office in the role of intermediary. He wasn't just a throwback to the 1970s. He was frequently in contact with the Kremlin. Kissinger had long-standing good relations with Russia's president and was treated as a VIP whenever he dropped into Moscow. This happened quite frequently, with Kissinger visiting in 2016. Like Trump, Kissinger had said favourable things about Putin. He had compared him to a character from Dostoevsky and said Putin possessed an "inward connection" to Russian history.

Additionally, Kissinger was a foreign policy realist. He believed—as did Putin and, seemingly, Trump as well—that deal-making rather than values should shape international relations. As the Russian opposition leader and former chess champion Garry Kasparov put it to me, Kissinger would like nothing better than to come out of retirement and broker a historic US–Russian concord. It would be his last service to diplomacy. The two states (together with, presumably, China) could divide the world between them into sovereign spheres. There could be a new Grand Bargain.

The "Russia thing," however, meant that rapprochement with Moscow was politically impossible. At least for now.

Meanwhile, for a president keen to dispel rumours of collaboration, the meeting was deeply unfortunate.

The *New York Times* put the photo of Trump and Lavrov on its front page. At the bottom of the photo taken inside the White House was a credit. It said: "Russian Foreign Ministry."

The day after his sacking Comey was at his home in Virginia. Photographers caught a glimpse of him in his driveway, wearing a white cap. It had been a bruising twenty-four hours. Comey's feelings at the time can only be guessed at—shock, righteous anger, a feeling that his collision with Trump was surely inevitable?

The situation, though, wasn't as grim as it seemed. The former FBI director had two things in his favour. One was his religious faith. The other was more tangible: a series of memos Comey had written setting down all his dealings with the president.

Certainly, his Christian belief was significant. In a profile, the *Guardian*'s Julian Borger described Comey as "a rare species in American politics, a public intellectual with a complicated personal history."

Comey had been born in Yonkers, New York, to an Irish Catholic and Democratic family. He had studied at the College of William and Mary in Virginia. There, Comey had turned away from his upbringing and embraced various kinds of evangelism. He wrote his thesis on how the evangelist teacher Jerry Falwell somehow embodied the teachings of Reinhold Niebuhr. Niebuhr was America's greatest mid-twentieth-century theologian. His work, *Moral Man and Immoral Society: A Study in*

Ethics and Politics, published in 1932, is a classic of Christian thinking.

Niebuhr's view of the world is pessimistic. He describes himself as a member of a "disillusioned generation" and writes from an age of war, totalitarianism, racial injustice, and economic depression. Individuals are capable of virtuous acts, he thinks, but groups and nations struggle to transcend their collective egoism. This makes social conflict inevitable.

Niebuhr is brutally honest about human failings. American contemporary culture is "still pretty firmly enmeshed in the illusions and sentimentalities of the Age of Reason," he writes. He doesn't see much room for goodness in politics. Instead, he identifies "greed, the will-to-power and other forms of self-assertion" at the level of group politics.

Comey's interest in Niebuhr remained constant, even as his church affiliation drifted from evangelicalism to Methodism. According to the magazine *Gizmodo*, Comey set up a personal Twitter account in Niebuhr's name. In party terms, Comey was of the political right and a movement Republican. Until Trump came along, this socially conservative faction dominated.

One imagines that Niebuhr wouldn't have been surprised by Trump or his unscrupulous brand of personal politics. (Instead, you can envisage the great religious intellectual saying: "I told you so.") The spectacle about to grip Washington in summer 2017 was certainly Niebuhrian. Here, after all, was an upright individual—a moral man—speaking truth to selfish power. Or in this case to a dishonest presidency.

Comey wasn't merely relying on providence or divine destiny to get him through his battle with the White House. He was relying on notes. These were his records typed up in the immediate aftermath of his interactions with Trump. There were nine of them—three face-to-face meetings and six telephone calls. They took place between January, when Trump was not yet president, and April. All these encounters were fraught, it would emerge.

Trump had underestimated Comey—by how much would soon become clear. The sacked FBI chief perfectly understood how Washington politics and bureaucracy interacted. The president didn't. Comey knew that DC was, as *The New Yorker* put it, a lawyer's town built on protocols and rules. His memos were an attempt to protect his own reputation and that of the FBI from subsequent smears. The goal was to proof his version of events from Trump's untruths.

"He [Comey] understands the system. He's played his cards perfectly at every turn," one seasoned Washington insider told me. The person added: "Trump has not got a clue. He has immense power as president. But he doesn't understand the operational issues and makes mistake after mistake after mistake."

Two days after Comey's firing, the *New York Times* published an account of a dinner Comey had with Trump on January 27. The venue was the White House. There were no other guests. According to the paper, the conversation began politely, with talk of the election and inauguration crowds. Then Trump turned to Comey and asked him, in effect, to pledge his loyalty. Comey declined, the report said.

The White House dismissed the story, with Trump telling NBC News the question of loyalty had never come up. The president's strategy must have confirmed what Comey had suspected: that Trump would simply lie about their conversations.

Trump followed this up with a threat and tweeted:

James Comey better hope there are no "tapes" of our conversations before he starts leaking to the press!

The tweet had the opposite effect to what Trump might have wished. As Comey would explain, a couple of days later he woke up in the middle of the night. There was now a distinct possibility that the White House had secretly bugged his conversation. This was good rather than bad: any tape would confirm his version. In the meantime, Comey needed to get out what had actually been said to the "public square," as he put it.

Comey turned to an old friend, Daniel Richman. Richman was a former federal prosecutor and a professor at Columbia University's law school. Richman had defended Comey when he'd come under fire in previous months—calling Comey's role at the FBI "apolitical and independent."

Comey instructed Richman: "Make sure this gets out." The professor contacted a reporter at the *New York Times*, Michael Schmidt. Richman offered details from another explosive Comey memo. It chronicled a meeting at the Oval Office on February 14, 2017. That was a day after Flynn had resigned for lying to Vice President Pence.

According to the memo, Trump had singled out Comey after the meeting. Trump then told him: "I hope you can see your way clear to letting this go, to letting Flynn go."

Trump added: "He [Flynn] is a good guy. I hope you can let this go."

There would be much future discussion of hope. Was this, as some Republican leaders suggested, an aspiration? Or was it a direct order from the commander in chief? Comey's reported reply to Trump was non-committal. Comey said: "I agree he [Flynn] is a good guy."

The FBI was investigating Flynn for various misdemeanours. None of them were trivial. They included alleged perjury committed by Flynn during his FD-302 interview. Comey was deeply concerned by Trump's comments. As Comey saw it, the president was asking him to shut down a criminal investigation. That amounted to obstruction of justice. It undermined the FBI's role as an independent investigative body.

What happened next was up to the Justice Department. When Sessions recused himself, it fell to the number two, Rosenstein, to respond to the *New York Times'* revelations. Democrats had been demanding that Rosenstein appoint a special counsel to oversee the Trump–Russia investigation. They argued that he—or she—would be independent of the White House and the Justice Department.

The answer from Republicans had been: there's no need. Now there was a shift, with some expressing misgivings at Comey's sacking. Rosenstein's dilemma was clear. If he agreed to a special counsel, this might redeem his reputation. But it would also attract the president's ire—and perhaps ultimately lead to Rosenstein's firing, too.

In an open letter to Rosenstein, the *New York Times* said that the deputy attorney general could safeguard democracy. He was uniquely placed to restore "Americans' confidence in their government. We sympathize; that's a lot of pressure," the editorial board said. It said that Trump had "exploited the integrity" Rosenstein had earned during three decades of public service, in the same careless way Trump liked to spend other people's money.

Rosenstein went for the "noble" and "heroic" *New York Times* option. He announced that it was "in the public interest" to appoint a special prosecutor. That didn't mean, he said, that he had determined a crime had taken place. Rosenstein signed his order without consulting Trump; it was left to White House counsel Don McGahn to carry the bad news to the Oval Office.

The president said he was innocent. According to several accounts, Trump was unusually non-combative. In a statement he again insisted there'd been no collusion between his campaign and "any foreign entity."

The episode illustrated Trump's capacity for self-sabotage. By firing Comey to "take the pressure off," he had made the crisis worse and hastened the appointment of a determined outside investigator. The new special counsel was Robert Mueller. Mueller had spent twelve years as FBI director under the Bush and Obama administrations, 2001 to 2013—the longest tenure of anyone in the job since J. Edgar Hoover. Comey had succeeded him. The two were allies.

Mueller had a tenacious reputation. Hayden—Mueller's former opposite at the NSA and CIA—described him to me as "a straight arrow. I'm trying to think of a good word for Bob. Formal, straight-laced, friendly, but governed by principle," Hayden said. Democrats and Republicans agreed. As did Comey, who would hail Mueller as "one of this country's great, great pros" and a "dogged, tough person."

Hayden predicted that Mueller would be scrupulously fair in performing his duties. He was sceptical Mueller would find Trump guilty of obstruction, the first article of impeachment drawn up against Nixon. "Which doesn't mean we don't have a really serious problem. I actually think the congressional investigations might be more important," Hayden suggested.

Thus far, Comey had got the better of Trump. He had out-intrigued and out-leaked the president, skilfully releasing information into the public domain that triggered Mueller's appointment. Comey had not yet given a complete version of events. That was coming: the Senate Intelligence Committee invited Comey to testify, this time in his capacity as a private citizen.

Would this actually happen? There was speculation that Trump might argue executive privilege, saying his conversations with Comey were classified. In theory, Justice might seek an injunction. But the White House had a problem here. During Watergate the courts established that privilege couldn't be used to cover up unlawful conduct by the executive branch.

Additionally, Trump's non-stop tweets about Comey meant that executive privilege on the grounds of confidentiality were pretty meaningless. Or as one Washington lawyer put it to me: "He [Trump] does these things that are unbelievably fucking stupid all the time."

By June, Washington was in a frenzy. There was a low but distinct rumble in the air: the sound of impeachment. This din was growing louder. There was discussion—in bars, cafés, and public squares—on whether Trump would complete his first term. And talk of the Twenty-fifth Amendment. This statute allowed for the removal of a president on the grounds of incapacity. Impeachment was slow and uncertain; might the vague Twenty-fifth be swifter?

Comey's upcoming testimony would be key. If his account of the Flynn conversation held up, then Trump was—or could be—in the frame for obstruction of justice. Republicans on the Hill were in no mood to dethrone their president: he was, after all, still the best hope of getting through their tax-cutting legislative agenda. But as Senator McCain observed, the situation was beginning to look like Watergate "in size and scale."

Comey had prepared well. On the eve of his appearance before the Senate Intelligence Committee, he released a statement, on the record, and drawn up for a non-classified hearing. It set out in calm tones his four-month-long interactions "with President-Elect and President Trump."

The document was a masterpiece of storytelling. It was lucid and sparse. There were flashes of reportorial colour. Best of all, it was authentic—a real-time account of what had transpired behind closed doors. Overall, one gets the impression of a master bureaucrat attempting to do the right thing—and of a wayward individual who happens to be president of the United States.

Comey's encounters with Trump, we learned, had been awkward from the start. The first was on January 6, 2017. The venue was a conference room in Trump Tower. US intelligence chiefs, including Comey, gave the briefing on Russian interference to the president-elect and his national security team.

The other agency chiefs exited and Comey stayed behind. He briefed the new president "on some personally sensitive aspects" of the information assembled during the assessment. That was the Steele dossier. The US intelligence community had decided to inform Trump for two reasons, Comey wrote, even though the Steele material was thus far "salacious and unverified."

One, it believed the media was about to leak the dossier, and publication was imminent. Two, it felt that by forewarning Trump it could "blunt" any effort to compromise him. The task fell to Comey by pre-agreement: James Clapper, the outgoing director of national intelligence, asked him to do the briefing alone because "the material implicated the FBI's counter-intelligence responsibilities." And to "minimize" any embarrassment to Trump.

Trump, it seems, didn't take the news well. His reaction isn't recorded. But it was such that Comey felt he had to assure Trump that he wasn't under suspicion.

Comey writes:

I felt compelled to document my first conversation with the President-Elect in a memo. To ensure accuracy, I began to type it on a laptop in an FBI vehicle outside Trump Tower the moment I walked out of the meeting. Creating written records immediately after one-to-one conversations with Mr Trump was my practice from that point forward.

Comey didn't "memorialize" his earlier discussions with President Obama. But this was a very different kind of president. That much became obvious during their second encounter on January 27, a week after Trump's inauguration. Comey said Trump rang him at lunchtime and invited him to dinner at 6:30 p.m. that evening. As Comey later explained, he had to cancel a date with his wife.

Comey assumed that there would be other guests. But, he wrote, when he arrived at the White House "it turned out to be just the two of us, seated at a small oval table in the center of the Green Room." Two navy stewards waited on Comey and Trump, only entering the room to serve food and drinks.

Trump began by asking Comey if he wanted to stay on as FBI director. Comey wrote that he found the question "strange" since Trump had twice previously told him that he hoped Comey would remain in the post. Comey said he'd already told Trump he intended to serve out his ten-year term. The president then said that "lots of people" wanted his job and he would understand if Comey decided to "walk away."

Comey's language here is neutral. But it's clear that the FBI director was horrified and appalled by Trump's blatant methods. Comey writes:

My instincts told me that the one-on-one setting, and the pretence that this was our first discussion about my position, meant that the dinner was, at least in part, an effort to have me ask for my job and create some sort of patronage relationship. That concerned me greatly, given the FBI's traditionally independent status in the executive branch.

Comey's forebodings turned out to be correct. He told the president that he wasn't "reliable" in the political sense but could always be counted on to tell the truth. This, he added, was in Trump's best interests as president. To which Trump replied: "I need loyalty, I expect loyalty."

It was a paralysing moment. "I didn't move, speak, or change my facial expression in any way during the awkward silence that followed. We simply looked at each other in silence," Comey reports.

Trump returned to this theme towards the end of the dinner. The bargain, as set out by Trump, was a classically transactional one: if Comey wanted to keep his job he had to serve Trump personally rather than his own institution. Trump repeated his demand: "I need loyalty." Comey replied: "You will always get honesty from me." Trump then said: "That's what I want, honest loyalty."

Comey agreed to this but said he had done so to terminate a "very awkward conversation." "My explanations had made clear what he should expect," Comey wrote.

There were further excruciating details. Trump delivered

his "I hope you can let this go" speech after deliberately cornering Comey in the Oval Office and sending everyone else out, including Kushner and Sessions. There were whining phone calls. During one, on March 30, the president likened the Russia thing to "the cloud." He denied being involved with Russia, or Russian hookers, and told Comey he'd always assumed "he was being recorded in Russia."

Twelve days later Trump rang again. He urged Comey to "get out" the fact that he, the president, wasn't personally under investigation. Comey refused. To do so, the FBI chief said, "would create a duty to correct" the record, should the situation change.

Comey's seven-page document was a stunning piece of contemporary history. It had everything—a timeline, detail, facts—except, perhaps, tone. Trump's final remarks to Comey on April 11 seem almost sorrowful, though it's hard to be sure. The president said: "I have been very loyal to you, very loyal; we had that thing, you know."

Comey writes:

> I did not reply or ask him what he meant by "that thing." I said only that the way to handle it was to have the White House Counsel call the Acting Deputy Attorney General. He said that was what he would do and the call ended.
>
> That was the last time I spoke to President Trump.

The line for public seats went on and on. The first person arrived at 4:15 a.m. By 7:30 a.m., three hundred people were queuing inside the Hart Senate Office Building. The human chain snaked along a corridor overlooking an airy atrium. The focus of its attention was room 216. It was here that Comey was due to give evidence.

Washington was used to big set-piece political events. But this occasion was special—a moment destined to feature in future accounts of Trump's doom-laden presidency. It had an elemental plot line: a wronged man, a renegade chief, an illegal (?) hint, cunningly delivered off-camera.

Twelve national networks were relaying Comey's testimony live. Sports bars and cafés, from Bond Street in Brooklyn to Sutter Street in San Francisco—were showing the event to customers. A Washington tavern offered FBI-themed sandwiches. There was even an early-morning Comey yoga party in West Coast LA.

America had experienced scandals before—Watergate, the Teapot Dome affair that shook Warren Harding's administration in the 1920s. But, as the *Guardian*'s Julian Borger noted as he scrambled for a hearing room seat, these were domestic squabbles. They featured one group of American politicians trying to smear another.

This scandal involved a foreign adversary. If Comey's statement was to be believed, it revolved around a president who was willing to abuse his power. In this case, that meant seeking to browbeat an investigator. The investigator—it appeared—was getting uncomfortably close to the truth. And so he was fired.

At 10:02 a.m. Comey entered. The buzz subsided, to be replaced by what sounded like a waterfall: the multi-click of cameras. The former FBI director looked grim, waxen, baggy-eyed. He sat behind a desk. Photographers were arrayed around him in a semicircle. There were senators and staffers and rows of reporters. Seen from above the tableau had the solemn sweep of a Renaissance picture.

It seemed likely Comey would criticize Trump. The extent of the former director's fury became evident immediately after he was sworn in. In his opening statement Comey said he accepted that Trump might fire him for any reason or none. But the official explanation "didn't make any sense to me," he said, especially after he learned from TV that Trump had actually done so because of Moscow.

"I was fired, in some way, to change—or the endeavour was to change the way the Russian investigation was being conducted. That is a very big deal, and not just because it involves me," he said.

The White House, he complained bitterly, chose "to defame me." It said the FBI was in disarray, poorly led, and with a workforce that had lost confidence in its boss. "Those were lies, plain and simple," Comey declared, "and I am so sorry that the FBI workforce had to hear them and I'm so sorry that the American people were told them."

Contrary to Trump's gloomy claims, the FBI was not in meltdown. Rather, Comey said, it was "honest" and "strong." "The FBI is, and always will be, independent," he stressed.

Trump had been expected to live-tweet the hearing to his 31.7 million followers. As the nation watched, gripped, the president was unusually silent. Comey said he had mistrusted Trump from the get-go. He told the committee he started making a record of their conversations because of the "nature of the person."

Fundamentally, he believed the president to be unethical. Mendacious even. "I was honestly concerned that he might lie about the nature of our [January] meeting, and so I thought it really important to document," he said.

There were other interesting details. The chairman of the committee, Richard Burr, asked if the FBI had been able to corroborate any of the "criminal allegations" contained in the Steele dossier. Comey passed on this, and remarked that he couldn't answer the question in an "open setting." The inference was clear: the FBI had managed to verify some of it. How much was secret information.

Comey said he passed on his Trump memos to Bob Mueller. It was Mueller, he said, who would now have to decide whether the president's comments on Flynn amounted to obstruction of justice. Comey said he took them as "direction." The episode had left him "stunned," he said. He hadn't told his agents, fearing a "chilling effect on their work."

Throughout Comey remained calm—which, if anything, made what he said more lethal. As the *Washington Post* columnist Eugene Robinson observed, there was a "welcome air of sobriety" about the session. The senators interrogating Comey had done so in a grown-up way. True, Democrats had gone for Trump and Republicans had sought to exonerate him, but all recognized what was at stake.

Comey's resolute appearance also earned him some unlikely plaudits. The *Daily Beast*'s Lizzie Crocker praised his "seductive integrity" and wondered whether the fifty-six-year-old fired FBI director was "hot":

Sure, he has a somewhat peaked complexion and under-eye bags that look like half-inflated tubular balloons. But he's handsome, and as with all sex symbols—both the unlikely ones and the obvious ones—he embodies certain qualities in society that we all lust after: integrity, emotional complexity, and quiet but certain confidence.

Hot or not, Comey's best speech came when he tried to put what had befallen America into context:

> We have this big, messy, wonderful country where we fight with each other all the time, but nobody tells us what to think, what to fight about, what to vote for, except other Americans, and that's wonderful and often painful. But we're talking about a foreign government that, using technical intrusion, lots of other methods, tried to shape the way we think, we vote, we act. That is a big deal. And people need to recognize it.

What struck me—watching on TV, like much of America—was the question that had prompted Comey's passionate words. Democratic senator Joe Manchin wanted to know, did Trump "ever show any concern or interest or curiosity about what the Russians were doing?"

The answer: no. Comey said Trump had asked a few questions during the January 6 briefing. Then nothing.

Trump, then, seemed profoundly unconcerned about Russia's attack on American democracy. As candidate, and even as president, he had stubbornly denied that Putin was involved. At the same time Trump insisted—to Comey, and to anybody who would listen—that he had nothing to do with Moscow.

This, too, was untrue. Trump's relationship with Russia went back a long way—to a trip almost certainly arranged by the KGB.

8

Collusion

1984–2017
Moscow–New York

A major effort is required in order to improve
performance in the recruitment of Americans.
—KGB ANNUAL REVIEW, 1984

It was 1984 and General Vladimir Alexandrovich Kryuchkov had
a problem. The general occupied one of the KGB's most exalted
posts. He was head of the First Chief Directorate, the prestigious KGB arm responsible for foreign intelligence gathering.

Kryuchkov was one of the USSR's success stories. His background was proletarian: father a worker, mother a housewife,
his first job in a factory. In the evenings he took correspondence classes. This led to a job in a provincial procurator's
office and then to a place at the Soviet foreign ministry's elite
training school.

From there his rise was swift. He spent five years at the
Soviet mission in Budapest under Ambassador Yuri Andropov,

at a time when Soviet tanks crushed the Hungarian uprising in 1956. In 1967 Andropov became KGB chairman. Kryuchkov went to Moscow, took up a number of sensitive posts, and established a reputation as a devoted and hard-working officer.

By 1984, Kryuchkov's directorate was bigger than ever before—twelve thousand officers, up from about three thousand in the 1960s. His headquarters at Yasenevo, on the wooded southern outskirts of Moscow, was expanding: workmen were busy constructing a twenty-two-storey annexe and a new eleven-storey building.

In politics, change was in the air. Soon a new man would arrive in the Kremlin, Mikhail Gorbachev. Gorbachev's policy of detente with the West—a refreshing contrast to the global confrontation of previous general secretaries—meant the directorate's work abroad was more important than ever.

Kryuchkov faced several challenges. First, a hawkish president was in power in Washington, Ronald Reagan. The KGB regarded his two predecessors, Gerald Ford and Jimmy Carter, as weak. By contrast Reagan was seen as a potent adversary. The directorate was increasingly preoccupied with what it believed—wrongly—was an American plot to conduct a preemptive nuclear strike against the USSR.

The general's other difficulty had to do with intelligence gathering. The results from KGB officers abroad had been disappointing. Too often they would pretend to have obtained information from secret sources. In reality, they had recycled material from newspapers or picked up gossip over lunch with a journalist. Too many residencies had "paper agents" on their books: targets for recruitment who had nothing to do with real intelligence.

Kryuchkov sent out a series of classified memos to KGB

heads of station. Oleg Gordievsky—formerly based in Denmark and then in Great Britain—copied them and passed them to British intelligence. He later co-published them with historian Christopher Andrew under the title *Comrade Kryuchkov's Instructions: Top Secret Files on KGB Foreign Operations 1975–1985.* (I read it in the British Library. It was fascinating. I bought my own copy.)

In January 1984 Kryuchkov addressed the problem during a biannual review held in Moscow and at a special conference six months later. The urgent subject: how to improve agent recruitment. The general urged his officers to be more "creative." Previously they had relied on identifying candidates who showed ideological sympathy towards the USSR: leftists, trade unionists, and so on. By the mid-1980s these were not so many. So KGB officers should "make bolder use of material incentives": money. And use flattery, an important tool.

The Centre, according to Andrew and Gordievsky, was especially concerned about its lack of success in recruiting Americans. The PR Line—that is, the Political Intelligence Department stationed in KGB residencies abroad—was given explicit instructions to find "US targets to cultivate or, at the very least, official contacts." "The main effort must be concentrated on acquiring valuable agents," Kryuchkov said.

The memo—dated February 1, 1984—was to be destroyed as soon as its contents had been read. It said that despite improvements in "information gathering," the KGB "has not had great success in operations against the main adversary [America]."

One solution was to make wider use of "the facilities of friendly intelligence services"—for example, Czechoslovakian or East German spy networks.

And: "Further improvement in operational work with agents calls for fuller and wider utilization of confidential and special unofficial contacts. These should be acquired chiefly among prominent figures in politics and society, and important representatives of business and science." These should not only "supply valuable information" but also "actively influence" a country's foreign policy "in a direction of advantage to the USSR."

There were, of course, different stages of recruitment. Typically, a case officer would invite a target to lunch. The target would be classified as an "official contact." If the target appeared responsive, he (it was rarely she) would be promoted to a "subject of deep study," an *obyekt razrabotki*. The officer would build up a file, supplemented by official and covert material. That might include readouts from conversations obtained through bugging by the KGB's technical team.

The KGB also distributed a secret personality questionnaire, advising case officers what to look for in a successful recruitment operation. In April 1985 this was updated for "prominent figures in the West." The directorate's aim was to draw the target "into some form of collaboration with us." This could be "as an agent, or confidential or special or unofficial contact."

The form demanded basic details—name, profession, family situation, and material circumstances. There were other questions, too: What was the likelihood that the "subject could come to power (occupy the post of president or prime minister)"? And an assessment of personality. For example: "Are pride, arrogance, egoism, ambition or vanity among subject's natural characteristics?"

The most revealing section concerned *kompromat*. The

document asked for "Compromising information about sub-ject, including illegal acts in financial and commercial affairs, intrigues, speculation, bribes, graft . . . and exploitation of his position to enrich himself." Plus "any other information" that would compromise the subject before "the country's authori-ties and the general public." Naturally the KGB could exploit this by threatening "disclosure."

Finally, "his attitude towards women is also of interest." The document wanted to know: "Is he in the habit of having affairs with women on the side?"

When did the KGB open a file on Donald Trump? We don't know, but Eastern Bloc security service records suggest this may have been as early as 1977. That was the year when Trump married Ivana Zelnickova, a twenty-eight-year-old model from Czechoslovakia. Zelnickova was a citizen of a communist country. She was therefore of interest both to the Czech intel-ligence service, the StB, and to the FBI and CIA.

During the Cold War, Czech spies were known for their professionalism. Czech and Hungarian officers were typically used in espionage actions abroad, especially in the United States and Latin America. They were less obvious than Soviet operatives sent by Moscow.

Zelnickova was born in Zlin, an aircraft manufacturing town in Moravia. Her first marriage was to an Austrian real estate agent. In the early 1970s she moved to Canada, first to Toronto and then to Montreal, to be with a ski instructor boy-friend. Exiting Czechoslovakia during this period was incred-ibly difficult, US intelligence sources suggest. Zelnickova moved to New York. In April 1977 she married Trump.

According to files in Prague, declassified in 2016, Czech spies kept a close eye on the couple in Manhattan. (The agents who undertook this task were codenamed Al Jarza and Lubos.) They opened letters sent home by Ivana to her father, Milos, an engineer. Milos was never an agent or asset. But he had a functional relationship with the Czech secret police, who would ask him how his daughter was doing abroad and in return permit her visits home. There was periodic surveillance of the Trump family in the United States, and when Ivana and Donald Trump Jr visited Milos in the Czechoslovak Socialist Republic, further spying, or "cover."

Like other Eastern Bloc agencies, the Czechs would have shared their intelligence product with their counterparts in Moscow, the KGB. Trump may have been of interest for several reasons. One, his wife came from Eastern Europe. Two—at a time after 1984 when the Kremlin was experimenting with perestroika—Trump had a prominent profile as a real estate developer and tycoon. According to the Czech files, Ivana mentioned her husband's growing interest in politics. Might Trump at some stage consider a political career?

The KGB wouldn't invite someone to Moscow out of reasons of altruism. Dignitaries flown to the USSR on expenses-paid trips were typically left-leaning writers or cultural figures. The state would expend hard currency; the visitor would say some nice things about Soviet life; the press would report these remarks, seeing in them a stamp of approval.

Despite Gorbachev's policy of engagement, he was still a Soviet leader. The KGB continued to view the West with deep suspicion. It carried on with efforts to subvert Western institutions and acquire secret sources, with NATO its number one strategic intelligence target. Nor did the KGB foresee imminent political upheaval; its officers assumed the USSR would go on for a long time. Meanwhile, the Soviet war in Afghanistan ground on.

At this point it was unclear how the KGB regarded Trump. To become a full KGB agent, a foreigner had to agree to two things. (An "agent" in a Russian or British context was a secret intelligence source.) One was "conspiratorial collaboration." The other was willingness to take KGB instruction.

According to Andrew and Gordievsky's book *Comrade Kryuchkov's Instructions*, targets who failed to meet these criteria were classified as "confidential contacts." The Russian term was *doveritelnaya svyaz*. The aspiration was to turn trusted contacts into full-blown agents, an upper rung of the ladder.

As Kryuchkov explained, KGB residents were urged to abandon "stereotyped methods" of recruitment and use more flexible strategies—if necessary getting their wives or other family members to help.

As Trump tells it, the idea for his first trip to Moscow came after he found himself seated next to Soviet ambassador Yuri Dubinin. This was autumn 1986; the event was a luncheon held by Leonard Lauder, the businessman son of Estée Lauder. Dubinin's daughter, Natalia, "had read about Trump Tower and knew all about it," Trump said in his ghostwritten 1987 bestseller, *The Art of the Deal*.

Trump continued: "One thing led to another, and now I'm talking about building a large luxury hotel, across the street from the Kremlin, in partnership with the Soviet government."

Trump's chatty version of events is incomplete. According to Natalia Dubinina, the actual story involved a more determined effort by the Soviet government to seek out Trump. In February 1985 Kryuchkov complained again about "the lack of appreciable results of recruitment against the Americans in most Residencies." The ambassador arrived in New York in March 1986. His original job was Soviet ambassador to the UN; Dubinina was already living in the city with her family, and she was part of the Soviet UN delegation.

Dubinin wouldn't have answered to the KGB. And his role wasn't formally an intelligence one. But he would have had close contacts with the power apparatus in Moscow. He enjoyed greater trust than other, lesser ambassadors.

Dubinina said she picked up her father from the airport. It was his first time in New York City. She took him on a tour. The first building they saw was Trump Tower on Fifth Avenue, she told *Komsomolskaya Pravda* newspaper. Dubinin was so excited he decided to go inside to meet the building's owner. They got into the lift. At the top, Dubinina said, they met Trump.

The ambassador—"fluent in English and a brilliant master of negotiations"—charmed the busy Trump, telling him: "The first thing I saw in the city is your tower!"

Dubinina said: "Trump melted at once. He is an emotional person, somewhat impulsive. He needs recognition. And, of course, when he gets it he likes it. My father's visit worked on him like honey to a bee."

This encounter happened six months before the Estée Lauder lunch. In Dubinina's account she admits her father was trying to hook Trump. The man from Moscow wasn't a wide-eyed ingenue but a veteran diplomat who served in France and Spain, and translated for Nikita Khrushchev when he met with Charles de Gaulle at the Elysée Palace in Paris. He had seen plenty of impressive buildings. Weeks after his first Trump meeting, Dubinin was named Soviet ambassador to Washington.

Dubinina's own role is interesting. According to the

Mitrokhin archive, the Soviet mission to the UN was a haven for the KGB and GRU. Many of the three hundred Soviet nationals employed at the UN secretariat were Soviet intelligence officers working undercover, including as personal assistants to secretary-generals. The Soviet UN delegation had greater success in finding agents and gaining political intelligence than the KGB's New York residency.

Dubinin's other daughter, Irina, said that her late father—he died in 2013—was on a mission as ambassador. This was, she said, to make contact with America's business elite. For sure, Gorbachev's Politburo was interested in understanding capitalism. But Dubinin's invitation to Trump to visit Moscow looks like a classic cultivation exercise, which would have had the KGB's full support and approval.

In *The Art of the Deal*, Trump writes: "In January 1987, I got a letter from Yuri Dubinin, the Soviet ambassador to the United States, that began: 'It is a pleasure for me to relay some good news from Moscow.' It went on to say that the leading Soviet state agency for international tourism, Goscomintourist, had expressed interest in pursuing a joint venture to construct and manage a hotel in Moscow."

Meanwhile, some colleagues disliked Dubinin. Andrei Kovalev—a Soviet diplomat who first met him in 1968—described Dubinin as "morally unscrupulous," "self-promoting," and vain about his ("admittedly handsome") appearance—a "preening peacock," keen to ingratiate himself with those in power at home. Dubinin would have been accompanied everywhere in the United States by a security guard who reported to the KGB, Kovalev told me.

There were many ambitious real estate developers in the United States—so why had Moscow picked Trump?

According to Viktor Suvorov—the former GRU military spy—and others, the KGB ran Intourist. It functioned as a subsidiary KGB branch. Initiated in 1929 by Stalin, Intourist was Moscow's official state travel agency. Its job was to vet and monitor all foreigners coming into the Soviet Union. "In my time it was KGB," Suvorov said. "They gave permission for people to visit." The KGB's first and second directorates routinely received lists of prospective visitors to the country based on their visa applications.

As a GRU operative, Suvorov was personally involved in recruitment, albeit for a rival service to the KGB. Soviet spy agencies were always interested in cultivating "young ambitious people," he said—an upwardly mobile businessman, a scientist, a "guy with a future."

Once in Moscow, they received lavish hospitality. "Everything is free. There are good parties with nice girls. It could be a sauna and girls and who knows what else." The hotel rooms or villa were under "twenty-four-hour control," with "security cameras and so on," Suvorov said. "The interest is only one. To collect some information and keep that information about him for the future."

These dirty-tricks operations were all about the long term, Suvorov said. The KGB would expend effort on visiting students from the developing world, not least Africa. After ten or twenty years, some of them would be "nobody." But others would have risen to positions of influence in their own countries.

Suvorov explained: "It's at this point you say: 'Knock, knock! Do you remember the marvellous time in Moscow? It was a wonderful evening. You were so drunk. You don't remember? We just show you something for your good memory.'"

Over in the communist German Democratic Republic, one of Kryuchkov's thirty-four-year-old officers—one Vladimir Putin—was busy trying to recruit students from Latin America. Putin arrived in Dresden in August 1985, together with his pregnant wife, Lyudmila, and one-year-old daughter, Maria. They lived in a KGB apartment block.

According to the writer Masha Gessen, one of Putin's tasks was to try and befriend foreigners studying at the Dresden University of Technology. The hope was that, if recruited, the Latin Americans might work in the United States as undercover agents, reporting back to the Centre. Putin set about this, together with two KGB colleagues and a retired Dresden policeman.

Precisely what Putin did while working for the KGB's first directorate in Dresden is unknown. It may have included trying to recruit Westerners visiting Dresden on business and East Germans with relatives in the West. Putin's efforts, Gessen suggests, were mostly a failure. He did manage to recruit a Colombian student. Overall his operational results were modest.

By January 1987, Trump was closer to the "prominent person" of Kryuchkov's note. Dubinin deemed Trump interesting enough to arrange his trip to Moscow. Another thirty-something US-based Soviet diplomat, Vitaly Churkin—the future UN ambassador—helped put it together. On July 4, 1987, Trump flew to Moscow for the first time, together with Ivana and Lisa Calandra, Ivana's Italian American assistant.

Moscow was, Trump wrote, "an extraordinary experience." The Trumps stayed in Lenin's suite at the National Hotel, at the bottom of Tverskaya, near Red Square. Seventy years earlier, in October 1917, Lenin and his wife, Nadezhda Krupskaya, had spent a week in room 107. The hotel was linked to the glass-and-concrete Intourist complex next door and—in effect—was under KGB control. The Lenin suite would have been bugged.

Meanwhile, the mausoleum containing the Bolshevik leader's embalmed corpse was a short walk away. Other Soviet leaders were interred beneath the Kremlin's wall in a communist pantheon: Stalin, Brezhnev, Andropov—Kryuchkov's old mentor—and Dzerzhinsky.

According to *The Art of the Deal*, Trump toured "a half dozen potential sites for a hotel, including several near Red Square. I was impressed with the ambition of Soviet officials to make a deal." He also visited Leningrad. A photo shows Donald and Ivana standing in Palace Square in what would become St Petersburg—he in a suit, she in a red polka-dot blouse with a string of pearls. Behind them are the Winter Palace and the State Hermitage Museum.

That July the Soviet press wrote enthusiastically about the visit of a foreign celebrity. This was Gabriel García Márquez, the Nobel Prize-winning novelist and journalist. *Pravda* featured a long conversation between the Colombian guest and Gorbachev. García Márquez spoke of how South Americans, himself included, sympathized with socialism and the USSR. Moscow brought García Márquez over for a film festival.

Trump's visit appears to have attracted less attention. There is no mention of him in Moscow's Russian State Library newspaper archive. (Either his visit went unreported or any articles featuring it have been quietly removed.) Press clippings do record a visit by a West German official and an Indian cultural festival.

The KGB's private dossier on Trump, by contrast, would have grown larger. The agency's multi-page profile would have been enriched with fresh material, including anything gleaned via eavesdropping.

Nothing came of the trip—at least nothing in terms of business opportunities inside Russia. This pattern of failure would be repeated in Trump's subsequent trips to Moscow. But Trump flew back to New York with a new sense of strategic direction. For the first time he gave serious indications that he was considering a career in politics. Not as mayor or governor or senator.

Trump was thinking about running for president.

The *New York Times* story appeared on September 2, 1987—less than two months after Trump's Intourist adventure. Its headline read: "Trump Gives a Vague Hint of Candidacy."

The article began:

Donald J. Trump, one of New York's biggest and certainly one of its most vocal developers, said yesterday that he was not interested in running for political office in New York, but indicated that the Presidency was another matter.

Mr. Trump, a Republican, bought full-page advertisements in three major newspapers around the country this morning to air his foreign-policy views. And an adviser disclosed that Mr Trump is planning a trip in October to New Hampshire, site of the first Presidential primary.

The advertisement was eye-catching. It appeared in the *New York Times*, the *Washington Post,* and the *Boston Globe.* It was addressed "to the American people" from "Donald John Trump" and headlined: "There's nothing wrong with America's Foreign Defense Policy that a little backbone can't cure."

It said:

For decades, Japan and other nations have been taking advantage of the United States.

The saga continues unabated as we defend the Persian Gulf, an area of only marginal significance to the United States for its oil supplies, but one upon which Japan and others are almost totally dependent. Why are these nations not paying the United States for the human lives and billions of dollars we are losing to protect *their* interests?

Trump took aim at Saudi Arabia—which had refused to lend the Pentagon a mine sweeper. He wrote that Japan, and "others," had got rich by taking advantage of American generosity. It was time, he wrote, to help "our farmers, our sick, our homeless. . . . Let's not let our great country be laughed at anymore," he concluded.

There's no doubt that Trump's message was authentic. He would return to these themes—of America first and freeloading partner nations—in his later actual campaign for the White House. At the same time Trump's public proclamation would have pleased Moscow.

General Kryuchkov was always keen to foster disagreement between the United States and its allies, as his secret 1984 work plan showed. The KGB's "global priorities" included a long list of active measures. These were to be done covertly. According to Andrew and Gordievsky, the second most important priority was to "deepen disagreements inside NATO over its approach to implementing specific aspects of the bloc's military policy." And "exacerbating contradictions between the USA, Western Europe and Japan on other matters of principle."

The *New York Times* reported that Trump had recently returned from Russia. It said that he had met with Gorbachev. (If he did, the Soviet press failed to report this.) The paper wrote: "The ostensible subject of their meeting was the possible development of luxury hotels in the Soviet Union by Mr. Trump. But Mr. Trump's calls for nuclear disarmament were also well-known to the Russians."

Trump's announcement remains puzzling. After all, he knew little of foreign policy. "The idea of doing it was his," ad executive Tom Messner told the *Post*. Messner had worked on Reagan's 1984 re-election campaign and said that his team had little input in Trump's letter. The advertisements cost Trump $94,801, paid for—the *New York Times* said—with his own money. They appeared in papers with a big New Hampshire readership.

As ever with Trump, at the time it was hard to tell whether his flirtation with a presidential run was another self-branding moment—or something more serious. Mike Dunbar, a prominent and eccentric Republican, invited Trump to visit New Hampshire and launched a "draft Trump movement." There was talk that Trump might secure the vice president slot, on a ticket with George H. W. Bush. In the end Bush picked Dan Quayle, the senator from Indiana.

Trump's subsequent attempts to build property in Moscow followed the same unsuccessful model: a bright fizz of publicity followed by nothing much. Were the Soviets stringing him along for their own reasons? Or were the visits to Russia simply Trumpian hyperbole, designed to project him as a global player, at ease with the capitalist West and communist East?

In December 1987 Mikhail and Raisa Gorbachev made their first trip to the United States. The visit was historic: the

American and Soviet superpowers had agreed to reduce their nuclear arsenals for the first time, with a landmark arms control treaty. Kryuchkov came with Gorbachev. It was the first time a First Chief Directorate boss had accompanied a general secretary on a trip to the West.

Trump told reporters that the Russians had called him and wanted him to show the Gorbachevs Fifth Avenue and Trump Tower. The Soviet first couple never showed up. Instead, Trump was pranked into meeting with a Gorbachev impersonator, hired by a US TV channel.

In Washington, Kryuchkov had dinner with Robert Gates, the CIA deputy director. Unbeknown to Gates, Kryuchkov's instructions to recruit Americans had got stunning results. The KGB had two moles inside US intelligence—the CIA's Aldrich Ames and the FBI's Robert Hanssen. Both gave secrets to Moscow and betrayed US agents.

In summer 1991—while Steele was working undercover in Moscow—Kryuchkov led a KGB coup against Gorbachev. The general believed this was the only way to preserve the Soviet Union. He was one of those arrested.

It would be another five years before Trump returned to post-communist Moscow. By this point his marriage to Ivana had ended. He had also survived the worst moment of his career, in 1990, when his credit-fuelled business empire fell apart, leaving him virtually bankrupt.

Trump's 1996 reappearance made the business daily *Kommersant*. It reported that the "famous businessman" who had been "wealthy, broke and made a fortune again" was interested in Moscow construction projects. Trump wanted to redevelop the Moskva and Rossiya hotels. The latter was a Soviet-era monster occupying a prime spot next to the Kremlin.

How serious was Trump's latest foray into Yeltsin's Russia? Not very, it appeared—though in 1996 Trump did begin registering trademark applications in Moscow for eight of his companies. In November that year he flew to Moscow with Howard Lorber, a businessman whose Vector Group had interests in Russia.

Trump met with Zurab Tsereteli, a Georgian-Russian sculptor. Tsereteli's overblown public works enjoyed official favour. According to *The New Yorker*'s Mark Singer, Trump discussed erecting a giant statue of Christopher Columbus on the Hudson River. It would be bigger than the Statue of Liberty. The mayor of Moscow would donate the statue to his New York counterpart, Rudy Giuliani, Trump told Singer.

The statue never arrived. Nor did Trump manage to close a hotel deal. And a year later the Russian economy crashed.

As an American and an outsider Trump was never likely to make money inside Russia or obtain favoured chunks of real estate. What counted in the lawless Moscow of the 1990s was connections—and buying off people at the top of state structures. What Trump needed was a Russian friend, a primary partner. Preferably one known to the Kremlin.

In October 2007 I was leafing through the morning papers. I was the *Guardian*'s Moscow correspondent. The newspaper's office wasn't much to boast about: two tiny low-ceilinged Soviet apartments knocked together to form a pair of dingy rooms. Mine had a bookshelf and a map of Russia. A mini-kitchen looked onto a strip of green. A short walk along Gruzinsky Pereulok took you to Belorussky train and metro station.

Although I didn't know it at the time, Steele had lived during his Moscow posting in the same building, used by journalists and diplomats. We were on the ground floor, apartments 75 and 76, entrance number three; Steele had lived two floors above us. We had shared a stairwell and a communal postbox. Not that letters ever arrived.

We assumed our office was bugged. Not from paranoia but because it was made obvious. Sometimes the FSB broke in and left the usual clues: an opened window (unlatched from the inside), a phone taken out of its cradle and left demonstratively on the desk in the early hours. There was electronic surveillance, too. Each time I made a joke about Putin, the landline was cut, replaced by an ominous crackle.

A branch of the Russian foreign ministry, UPDK, managed our apartment. Like Intourist, UPDK used to be KGB. Presumably the FSB had its own set of keys.

I found an article in the *Moscow Times* with a familiar subject: the antics of the capital's super-rich. It mentioned a new exclusive club at the National Hotel, where Trump had stayed. At this time, according to *Forbes* magazine, Russia had fifty-three billionaires, a lot of "minigarchs," and tens of thousands of millionaires. I read on.

The story reported that one wealthy individual—property developer Aras Agalarov—was planning to make something extraordinary.

Agalarov was building a luxury housing estate on the outskirts of Moscow. It would be a sort of oligarch utopia, with houses costing around $25 to $30 million each, and a gilded retreat from which the poor were invisible. There would be two hundred and fifty high-end properties, a golf course and club house, a lake, and an artificial beach decked out with white sand imported from Thailand.

I picked up the phone.

Arranging an interview with Agalarov was easy. A few days later I got a lift up to the Istra region, west of Moscow, to a rustic spot dotted with fir trees and white camomile flowers. Several villas had been completed. Others were being built. Each was different. A Scottish baronial mansion rose above a line of newly planted birch trees. Nearby was a neoclassical palace, a froth of concrete pillars, acanthus capitals, and Greek fluting.

In person, Agalarov was jovial and welcoming. He spoke fluent English. The tycoon was a figure of medium height, at this point in his early fifties, wearing a sports jacket. *Forbes* had dubbed him the "vainest of the Golden Hundred," its list of the top one hundred richest Russians. Actually, he was quite charming.

Agalarov gave me a tour. We climbed into a dark blue Land Rover. On the vehicle's door, I noticed, were the initials *AE*, approximately a foot and a half in height, standing for Agalarov Estate. A dainty crown floated above the monogram. Agalarov drove; I sat in the front passenger seat.

Agalarov's son Emin had given him the British-made jeep as a present, he said. Emin was a well-known pop star married to one of the daughters of Ilham Aliyev, the president of Azerbaijan, he explained. Agalarov was Azeri-Russian. He was born in Azerbaijan's capital, Baku, in 1955 and moved to Moscow in 1981, he told me. He obviously moved in the right circles: Aliyev's late father, Heydar, was Soviet Azerbaijan's KGB chief and—like Kryuchkov—an Andropov protégé. In 1993 Heydar became Azerbaijan's president.

We went past a waterfall. Agalarov's bodyguards followed us in a sleek black Mercedes, keeping a respectful distance. The tycoon said he'd studied business and economics. He was the first person in Russia to organize international exhibitions—this would become his Crocus Group. He started a chain of shoe stores, he said. There were setbacks: "I lost everything in the crisis of 1997. I closed all my stores. I had a $100 million loan."

By 2000 Agalarov had bounced back. The same year he built Crocus City—a vast shopping centre and exhibition space next to Moscow's churning MKAD outer ring road.

The idea of an exclusive estate for the rich had come from the United States, I discovered. Agalarov said he'd seen "proto-types" for the kind of community he wanted to create during trips to Alpine in New Jersey and Greenwich in Connecticut. Alpine was an exclusive cliff-top village, twenty miles north of New York, with property prices greater than West Palm Beach or Beverly Hills. It would shortly become the United States' most expensive address.

"I had a kind of jealousy. Why can't we do this in Russia? This was the source of the idea," Agalarov said. "Then I started to buy land." As Agalarov's land holding grew—he would accumulate 320 hectares—so did his vision, to encompass fourteen lakes ("the length of these lakes is 3.5 kilometres"), an eighteen-hole golf club ("designed by a US consultant"), and Agalarov's personal mansion ("I have not started building my house").

There were a few wrinkles along the way. Agalarov was keen to demolish properties in the nearby village of Vorinino, believing they spoiled the view. Some villagers didn't want to sell. The man at number 54—a decrepit redbrick cottage—was holding out despite being offered $1 million. "He'll sell in the end," Agalarov told me.

Then there were the customers. As part of his social experiment, Agalarov said he'd drawn up a set of rules for anyone wishing to buy one of his properties. First, bodyguards were banned. They were banished to a purpose-built house on the periphery of the estate, complete with billiard table. Second, residents weren't allowed to shoot at birds, let off fireworks, or hang out washing. Third, no dogs.

"We want normal rich people here," Agalarov said. He personally vetted all applicants. "One told me he had an Afghan shepherd dog. I wouldn't sell him a house. I lost $30 million because of a dog!" When complete, the estate would be the "most beautiful place in Moscow"—superior even to Rublyovka, the exclusive dacha colony set in pine forests west of the capital, where Putin resided.

The migrant workers building Agalarov's dream came from China, Tajikistan, and Belarus. The country that loomed large in Agalarov's thinking, however, was America. Agalarov said his nineteen-year-old daughter, Sheila, was studying in New York, at the Fashion Institute of Technology. His wife, Irina, "stayed with her." Agalarov had a "small house in the United States." He preferred to live in Russia.

"I don't like big words like 'patriotism.' You don't show it. But everything I do is connected to Russia," he told me. "I can't stay there [in the United States]. I don't have anything to do there. My work is here. My life is here. My circle is here." He spent each day on site ("Saturday and Sunday I'm here"), viewing his bold architectural creation not as toil but as "a hobby."

Agalarov has been described as Russia's Trump. Certainly, there were points of overlap: like Trump, Agalarov believed that *Forbes* wilfully understated the size of his fortune. In

2007 he was ninety-fifth on its rich list, worth $540 million. Agalarov told me the real figure was more like $10 billion. His land assets alone "came to $6 billion. . . . It's wrong for everybody," he grumbled.

Not that this cash was an end in itself. "For me money is nothing. It's like an instrument to make something crazy," Agalarov said. And—again like Trump—Agalarov believed in showmanship and visible excess. I asked Agalarov if Moscow's rich were slowly developing subtler tastes. "No. It's still about show. Show is continuing," he replied.

Despite these similarities there were differences. Unlike Trump, Agalarov existed in a stark political space in which the Kremlin made the rules. Being a member of the Russian elite brought privileges—and obligations. If the presidential administration wanted you to do something, you delivered. The Crocus Group built a federal university near Vladivostok; Agalarov would later agree to construct two soccer stadiums for Russia's 2018 World Cup, in Kaliningrad and Rostov.

Agalarov's wealth was provisional, then. Much of his income came from state contracts. If he fell from favour, someone else would take everything away, including his beloved estate and its designer boulders.

Towards the end of my tour, I asked Agalarov if he'd ever paid bribes. He said not. He had, he said, impeccable relations with the Moscow region—its ministers and governor—where his utopia was being shaped. The region was separate from Moscow City Hall and had its own HQ next to Crocus City. It was more dynamic, with "one and a half times" more construction, he said.

Though he didn't mention her by name, one of Agalarov's lawyers was the region's top attorney. Her name was Natalia

Veselnitskaya. Veselnitskaya's former husband, Alexander Mitusov, was a former prosecutor who had become the region's deputy transport minister. Veselnitskaya worked in turn for Mitusov's boss, Pyotr Katsyv.

It was Katsyv's son, Denis, who would shortly find himself at the centre of an international scandal. He was one of a series of Russian officials accused of involvement in the case of Sergei Magnitsky. At this point Magnitsky, an accountant, was in prison. He had investigated and discovered a $230 million tax fraud scheme, involving Katsyv and others. They had allegedly stolen taxes paid by Hermitage Capital, an investment fund run by a US-born British CEO, Bill Browder.

In 2009, Magnitsky died in custody—murdered, Browder said, by the Russian state. Veselnitskaya would expend much effort seeking to overturn a US law that punished the Russians allegedly involved, including Katsyv. This was the Magnitsky Act. Fusion GPS—the same outfit that commissioned Steele—provided litigation support to Katsyv, who fought a civil forfeiture case.

The Moscow region functioned at a level well below the Kremlin. But Veselnitskaya was known to be close to Russia's prosecutor general, Yury Chaika. Agalarov would later defend Chaika publicly when he was accused of corruption. According to one person who worked with her, Veselnitskaya was "fastidious" and "extremely smart." And, the person said, "would never act without authority." Another associate described her as ambitious and capable, adding: "She wasn't a Kremlin insider. She deeply wanted to be one."

Putin was furious about the passage of the Magnitsky Act. He retaliated by banning the adoption of Russian babies by US couples. The Kremlin launched a campaign to overturn the act. It frequently lobbied on the issue of "adoptions"—Kremlin-speak for lifting US sanctions.

So Putin's interests and Veselnitskaya's interests neatly coincided. Their common goal: the removal of American sanctions.

Trump made further attempts at doing business in Russia. In 2007 he launched his latest product at the Millionaire Fair. This was annual event for the rich and the aspirational, held at Agalarov's Crocus City Mall. The product was vodka—specifically "super premium" Trump vodka. Around this time Trump sought to patent the following brands in Russia: Trump, Trump Tower, Trump International Hotel and Tower, and Trump Home.

The vodka was another commercial flop. By the time I visited the fair in 2008, it was nowhere to be seen. There were plenty of other things on offer: a beachside villa, for example, and a helicopter to take you there with an interior designed by Versace. I found a luxury German dental clinic, a sculptor selling bronze female nudes, and a yacht stand displaying a UK-made Princess yacht, complete with double bed and plasma TV.

For millionaires entry was free. Everybody else had to pay $64 admission. Many of the men drifted round in tuxedos; young women wore cocktail dresses. "I'm not looking for a rich husband. I'm looking for someone with a big personality," said Irina, twenty-six, photographing her friend Olga in an Aston Martin car. (After a few seconds of reflection she conceded: "Obviously, if he was an oligarch with a big personality that would be okay.")

After vodka, Trump tried something else in Russia. From 1996 to 2015 he co-owned with NBC the rights to the Miss Universe beauty contest. According to the Russian press, Trump had been thinking about holding the 2013 contest in Paris. It was at this point that Agalarov's son Emin—a fan of Trump's TV show *The Apprentice*—persuaded Trump to bring the contest to Moscow.

Emin had New York connections: he had studied in Switzerland and at New York's Manhattan Marymount College. In January 2013 the Agalarovs flew to Las Vegas to meet with Trump at the Miss America beauty pageant.

Agalarov Sr backed Miss Universe in Moscow—offering to pay Trump around $14 million in rights to host the contest. Why? The event worked on several levels. There was a state-friendly dimension. It showcased Russia ahead of the Winter Olympic Games in Sochi, hosted by Moscow. It was good PR at a time when Putin faced Western criticism over his clamp-down on civil society.

The contest was also an opportunity to show off the Agalarov brand and to boost Emin's career as a pop artist. Emin would perform before a global TV audience. Finally, according to the Steele dossier, the Kremlin was actively cultivating Trump—an on–off process that had seemingly begun back in 1987 and resumed, the dossier said, around 2008. The FSB would have known of Trump's arrival and Ritz-Carlton stay.

Trump offered plenty of possibilities. He was in the midst of an ugly public campaign questioning Obama's citizenship and demanding the release of his birth certificate. Even if Trump didn't meet the KGB standard for a target in the 1980s, he sure did now.

Ahead of the contest, in June, Trump tweeted:

Do you think Putin will be going to the Miss Universe Pageant in November in Moscow—if so, will he become my new best friend?

Some eighty-six Miss Universe contestants spent three weeks in Moscow. They saw Red Square and the Bolshoi Theatre. They visited the Agalarov estate, shot a round of golf there, and posed in bikinis. Trump arrived in Russia with his Las Vegas business partner, Phil Ruffin. After checking into the Ritz-Carlton, Trump had lunch with the Agalarovs.

The Miss Universe contest took place in Crocus City Mall. The VIPs watching from the balcony formed a microcosm of Putin's Russia. They included Vladimir Kozhin, Putin's aide; Leonid Fedun, the vice president of Lukoil; and Alexsey Mitrofanov, an outspoken nationalist deputy in the state Duma. Plus an alleged gangster, a vodka baron, a singer, and the boss of a state-connected media holding company.

Miss Venezuela, Maria Gabriela Isler, won. According to *Kommersant*, Trump spent the after-party talking to the Miss Universe contestants: "For every girl wearing a sash he found a special word, which he whispered in her ear amid the surrounding disco."

Agalarov was in another VIP zone, talking to Kozhin, Putin's representative, the paper reported. A few days before the pageant, Putin presented Agalarov with one of Russia's highest civilian awards, the Order of Honour. Agalarov posed with Russia's president. He looked pleased. The medal hung from a sky-blue ribbon.

Trump spent November 8 and 9 in Moscow. He didn't manage to see Putin. (According to the Agalarovs, Putin sent Trump a friendly note.) A source told the *Guardian*'s Shaun

Walker that a meeting with Trump had been pencilled into Putin's diary by aides. It fell off the schedule a few days before the event.

Trump did have dinner at the Agalarov-backed restaurant Nobu with a group of Russian businessmen, including Herman Gref, a former economics minister. Gref—the CEO of state-controlled Sberbank, Russia's biggest bank—described Trump as "very lively." Trump had a "good attitude towards Russia," Gref said.

It was the Agalarovs who became Trump's new buddies. On November 9 Trump made an early-morning appearance in Emin's latest music video. Trump reprised his *Apprentice* role, mock-firing Emin, who performed with Miss Universe models. The shoot took place at the Ritz-Carlton.

There was further talk of Trump's long-unfulfilled project: a skyscraper in Moscow bearing his name. According to Emin, speaking to *Forbes*, the idea was to build a Trump Tower and an Agalarov Tower side-by-side. Back in New York, Trump tweeted:

I had a great weekend with you and your family. You have done a FANTASTIC job. TRUMP TOWER-MOSCOW is next. EMIN was WOW!

But then Trump suddenly had bigger plans than a mere tower. After this trip he was running for president for real. The Agalarovs were enthusiastic supporters of his White House bid, as were other forces in Moscow.

It was alleged the Agalarovs also knew things about Trump that could damage him very badly, were they to be released.

Steele's dossier read:

> AGALAROV . . . has been closely involved with TRUMP in Russia and would know most of the details of what the Republican presidential candidate had got up to there.

Thirty years ago Birmingham was a city of browns and greys in the West Midlands. From a concrete tower at its centre one could see a metropolis that was industrial, unlovely, depressed. The Victorians had made Birmingham into a place of commerce and prosperity, but by the 1980s much of its heavy industry had vanished.

There was poverty, unemployment, and community tension—which, in the summer of 1981, flamed into race riots in the suburb of Handsworth, home to several ill-sorted ethnic communities. The police raided a pub; locals responded by looting and trashing property and hurling firebombs. Elsewhere—in Balsall Heath, for example—prostitution was rife. As was crime.

The tower belonged to the *Birmingham Post and Mail*, the city's paper. Built in the 1960s, it was a modernist slab stuck on a podium. Below, cars, vans, and double-deckers streamed through Colmore Circus. The city's economic woes and blight were a source of misery, but they provided plenty of fodder for the journalists working in the building's open-plan office.

In 1983–1984 one of them was Rob Goldstone. Born in Manchester, and in his twenties, Goldstone was an easy-to-spot figure—charming, highly disorganized, and endlessly talkative, in the words of Owen Bowcott, a former *Post and Mail* colleague. "He was a lovely man, and cheerful. He would generate an enormous amount of chat. A motormouth. He could spout for Britain," Bowcott said.

True, Goldstone looked as if he'd never seen the inside of a gym. But he had a gift for making contacts and an enthusiasm that made his subjects talk, open up. From Birmingham he moved to London, working on Fleet Street tabloids and the celebrity beat. And he became a music promoter and publicist, based in Sydney, London again, and New York.

One of his clients was Emin Agalarov. Agalarov's sugary music career had never quite taken off outside Azerbaijan. This wasn't really Goldstone's fault. He was an assiduous representative. He plugged Emin's tours on Facebook, promoted his European concerts, and celebrated Emin's birthday with him in Baku.

Goldstone's now-deleted Instagram profile revealed a luxurious lifestyle—fancy dinners, five-star hotels, cocktails, photos with a procession of young companions whom Goldstone dubbed "muppets." There were numerous trips to Moscow. And a lot of Trump.

The publicist was heavily involved in organizing Miss Universe. In May 2013 he met the Miss Universe team. He returned to Moscow in September and attended the pageant through October and November, posting a photograph of himself in a garish tie.

In February 2014 he was back in Russia again, one of five or six trips that year, this time with Ivanka Trump and Emin. The Agalarovs and the Trump kids became friends. In May 2015 Emin and Goldstone were back at Trump Tower; the tycoon and the singer posed with upturned thumbs. In March 2016 there was another dinner with Trump in Las Vegas.

In fact, Donald Trump Jr spent more time in Moscow than

his father. He was an enthusiastic visitor—flying in repeatedly from 2006 onward. He attended a real estate conference in Russia two years later and was at the Miss Universe pageant. He was meant to oversee Dad's Moscow tower. It was therefore logical that when Goldstone—in June 2016—needed to get in touch with Trump on a delicate matter, he went via Trump Jr.

Goldstone sent him a series of emails. On June 3, 2016, at 10:36 a.m., he wrote:

Good morning.
Emin just called me and asked me to contact you with something very interesting.

The Crown prosecutor of Russia met with his father Aras this morning and in their meeting offered to provide the Trump campaign with some official documents and information that would incriminate Hillary and her dealings with Russia and would be very useful to your father.

This is obviously very high level and sensitive information but is part of Russia and its government's support for Mr Trump—helped along by Aras and Emin.

What do you think is the best way to handle this information and would you be able to speak to Emin about it directly?

I can also send this info to your father via Rhona [Rhona Graff, Trump's long-time assistant] but it is ultra-sensitive so I wanted to send it to you first.
Best
Rob Goldstone

The email was unequivocal. The Russian government was offering Trump damaging material on Clinton as part of its efforts to make Trump president. These "official documents" were arriving through the back door. Naturally enough, this operation was "sensitive." In classic espionage fashion, the approach was done via intermediaries—a chain stretching from the Kremlin, to Russia's prosecutor Yury Chaika, to the Agalarovs, to Goldstone, to Trump Jr, to the candidate himself.

At this point Trump Jr might have notified the FBI. And declined to co-operate with Goldstone, who was acting as emissary for a power with its own agenda.

Instead, Trump Jr answered:

> Thanks Rob I appreciate that. I am on the road at the moment but perhaps I just speak to Emin first. Seems we have some time and if it's what you say I love it especially later in the summer. Could we do a call first thing next week when I am back?

Later in the summer meant closer to the election—to a time when Moscow-supplied *kompromat* might cause maximum damage to Clinton. A weekend passed. Then, on Monday, June 6, Goldstone emailed again, this time with the unambiguous subject line "Russia–Clinton—private and confidential."

> Let me know when you are free to talk with Emin by phone about this Hillary info—you had mentioned early this week so wanted to try to schedule a time and day. Best to you and your family.

Trump Jr messaged back—"Rob could we speak now?" Goldstone tracked down Emin, who was onstage in Moscow, and arranged for him to ring Trump Jr on his cell phone.

The following day, June 7, Goldstone emailed again:

Hope all is well. Emin asked that I schedule a meeting with you and the Russian government attorney who is flying over from Moscow for this Thursday. I believe you are aware of this meeting—and so wondered if 3 p.m. or later on Thursday works for you? I assume it would be at your office.

Trump Jr:

How about 3 at our offices? Thanks Rob appreciate you helping set it up.

Goldstone:

Perfect . . . I won't sit in on the meeting, but will bring them at 3pm and introduce you etc. I will send the names of the two people meeting with you for security when I have them later today.

Trump Jr:

Great. It will likely be Paul Manafort, my brother in law [Jared Kushner] and me. 725 Fifth Avenue 25th floor.

The next day, June 8, Goldstone sent another email, postponing the meeting by one hour to 4 p.m. since the "Russian attorney is in court." Trump Jr offered to bring the meeting forward by a day. Goldstone replied that the attorney—Natalia Veselnitskaya, who worked for Agalarov—hadn't arrived yet from Moscow. Trump Jr forwarded the whole exchange with its damning subject line to Manafort and Kushner.

Goldstone didn't act much like an undercover operative. When he arrived at Trump Tower on June 9, he posted his location on Facebook. Veselnitskaya brought several people with her to the meeting. One of them was Rinat Akhmetshin. Akhmetshin was a lobbyist and US citizen who had previously campaigned against the Magnitsky Act.

He was also a former Soviet intelligence officer who had served in Afghanistan. Akhmetshin insisted he was never GRU and had merely worked for a branch of the army that supported the Special Department, a KGB unit attached to the military. But he made no secret of the fact that he was still in contact with people from Russian intelligence. One associate described Akhmetshin as fun, charming, erudite, a gastronome, and "a total sleazebag" who would work for anybody, regardless of whether they were pro- or anti-Kremlin. Indeed, Akhmetshin told the *Financial Times* that his spy contacts in Moscow didn't trust him because "they know I'm a mercenary."

Also in the room was a translator, Anatoli Samochornov, since Veselnitskaya didn't speak English. Plus Ike Kaveladze, the US-based vice president of Agalarov's Crocus Group.

Akhmetshin turned up to the meeting in sneakers and jeans. He later said Veselnitskaya handed over a folder of documents to the Trumps—"lawyerly stuff," as he put it. It concerned a firm linked to Browder's Hermitage Capital that had donated to Bill Clinton's foundation. This could be "a great campaign issue," Veselnitskaya said, according to Akhmetshin.

Veselnitskaya had hired Fusion GPS in 2014. It had supplied her with some of the material on Browder. (Glenn Simpson saw no conflict of interest between the Magnitsky project and his work beginning a year later on Trump. His view: he wasn't a political activist or a crusader; he was an investigator.)

What was going on at this meeting? Veselnitskaya and Akhmetshin had been lobbying against the 2012 Magnitsky

Act for some time. They had originally hoped to give evidence in Washington to Congress and its foreign affairs subcommittee. This fell through after Republicans scheduled a full committee hearing. In the meantime, Trump's political ascent elevated their efforts to a new level.

Alex Goldfarb—a friend of Litvinenko's—spotted Veselnitskaya and Akhmetshin four days after the Trump Tower meeting. This was in DC. They were at a special screening of *The Magnitsky Act*, a documentary by the Russian filmmaker Andrei Nekrasov.

The film was bitterly critical of Browder and suggested that his version of Magnitsky's death was wrong. Goldfarb exchanged a few words with Akhmetshin—a relatively small guy, as he put it, and chubby, who spoke English with some accent but not much. Goldfarb saw Veselnitskaya mingling with guests. The event at Washington's Newseum ended in a shouting match. Much of the audience interpreted the film as little more than anti-sanctions propaganda.

Formally, Veselnitskaya wasn't in the United States on a government mission, Goldfarb acknowledged. But he said this distinction was meaningless since the lawyer and the people she represented back in Moscow were "all part of the same octopus. . . . It's a big conglomerate, Kremlin Inc., based not on power but on money. They are part of the same club," he told me.

Why had the Kremlin picked a mid-level lawyer as emissary to the Trumps? "It was purely opportunistic," Goldfarb said. "You don't send a gangster like Mogilevich. She had access."

Donald Trump Jr's emails emerged in July 2017. Before that, Trump Jr had dismissed the suggestion that his father had received furtive help from the Russian government as "disgusting" and "phony." Now there was proof of collusion.

When the *New York Times* first contacted Trump Jr over the emails, he was evasive. He claimed the meeting with Veselnitskaya had been to discuss something else: the Kremlin's decision to ban the adoption of Russian babies by US couples. If it was not clear before, "adoption" was Moscow code for lifting sanctions, and it would come up again.

When it emerged that the *New York Times* had the emails, Trump Jr's explanation changed. He admitted that an acquaintance—Goldstone—had asked him to meet someone who "might have information helpful to the campaign." Trump Jr then characterized the meeting as a zero, "the most inane" nonsense—an unevent that left him "actually agitated," with nothing handed over. Manafort and Kushner claimed not to have read the email chain or clocked its incendiary offer.

What mattered here, though, was *intent*. Trump's two relatives and his campaign manager must have believed they might receive covert information from a foreign government. They seemed willing and ready to accept it—and, it appeared, to conceal its provenance. This would be a textbook definition of collusion. It was further material for Bob Mueller, the special prosecutor. Trump said he knew nothing about it. Like most of Trump's denials—he was in Trump Tower at the time—it didn't convince.

Trump Jr said he was disclosing the emails in order to be "totally transparent." But in an interview with Fox's Sean Hannity he kept quiet about some of the other characters in the room. He said nothing about Akhmetshin, the former counter-intelligence officer.

In the wake of these embarrassing disclosures, the White

House's explanations for its dealings with Russia mutated. First, there were flat denials—there had been no meetings. Then, there were meetings, but nothing of importance transpired. Finally, we were offered material, but this was standard political opposition research. By the summer of 2017 Trump's message amounted to this: Sure, we cheated. But what are you going to do about it?

It had been a long road to get to that point. Putin may not have had much luck in recruiting students from South America. But now—three decades later—he was finally going to meet someone the KGB had talent-spotted all those years ago. Putin was meeting President Trump.

9

Thraldom

Summer 2017
Hamburg–Washington

The Russian leadership did not interfere
in these elections. He [President Trump]
accepts these statements.
—SERGEI LAVROV, speaking at the
G20 summit in Hamburg

It looked like a war zone. Smoke, the sound of breaking glass, burning vehicles, sirens. A sinister procession of masked men dressed entirely in black, advancing through a city with evil purpose. Gaza? Aleppo? Mosul? A parade by ISIS fighters? Or perhaps a pyrotechnic film set built for a Hollywood fantasy movie pitting humans against some mythical fire monster?

Nope. The apocalyptic scenes were taking place in Hamburg, one of Germany's most civilized northern cities. The men in black were left-wing protesters. They belonged to a radical autonomous faction known as the Schwarzer Block. The Black Bloc. And the reason for their protest was the arrival in Hamburg of global capitalism—or at least its best-known politician representatives.

The G20 summit hadn't even officially started. Nevertheless, the Schwarzer Block were up and about. While most residents in the Altona district were having breakfast, the activists were already creating carnage. They moved on Elbchaussee, a sinuous street of bourgeois villas overlooking the Elbe River and Hamburg's port. There they started smashing stuff.

The destruction was methodical, efficient. One protester would stave in a car window. Seconds later another would chuck in a flare. Shadowy figures overturned al fresco café tables, dragged plant pots into the middle of a pedestrian shopping precinct, and sprayed graffiti on walls. The group, an ambulant ant army, then passed on.

Video taken from a balcony shows the protesters advancing towards a blue-and-yellow symbol of capitalist hegemony—Ikea. Behind them thick grey smoke fills the air. Some of their targets seem distinctly underwhelming. They include cars parked outside an old people's home and a local pharmacy.

You had to feel a stab of sympathy for Angela Merkel, the G20's host. Dozens of anti-G20 demonstrations were taking place, one called appropriately "Welcome to Hell." Some of her least favourite people were coming: Trump, Putin, and Turkish president Recep Tayyip Erdoğan, as well as more sympathetic faces such as France's Emmanuel Macron and Canada's Justin Trudeau.

German officials had spent a year preparing the agenda. It encompassed trade, migration, climate change, a compact to build private investment for Africa. It was an opportunity for world leaders to overcome their differences and make common cause.

The five thousand members of the press accredited for the two-day event, however, were mainly focused on one question:

How would Trump get on with Putin?

It turned out: just great. The two met at a summit get-together that morning and at bilateral talks in the afternoon. This second encounter coincided with a plenary session on climate change. The schedule clash seemed deliberate: the German media suggested that Trump and Putin had "bunked off" the session, following Trump's exit from the Paris accord.

The American and the Russian sat down together on white leather chairs. There had been phone calls, three of them, and long-distance blandishments, delivered by Trump to Putin and Putin to Trump. Now, at last, they were meeting face-to-face. Before the cameras Trump said it was an "honour" to meet Russia's president. He added that he looked forward to "a lot of very positive things happening for Russia, for the United States, and for everybody concerned."

Putin sat impassively. He waited. Then it came—Trump extended his hand. Putin paused for a fraction of a second, his left hand clasping his right. And then he took Trump's out-stretched palm.

The resulting photo was what Putin had surely intended. Russian state media adopted it joyfully. It depicted the US president, hand out in greeting, as a petitioner, a junior player—seeking approval from the world's pre-eminent statesman. Putin looks Trump coolly in the eye. As told by Moscow, here was Russia's leader dominating the international stage again.

Putin made a few comments in Russian on how a personal meeting was better than a phone call. He gestured to the TV cameras and journalists with his right thumb and whispered to Trump, in what looked like solidarity:

"Are these the ones who insulted you?"

*

This was a cosy affair. The restricted discussion format suited Moscow perfectly. Taking part in the talks were Putin, Trump, and just two other principals: Lavrov and US secretary of state Rex Tillerson.

Putin may not have met Trump before but he went back a long way with Tillerson. In 2013 Russia's president pinned a prestigious state medal to the oilman's chest—the Order of Friendship. Tillerson described his relationship with Putin as "great." It dated back almost two decades. They met in 1999, when Tillerson was an executive at Exxon Mobil and seeking to develop an oil field on Sakhalin Island.

Tillerson succeeded where other foreigners failed by striking a deal with Rosneft and Igor Sechin. Rosneft got a controlling stake in what would become the Sakhalin-1 project. Tillerson's partnership with Sechin—who talked of wanting to ride motorbikes in the United States with Tillerson—continued when in 2006 Tillerson became Exxon Mobil's chief. It would lead to a further agreement in 2012 to co-develop Russia's Arctic.

Of all the CEOs in America, it was Tillerson who had the best contacts with senior Russians. Sechin was at Tillerson's elbow when the American got his Kremlin medal. Putin, Sechin, and Tillerson celebrated with champagne.

Was it this—rather than Tillerson's passion for diplomacy—that led Trump to name him unexpectedly as secretary of state?

Trump's national security adviser, H. R. McMaster—a serving general sceptical of Russia, appointed after Flynn's departure—was missing from the Hamburg bilateral. Also excluded was Fiona Hill, the president's senior Russian adviser. Hill is a career academic and Russia scholar with a PhD from Harvard. As a director of the Brookings Institute she had co-authored a book titled *Mr. Putin: Operative in the Kremlin.* In 2014 Hill published an updated edition after Russia took Crimea.

It was safe to say that Trump hadn't read it.

With or without his senior advisers, this was the moment for Trump to make the American view clear—namely, that the Kremlin's hacking of the election amounted to ill-considered interference. And that any attempt by Moscow to do the same in 2018's mid-term elections or 2020 would lead to a stringent US response—more sanctions, travel bans, even a cut-off of Russia's access to the SWIFT banking payments system.

Putin would interpret anything less than this as American weakness. And, practically, a green light for his operatives to tamper again in Washington's affairs. All done, of course, under the same cover of plausible deniability. There was no *official* hacking, the *government* wasn't involved, etc.

Apparently, Trump said none of this. The discussions went on for two hours and sixteen minutes. At one point Melania came in to break up the talks, only to exit again, Tillerson said. The time went well beyond the allotted slot. A record of what was discussed would have been illuminating—but there wasn't one.

Afterwards, Tillerson hailed the talks as successful and said "there was a very clear positive chemistry" between the two. He said that the White House had demanded a future commitment from Moscow that it wouldn't interfere in US politics. But, he said, neither side saw much value in "relitigating" the past.

There were positive outcomes, Tillerson said, including a ceasefire in southwest Syria. And a new US–Russian working group on . . . how to prevent cyber crime. This second announcement lit up Twitter. Trump had agreed to co-operate with the Kremlin on preventing election hacking and to form an "impenetrable" joint team. (The plan—akin to inviting in your burglar to discuss home security—was soon dropped.)

Lavrov gave a Russian account of what happened. According to him, Putin told Trump that the Kremlin hadn't interfered and had nothing to do with hacking or the "strange" incidents in the lead-up to the US vote. Trump "accepted" this statement, Lavrov said in Russian. The verb in the original—*prini-mat*—has a definitive ring to it.

If Lavrov's report were accurate, it meant that Trump had chosen to believe Putin over his own intelligence community. For months, Trump had equivocated about Moscow's involvement. Twenty-four hours earlier, during a visit to Poland, he had said, "I think it was Russia," but added that "nobody really knows" and "it was probably other people or countries."

Now he was signing off on Putin's Big Lie.

Outside the G20 security zone, there were chaotic scenes. The Hamburg police were overwhelmed. The summit was taking place next to the Schanzenviertel district, a traditional bastion of left-wing activism and dissent. Protests were always likely. Some residents felt that the police's heavy-handed tactics made the situation worse.

Hamburg's Social Democrat-run city hall was having a lousy time. It would face criticism—from the owners of torched cars and broken corner shops—that it had mishandled everything. The Schwarzer Block succeeded in alienating left-leaning residents who might have otherwise sympathized with its stance on neoliberalism.

One of the city's headaches was finding accommodation for heads of state. Hamburg's senate put Trump in a nineteenth-century neoclassical villa located between the Alster River and a pond, the Feenteich. If Trump had got into a boat and rowed across, he would have received a warm reception. There was the Russian consulate.

The *Guardian*'s Berlin correspondent, Philip Oltermann, tried to visit the temporary presidential guesthouse, only to find the road blocked. He met an old man on a bike, standing next to a security barricade. Looking at the port city—wreathed in black smoke and with a helicopter patrolling ominously in the sky above, the man remarked:

"This must be the end of the world, then?"

On the eve of the summit riot police had intercepted one group of protesters determined to march to the G20 entrance. The authorities broke up the protest next to Hamburg's fish market using water cannon, baton charges, and pepper spray. By Friday afternoon, July 7, the demonstrators were regrouping and attempting to reach another Hamburg venue—the Elbphilharmonie.

The undulating concert hall on the north bank of the Elbe was hosting the G20 participants and delegates. The programme included a gala performance and dinner. Putin and Trump were guests. So were Ivanka Trump and Jared Kushner, who had travelled to Germany as part of the official US delegation.

Oltermann witnessed the surreal occasion. "It was like something out of a dystopian science fiction film. You had the most powerful people in the world eating canapés in an ivory tower and listening to Beethoven. And then outside you had thousands of anarchists, covered in blood, battling with police."

He watched as Greenpeace tried to reach the hall on speed-boats. They were stopped. About twenty activists then plunged into the water and started swimming frantically towards the venue; the police fished them out. One protester managed to smash the window of a US delegate's car. Oltermann likened what he saw to a hellish and watery vision by the medieval painter Hieronymus Bosch. "It looked like the End of Days," he observed.

Unseen by those outside, something strange was going on inside.

During the concert the Trumps sat next to the Macrons. At dinner spouses were separated. Melania was placed next to Putin; Trump alongside Juliana Awada, the wife of Argentina's president. At some point Trump got up. He sat down again—next to Putin. For the next hour Trump and Putin were deep in conversation. Only one other person was with them: Putin's personal interpreter.

What they discussed was a mystery. Trump left his own interpreter behind, in a breach of national security protocol. G20 leaders looked on in amazement. Circulating at these high-level events was normal. But the US president who had skipped most of the plenary sessions only appeared to want to talk to one person.

The White House kept quiet about the meeting. It was revealed only after two people who were there tipped off Ian Bremmer, the president of the Eurasia Group.

Bremmer said his informants were "startled" by what they witnessed. "It's very clear that Trump's best single relationship in the G20 is with Putin. US allies were surprised, flummoxed, disheartened," he said. "You've got Trump in the room with all these allies and who's the one he spends time with?"

Trump dismissed claims he tried to conceal the chat as "ridiculous." He told the *New York Times* that the meal was "going toward dessert" when he decided to say hello to Melania and sat with Putin: "It was not a long conversation, but it was, you know, could be fifteen minutes. Just talked about things."

The things, Trump clarified, included "adoptions"—that is, sanctions. And, uncannily enough, the same subject discussed during the closed meeting between Donald Trump Jr, Veselnitskaya, and a former Russian spy. Putin wanted them gone. They were still in place.

If Trump failed to remove them, how might Putin respond?

This question was unanswerable, not least because there was no government record of this private conversation. Trump's critics sniffed conspiracy. The columnist David Frum tweeted that the president had things to say to Putin that "he wants literally nobody in the US govt to hear, very much including his own National Security team." Garry Kasparov said Trump was meeting his "KGB handler."

Such assertions were unverifiable. But six months into his presidency Trump's weirdly deferential behaviour towards Putin—his singular reluctance to criticize, his boundless willingness to appease, his desire for face time—were there for all to see.

It looked like a kind of thraldom.

One of the KGB's long-standing goals was—as one secret memo put it—to "aggravate disagreements" between the United States and Western Europe. As Kryuchkov's instructions showed, Moscow wanted to "deepen division" within NATO and to cleave the United States from its allies.

Until the election of Trump, this strategy had never quite worked. The EU and the Obama administration had co-ordinated their responses to Russia's assault on Ukraine, for example. There were differences, for sure. But the post-war transatlantic relationship was solid.

It was based on values, even if the practice of them was often flawed. They included international institutions, NATO and its mutual defence pact, the global rule of law, human rights, and basic decency.

Now the Atlantic alliance was in trouble. For the first time in more than seventy years European states were beginning ask a question that in previous times might have seemed ridiculous.

It was this: is the US administration as led by Trump actually an ally?

These doubts had several dimensions. First, Trump seemed to prefer the company of autocrats—Putin, the Saudis—to that of his own democratically elected peers. Second, there was Trump's ill-informed commentary on Twitter. Often he criticized the Europeans, and in particular the Germans.

This did not mean the Atlantic alliance was finished. Mike Hayden, the former CIA director, observed that the partnership had such strong historical roots it would survive, despite suffering heavy "blows" from Trump.

But there was a rift. Its scale was apparent before the Hamburg summit, when Trump made his maiden trip as president to Europe. As an exercise in diplomatic outreach, the trip in May was a disaster. In Brussels, the president unveiled a memorial to 9/11, the one occasion when NATO's collective defence principle, article 5, was invoked. His speech, however, made no mention of the United States' commitment to it.

Instead, Trump used his speech to reprove other countries for "not paying what they should be paying" into the NATO budget. He said they owed "massive amounts." (Not true: NATO's spending rules were domestic guidelines.)

In the case of Duško Marković, the prime minister of Montenegro, this low-grade hectoring went a step further. On the way to a NATO summit photo shoot Trump pushed Marković aside. Probably Trump had no idea who Marković was. Yet if Putin had been able to choose which man in a suit to shove, he would surely have chosen Marković.

To the intense displeasure of Moscow, Montenegro was joining NATO. Russia views the western Balkans as its zone of influence. According to Montenegrin officials, Russian intelligence had recently tried to stage a coup in the capital, Podgorica, with a view to halting its NATO accession. The plot—allegedly involving a GRU officer—failed.

There was more physical theatre during Trump's first meeting with Macron, which featured an extended—and arguably victorless—handshake war. Then there was a meeting with the EU's executive leadership, in which Trump complained about Germany's trade surplus with the United States.

"The Germans are bad, very bad," Trump said, according to one participant who spoke to *Der Spiegel.* Trump added: "See the millions of cars they are selling to the United States. Terrible. We will stop this."

Trump's behaviour at the G7 summit, hosted by Italy the same week, was scarcely an improvement, from the European perspective. The venue was the town of Taormina in Sicily. There was disagreement over climate change, with six countries opposing one country, Trump's.

Then there was the president's aloof style. The leaders strolled seven hundred yards together to the town's hilltop piazza. Minus Trump, who took a golf cart.

No wonder, then, that in a speech launching her bid to be re-elected chancellor for the fourth time, Merkel noted that the

EU was now on its own. It could no longer rely on the United States or post-Brexit Britain. Merkel implied that she'd come to this conclusion following her recent brushes with Trump. "I've experienced that in the last few days. We Europeans truly have to take our fate into our own hands," she said, speaking in Munich.

Trump was unpopular in Germany. For Merkel to distance herself from his administration made electoral sense.

At the same time Merkel's negative view of Trump might be explained by other factors. In 2016 the BND, Germany's foreign intelligence agency, supplied material to the Obama administration concerning contacts between the Trump team and Russians. The BND reported directly to Merkel's office. It had inside knowledge of Trump's business transactions, many of them conducted via German banks.

One former senior director on the US National Security Council speculated: "Merkel knows how bad Trump is. She's been briefed [by her agencies]."

The ex-director said that as someone who grew up in communist East Germany, Merkel—the daughter of a pastor, a one-time research scientist, and a fluent Russian speaker who visited Soviet Moscow—had little tolerance for lying. "She lived through that. She's almost Calvinist," the former official said.

Beyond the atmospherics, and Trump's boorish habits, there were substantial foreign policy differences—most of all over Russia.

Evidently, Trump chose to believe Putin's assurances of Russian non-involvement in hacking. The Europeans knew better. The Kremlin's interference in the US election was merely the latest manifestation of a deliberate attempt to distort democracy, often involving cyber attacks. It had been going on across Europe for some time.

In 2007 Moscow staged its first major external web attack against Estonia. Since then, suspected Russian hacking teams had targeted EU institutions and, in 2015, the German parliament. Like the DNC hack, the apparent goal was to gather data with a view to influencing Germany's elections. And to damage Merkel, Europe's most powerful leader and a proponent of Crimea-related sanctions.

The Russian hackers struck France, too. In April 2015 they breached the television network TV5Monde. The hackers suspended programming for three hours. According to the French government's cyber agency, they were from the same group that would later be designated as Fancy Bear. The attack was a warm-up. On the eve of the 2017 French general election, hackers dumped tens of thousands of emails and other documents from the systems of Macron's political party, En Marche!

The breach came too late to affect the result. But the method—an anonymous cyber raid, the material linked to by WikiLeaks—was redolent of the DNC hack.

As EU spy chiefs warned, cyber attacks were part of a hybrid Russian strategy. Another plank was to support far-left and far-right parties across the European continent. This could be political and financial. In Soviet times, Moscow helped and sponsored Western communist parties and friendship societies. Now it was cultivating a soft-power network of radical nationalist groups opposed to the European Union and friendly to Putin.

One beneficiary was Marine Le Pen, whose far-right National Front received a €9.4 million loan from a Russian bank. Le Pen backed Trump's White House bid and received an implicit endorsement in return, when Trump described her ahead of the French presidential election as the "strongest" candidate on borders and terrorism. In January Le Pen visited Trump Tower (without, apparently, meeting Trump). In March she held talks at the Kremlin with Putin.

The Europeans viewed Putin with scepticism and foreboding.

Trump, seemingly, saw Moscow as his nearest G20 ally. But if Putin did something that directly damaged and offended US interests, Trump would rebuke him. Wouldn't he?

The Harry S. Truman building in Foggy Bottom is a piece of monumental architecture. Its white classical lines radiate calm and austere grandeur. In the years after World War II, the US State Department was the planet's most consequential foreign ministry. Its soft power was enormous.

The State Department's officers were a dedicated bunch. In 2010 diplomatic cables sent by US missions around the world were leaked. This was embarrassing for Hillary Clinton. Paradoxically, these on-the-ground reports enhanced her department's reputation. They offered frank, and sometimes unflattering, assessments of world leaders; analysis, much of it of high quality; and some entertaining gossip. A few were written with literary flair.

Seven years later, and the State Department was—in the words of one DC insider—"being gutted." Senior posts requiring Senate confirmation remained unfilled, the Trump administration was proposing a 32 percent cut in the budget, and around a third of ambassadorial jobs were vacant. Scandinavia was a black hole: no head of mission in Oslo, Stockholm, or Helsinki. Or Berlin or Brussels or Canberra.

Veteran diplomats were heading for the door, off and out after long careers. Principal assistant deputy secretaries were being thinned out.

One explanation for this was new management. Tillerson was an aloof and inscrutable figure who made little or no effort to communicate with his seventy-five thousand employees. During the early months of the Trump administration, Tillerson was practically invisible. According to the rumours, he was deeply at odds with his boss and being constantly undercut by the White House, a few blocks away.

There was proof of this following the wretched events that summer in Charlottesville, Virginia. One person was killed and others injured when a suspected white nationalist drove into a group of activists protesting at a neo-Nazi rally. Trump's response was to condemn violence on "many sides." There were many "fine people" among those who had attended the far-right rally, the president said. His sympathies, evidently, were with the white supremacists, some of whom had marched in Charlottesville waving torches and chanting: "Jews will not replace us."

In a Fox interview, Tillerson was asked if Trump's comments made it harder for him to represent America abroad. Were US values Trump's values? Tillerson's damning answer: "The president speaks for himself."

There was a fundamental problem, too: What, in the age of Trump, was the State Department's mission? Was it to uphold American principles abroad? Simply to deal with bad people (terrorists, Islamist radicals) and China? Or to cultivate warm relations with authoritarian kingdoms where Trump had hotels and branded golf resorts? Was Trump an America First isolationist or an interventionist?

As a candidate Trump had disdained internationalism, condoned the use of torture, and declared climate change "a hoax." His worldview, if you could call it that, was unashamedly inward-looking.

This nativist creed appeared to be for real—at least until August. In a major speech Trump announced that he was increasing the number of American troops in Afghanistan. The president said he was no longer interested in nation-building. Even so, Trump's new strategy looked remarkably like Obama's. It marked defeat for Breitbart and a victory for Trump's generals, plus the US intelligence agencies, all of them believers in the use of American force abroad.

Friends of State watched the president's flip-flop with confusion and dismay. Writing in the *New York Times*, Roger Cohen called Trump's determination to chop the State Department a "strange act of national self-amputation." Cohen offered reasons for its dismemberment. They included the president's love of military leaders, Steve Bannon's plan to "deconstruct" the administrative state, and revenge on a bureaucracy that was once Hillary's. It appeared that State's woes couldn't get worse.

But they did.

According to the investigative journalist Michael Isikoff, the Trump administration in its early weeks had tried to "normalize" relations with Russia. Officials asked State Department staffers to come up with a plan that would see the diplomatic compounds closed by Obama given back to Moscow. And a conciliatory US package scrapping the sanctions introduced over hacking. The goal was a "grand bargain" with the Kremlin. It was unclear what, if anything, Russia would have to offer in return.

The plan ran into immediate opposition on Capitol Hill and

was abandoned after Flynn's resignation. In fact, Congress was moving in the other direction. Two weeks after the G20 summit it passed a comprehensive new sanctions package, designed to censure Russia for its interference in the United States and Ukraine. The bill was passed by the House of Representatives by 419 votes to 3, and by the Senate by 98 votes to 2. This left Trump little option but to sign it into law.

This he did, grudgingly. At the same time he made clear that he believed the legislation to be "seriously flawed" and a curtailment of his executive right as president to decide foreign policy. In short, he didn't like it.

The Kremlin's reaction was icy. The foreign ministry said it was closing down the US embassy dacha, spared in December, and rescinding access to warehouse space. And cutting the number of diplomats and support staff at US missions in Russia. Not by thirty-five, as Obama did, but by 775. This, the ministry said, would bring the number of American personnel in Russia in line with the number of Russians in the United States.

Russian officials sought to absolve Trump of blame for this "countermove." They portrayed the US president as a victim of a ploy by "the deep state," abetted by the fake news media to prevent the normalization of ties. As Dmitry Medvedev put it on Twitter:

The US establishment fully outwitted Trump. The president is not happy about the sanctions, yet he could not but sign the bill.

However the Russian media might spin it, the expulsions were a hostile and provocative move. They damaged the

United States' ability to conduct diplomacy and, on a basic level, to provide visas to ordinary Russians seeking to travel to the United States. Trump's reaction, then, should have been obvious: to protest, lament, and condemn.

Instead, when asked about the expulsions, Trump said: "I want to thank him [Putin], because we're trying to cut down our payroll and as far as I'm concerned, I'm very thankful that he let go of a large number of people because now we have a smaller payroll. There's no real reason for them to go back. I greatly appreciate the fact that we've been able to cut our payroll of the United States. We're going to save a lot of money."

Even by Trump's standards, the remarks were a surprise. He was *thanking* Putin. Expressing gratitude to Russia's president for upending the careers of loyal American diplomats and wrecking those of officers preparing for a Moscow posting.

Trump's comments—made from his golf course in Bedminster, New Jersey—weren't even true. Foreign Service staff evicted from Moscow would remain on the federal payroll and work elsewhere. State Department employees were left appalled and angry by Trump's failure to defend them, and by Tillerson's feeble silence.

A day later Trump said his comments were sarcastic. But he offered no criticism of Putin.

When it came to Trump and Putin, one person was stronger, one weaker. Putin knew the full extent to which Trump and his entourage had—or hadn't—collaborated with Moscow. This gave the Kremlin leverage.

Putin's usual method in these circumstances was to exploit the situation to his advantage. He could turn the pressure on Trump up or dial it down. Either way, the president was helpless.

*

By the summer of 2017 two processes were taking place in Washington. They were opposites. One involved discovery: finding leads, turning over stones, following evidence. The other: hiding tracks, making false or misleading statements, and generally covering up.

The second process of concealment appeared to be led, erratically and impulsively, by the president himself; the first by Trump's most dangerous adversary—not Congress or the Democratic Party but Bob Mueller, whose inquiry into alleged collusion between the Trump campaign and Russia was gaining speed and force.

The Hamburg summit had a final chapter. The *New York Times* discovered the Veselnitskaya meeting, featuring Trump Jr, Kushner, and Manafort. It asked the White House for comment. According to the *Washington Post*, Kushner and Ivanka held discussions with their lawyers on the sidelines of the G20, to plot a way forward.

It was unclear at this point how much the *New York Times* had. One version said that Trump Jr wanted to give a full explanation; another that he was opposed. Kushner was in favour of transparency, believing that it would be better to give details and release the relevant emails to the media. His view: sooner or later the story would come out. The president's legal team, led by Marc Kasowitz, agreed, as did Josh Raffel, a White House spokesman who works closely with Kushner, the *Post* reported.

The consensus lasted until Trump climbed aboard Air Force One. Sitting in a forward cabin and en route to Washington from Hamburg, Trump rewrote his son's press statement. What emerged was a minimal four-line version. Trump Jr said:

"It was a short introductory meeting. I asked Jared and Paul to stop by. We primarily discussed a program about the adoption of Russian children that was active and popular with American families years ago and was since ended by the Russian government, but it was not a campaign issue at the time and there was no followup."

This was erroneous—a lie, in fact.

There was no mention of the fact that the Kremlin had pre-promised "sensitive" material on Clinton that could help the Trump campaign. Instead, the president made out that the meeting was exclusively about adoptions. It happened following an approach from an unnamed "acquaintance," Trump dictated.

Here, then, was the president's method: to conceal and to obfuscate, even if others thought this poor strategy. It appeared to flow from Trump's belief that he was his own best adviser and tactician. In this case, Trump's actions were counterproductive. As with his firing of Comey, it looked as if Trump was trying to impede justice. Or—if not that—to throw dirt in the face of those who would investigate him.

The special counsel's probe began in May. It was based in a nondescript office in Washington, where more than a dozen attorneys, investigators, and support staff were busy at work. These were Mueller's staff. According to CNN, the atmosphere was akin to that of a small attorney's office, with FBI agents and prosecutors examining different aspects of a growing investigation.

There was the core collusion inquiry and the possible obstruction of justice from within the White House. Plus the roles of Manafort and Flynn, both of whom had initially hidden their true roles and failed to register as foreign agents.

There were few hard facts. As Scott Horton, a lecturer at Columbia Law School, put it to me: "Mueller is famous for managing an extremely tight ship in terms of leaks." His inquiry was being conducted against the backdrop of "an incredible storm" inside the FBI. Staff were furious at the way Trump had treated Comey, Horton said, with the mood one of unprecedented "hostility" towards the White House.

Mueller may have been tight-lipped but his choice of team gave clues. His investigation was moving in a classic manner. It was following the money—in this case, the flow of cash from Russia and Eastern Europe. One of those hired by Mueller was Andrew Weissmann, a New York federal prosecutor known for going after mafia families in the city with Russian ties. Mueller—who also investigated Enron—had come from the Justice Department, where he headed up the criminal fraud section.

Another recruit was Lisa Page. Page was a Justice Department trial attorney who had been based in Budapest. There she had pursued Russian organized crime and Semion Mogilevich, the mobster allegedly under FSB protection. Budapest was an important FBI centre and a hub for Russian intelligence.

Other high-powered names included Elizabeth Prelogar, a fluent Russian speaker who had studied in Russia as a Fulbright scholar. Plus Michael Dreeben, a former deputy solicitor general described in the blog Lawfare as "quite possibly the best criminal appellate lawyer in America." And James Quarles, a veteran attorney who worked as an assistant prosecutor during the original Watergate investigation.

It was a formidable team. No surprise, then, that the White House was keen to discredit Mueller and slime the FBI.

Trump decried the investigation as a political witch hunt. He indicated that he might consider firing Mueller and attacked

Jeff Sessions. In an interview with the *New York Times* Trump said that if he had known Sessions would recuse himself over Russia—an act that led indirectly to Mueller's probe—he would never have made him attorney general. Trump said his own financial affairs were irrelevant to the Russia thing and a "red line."

These public hostilities appeared not to deflect Mueller from his job. Without fuss, he relocated to a secure suite of offices better equipped to handle secret and classified material. Mueller was an obvious target for Russian espionage and technical collection measures such as bugging. His office grew. It had sixteen attorneys, with Greg Andres, a fraud specialist and expert on foreign bribery, the latest.

When it came to collecting evidence, Mueller had different tools in his box. He could informally request documents, issue subpoenas, or—the legal equivalent of a big hammer—carry out raids on a suspect's property.

In late July FBI officers gathered outside an innocuous-looking residential building in Alexandria, Virginia. It was early. They didn't have an appointment. Dozens of agents burst into an apartment and carried away documents.

The home belonged to Manafort. Later the same day, July 26, Manafort had been due to testify before the Senate Judiciary Committee. The FBI pre-empted this by going before a judge and obtaining a search warrant. The bureau had to offer evidence that a crime had likely taken place to persuade a judge that its actions were proportionate.

The raid was a stunning sign to the White House that Mueller's inquiry was in earnest. Moreover, it implied that FBI investigators weren't fully confident Manafort would tell them everything he knew.

It's unclear what the FBI took. Manafort had already turned over three hundred pages to congressional committees, including notes taken during his Trump Tower sit-down with Veselnitskaya. A similar request was made to the White House, asking for records from the meeting. Manafort denied collusion and said via his lawyer that he was co-operating with law enforcement.

Investigators also zeroed in on Flynn. They asked the Trump administration to hand over material concerning Trump's former national security adviser. Witnesses were also questioned in connection with Flynn's lobbying activities, the *New York Times* reported. Mueller's focus was on whether the Turkish government was secretly behind the payments made to Flynn via a Turkish businessman.

Steele declined to say whether Mueller had been in touch with him. But it would be logical for Mueller to establish a channel of communication with him in London. And for Steele to help the investigation where possible.

When Mueller took over, he used a grand jury in Virginia, set up by his predecessor, to execute his requests. His next step was to convene a dedicated grand jury in DC, a few blocks away from the suite of offices where he and his team were working. This indicated that Mueller intended to use the jury to make extensive requests for documents.

As the *Guardian*'s Julian Borger noted, this was inhospitable terrain for the president. Republicans were an endangered species in the District of Columbia, where Trump won just 4 percent of the vote. It was a nightmare jurisdiction for him politically—unlike Virginia, where Republicans were more prevalent—and the place from where any indictments would be issued. And where potential criminal trials could be held.

All of this was ominous for Trump and his beleaguered presidency. There were further unhappy rumours sweeping Washington—that either Manafort or Flynn, and possibly others, had been "flipped." This meant that they had agreed with the FBI to become co-operating witnesses in exchange for leniency down the line.

There was no proof of this. And it was unclear when Mueller would report or if the evidence his team was accumulating in painstaking fashion would ever lead to criminal charges. The big question—as one former national security adviser put it to me—was whether Mueller's "arrows would impale Team Orange."

But the legal net appeared to be tightening. Of its own accord Trump's administration was freely imploding. First Flynn, then Spicer and Priebus, and then Bannon—by mid-summer all were sacked and out.

Trump repeated his claim that he had no investments in Russia, no deals, no loans. This was formally true. But as Mueller was discovering there was plenty of flow in the other direction—of Russian money *into* Trump real estate and related entities. Going back several decades.

There was also the matter of the oligarch who bought Trump's former Florida house. The purchase left Trump with a $50 million profit. Why would a Russian do that?

10

From Russia with Cash

1984–2017
Perm–Florida–Monaco–Cyprus–New York

Russians make up a pretty disproportionate
cross-section of a lot of our assets. We see a lot
of money pouring in from Russia.
—DONALD TRUMP JR, speaking in Moscow
in 2008 about the Trump Organization

Perm, 1984. It was the beginning of term at Perm's medical academy. Student doctors were queuing up for registration. One of them was Dmitry Rybolovlev, the son of accomplished local medics.

Rybolovlev couldn't help but notice the girl standing immediately behind him in the line. She was blonde, blue-eyed, and—as he would soon discover—smart, a whizz at maths, the daughter of an engineer. The girl's name was Elena. Dmitry and Elena took the admissions test together. They found themselves in the same class for cardiology.

Their teenage romance was a *coup de foudre*. Over the next six years they passed all of their exams together. Elena won the

Lenin Prize, three times. As well as study, the young couple explored the subsidized cultural life on offer in the late Soviet Union. There were weekly trips to the city's opera house and ballet, to museums and to the theatre.

It was a modest lifestyle—but who lived better?

At the age of twenty-one they married. The first of two daughters, Ekaterina—Katia—arrived two years later. By this point Rybolovlev was considering his options. He could pursue the same steady career as his father, Evgeny, a cardiologist. Or he could move to Moscow, learn about finance, and plunge into the untried world of Russian capitalism. He chose the second.

What happened next resembles a dark fairy tale. In 1992 Rybolovlev went on a business course in the capital. He returned to Perm, set up an investment bank, and applied what he knew about privatization to the region's Soviet-era chemical factories. He acquired a stake in Uralkali, Russia's biggest producer of potassium-based fertilizer. By 1996 he had control.

Rybolovlev would insist that unlike other tycoons he received no leg up from the state. Apparent proof of this came the same year, when he spent eleven months in jail, accused of murdering a rival factory executive. After getting out, exonerated, he joined his family in Switzerland and the safety of Geneva. Uralkali expanded. So did Rybolovlev's fortune.

In 2007 Uralkali floated on the London Stock Exchange. By the spring of 2008, according to *Forbes,* Rybolovlev was the world's fifty-ninth richest man. He was worth $12.8 billion, the magazine said. He was considerably better off than Trump.

It was at this point, in July, that Rybolovlev purchased Trump's Palm Beach mansion for a staggering $95 million. The mansion had seventeen bedrooms, Greek fountains, a hundred-foot swimming pool, a cavernous underground car park, and a jacuzzi overlooking the ocean. And a French name—Maison de l'Amitié. Rybolovlev managed to knock $5 million off Trump's original $100 million asking price.

Even so, the purchase raised eyebrows. First, the Florida property market had been cooling for some time. Second, the house had been on the market for two years. Third, Trump had paid $41.4 million for it less than four years earlier. Fourth, subsequent renovations were modest. Fifth, Rybolovlev had never set foot on the estate, although he did once visit to take a look and paddled on the edge of the territory. Sixth, the house had mould.

The Palm Beach home would feature in a spectacular divorce action brought in December 2008 by Elena against her husband after two decades of marriage. In court papers, she accused him of infidelity. She alleged that Rybolovlev had secretly shipped off their art collection to warehouses in London and Singapore.

This was no trivial matter. The Rybolovlevs, the papers said, owned several Picassos and Modiglianis, together with two Monets, a Gaugin, a Van Gogh, a Degas, and a Rothko. Plus a collection of rare furniture, much of it from Paris. (One piece, a circular-top table, or *guéridon*, was decorated with mythical figures celebrating the history of love.) There was a yacht, bought for $60 million and named *My Anna* after the couple's second daughter. And other assets.

In 2015 they reached a private settlement. As for the Palm Beach mansion, Rybolovlev showed little interest in it.

He never lived there.

He eventually demolished it.

According to the French sports writer Arnaud Ramsey,

Rybolovlev was not an idiot or the kind of person to throw money away. Rather he was intelligent—"his brain is really quick"—shy, modest, lacking in ostentation or bling-bling." His appearance was unremarkable. When Ramsey met him, he was wearing a tracksuit.

At the same time Rybolovlev had an aura of "being the boss" and "not being afraid of anybody," Ramsey said.

The Russian wasn't a fan of the media. It took Ramsey several attempts before Rybolovlev finally agreed to an interview. They met at Rybolovlev's penthouse mansion in Monaco. The flat had a private lift, terrace, spa, and library. And a backstory: its previous owner, the Lebanese-Brazilian financier Edmond Safra, burned to death in it in 1999 in a grisly case of arson.

The oligarch acquired another local asset, Monaco's soccer team. In 2011 he became the majority owner of AS Monaco FC, which soon scaled the French premier league. One person who had lunch with him in his penthouse around this period told me that Rybolovlev said he was looking at productive ways of investing in the United States. The billionaire was on a diet and "ultra-thin," the person said.

Ramsey interviewed Rybolovlev again on the Greek island of Skorpios. They talked about AS Monaco's prospects while sitting on the Russian's yacht. The island used to belong to shipping magnate Aristotle Onassis and was now owned by Rybolovlev's daughter Katia. Her other assets included an apartment overlooking Central Park, which she bought at the age of twenty-two for $88 million—a New York record.

Ramsey turned his encounters with the publicity-shy billionaire into a lyrical French-language biography. Its title was *The Russian Novel of the President of AS Monaco*.

In fact, aged twelve or thirteen, Rybolovlev was inspired not by Russian literature but by the books of an American writer, Theodore Dreiser. As a Soviet teenager he read Dreiser's novel *The Financier*. It was from this portrayal of nineteenth-century capitalism, set in Philadelphia, that Rybolovlev learned about speculation and profit, taking inspiration from Dreiser's youthful hero, Frank Cowperwood. The fictional Cowperwood and the future oligarch both spent time in jail.

Rybolovlev said his success, like Cowperwood's, was self-made. This was true. But getting rich in Russia and—more importantly—protecting what you owned from predatory external attack required connections, as Agalarov and other oligarchs well understood.

In 2000 the Perm region held an election for governor. It was assumed that the liberal incumbent, Gennady Igumnov, would win. Instead, Rybolovlev unexpectedly backed another candidate, Perm's mayor Yuri Trutnev. Trutnev was duly elected.

This was a shrewd move. Four years later Trutnev was due to go on vacation when he got a phone call from Moscow. It was the Kremlin. Trutnev had hosted Putin when the president visited Perm. They had got on. Both were practitioners of martial arts: for Vladimir, judo; for Yuri, karate. Putin summoned Trutnev and appointed him minister for the environment and natural resources.

This was a key post. Trutnev was now in a position of overseeing Russia's oil and gas sector. He could find environmental violations—or not.

One of Trutnev's allies was Igor Sechin, the head of the major oil company Rosneft and Putin's powerful ally. The two sometimes had bureaucratic squabbles. But Trutnev consistently backed Sechin in his conflicts with other oil firms. For example, Trutnev's ministry supported Rosneft when it took over the assets of Yukos. (In 2003 Putin jailed Yukos's billionaire owner, Mikhail Khodorkovsky.) Inside Russia's power structures Trutnev's reputation was unwavering—he was the president's loyal creature.

The Russian press wondered whether Trutnev had an interest in Uralkali. Was he Rybolovlev's shadow partner? All sides strongly denied this. The speculation came about after a disaster in 2006 threatened to wipe out Rybolovlev's entire business.

His potash mine was located in the Urals, in the city of Berezniki, on the banks of the Kama River. Gulag labourers had originally dug the mine and propped up its tunnels with salt pillars. The city sat on top. A flood caused the walls and supports to dissolve—and opened a giant municipal sinkhole. The hole swallowed up the railway line and menaced the inhabitants.

It was entirely possible that the state would impose punitive fines on Uralkali or seize its Mine-1. Sechin threatened as much. Mysteriously, the state did nothing. Four months after Rybolovlev bought Trump's mansion, Trutnev issued the government's verdict.

"I think the investigation into Uralkali's fault is inappropriate," Trutnev declared mildly.

He blamed the problems on Stalin-era planners, who were conveniently dead. Uralkali's share price soared.

For Rybolovlev, 2008 was a hell of a year. His company won a dramatic reprieve, his wife sought $6 to $12 billion, and he acquired an interesting piece of south Florida real estate from a celebrity American TV star. Trump's profit was in the region of $50 million.

According to the Steele dossier, it was around this time that the Kremlin and the Trump campaign began what the dossier called a "regular exchange" of information.

It was November 3, just five days before the US election, and Anna-Catherine Sendgikoski was waiting for a client. Sendgikoski was a limousine driver. And an ardent Democrat who hated all things Trump. Her station was Charlotte International Airport in North Carolina—specifically the terminal used by private jets.

At around 2:00 p.m. Sendgikoski noticed a newly arrived plane. It had come in at lunchtime. Even by the standards of personal aviation the jet was a head-turner—a sleek Airbus A319, painted in flowing lines of teal, cream, and ink black. There was nothing to identify it apart from a handful of letters on the tail fin. Painted in white capitals they read: M-KATE. The *M* meant the plane was registered in the Isle of Man.

Sendgikoski snapped a photo. A perimeter fence with barbed wire and a yellow fire truck half obscured the plane, but the call sign was clearly visible. Some twenty minutes later another private jet came in to land. This one wasn't bashful about its proprietor. Giant letters behind the cockpit screamed out a familiar name: TRUMP. She took another picture and posted the two planes on Twitter.

The man himself walked from the jet and got into a waiting motorcade. Sendgikoski said she didn't see anyone emerge from the mystery plane. She did look up its owner—Rybolovlev. The Russian had named his jet after his daughter Katia. It was parked around three hundred feet away from Trump's. The coincidence struck her as "suspect" and "strange," she told the *Charlotte Observer*. Rybolovlev had turned the inside of his plane into a cosy home. It had a bed, shower, table, and state-of-the-art TV.

North Carolina was a battleground state and both Trump and Clinton had been making frequent trips there. At a rally in Charlotte that afternoon Trump accused Hillary of "far-reaching criminal conduct" and said a Clinton victory would create "an unprecedented constitutional crisis." But why was a Russian billionaire in town?

Over the next months, investigative reporters would spend hours combing through flight records. The White House dismissed their efforts as a conspiracy theory and said that Trump and Rybolovlev had never met.

This appeared to be true.

Still, M-KATE's hyperactive flight schedule raised more questions than answers. In 2016 and early 2017 Rybolovlev's jet made seven trips to New York, for several days each, usually at a time when the candidate was there. It flew twice to Miami when Trump was at Mar-a-Lago. And it made seven trips to Moscow, mostly preceding or following flights to Florida or New York.

The simplest way of getting an explanation for these movements was to inquire. I emailed the billionaire's adviser, Sergey Chernitsyn, asking if I could interview Rybolovlev. We might speak in Russian, if he preferred, and I was ready to head off to the south of France or any location that suited him. My email said: "The big question, I guess, is why Dmitry's jet is often in the same place as Donald's?"

Chernitsyn's answer was friendly. Regrettably, there would be no interview. He confirmed that Rybolovlev hadn't met Trump. And "D [Dmitry] often goes to the States—so it's not so strange that the planes were at the same time at the same place." The purchase of the Trump mansion was a "good enough investment done," with the land on sale in three parcels, he wrote.

Okay, but what was Rybolovlev doing in the United States? Chernitsyn: "He travels for business and pleasure. He always travels a lot as you can see from the plane records."

The answer made a kind of sense but was couched in language so vague as to be meaningless. It left open the question of whether Rybolovlev might have been delivering something. Or had he perhaps met someone else from Trump's entourage during his travels? Like, for example, Trump's personal lawyer, Michael Cohen.

The Steele dossier alleged that Cohen played a role of secret intermediary. It said that Cohen made a clandestine trip to Europe in August 2016. The goal was to "clean up the mess" left by media revelations concerning Manafort and Carter Page. The meetings were originally scheduled to take place in Moscow but were shifted to an "operationally soft" EU country "when it was judged too compromising for him [Cohen] to travel to the Russian capital."

Steele's sources told him the meeting took place in Prague, the Czech capital. The location may have been the premises of the Russian state cultural organization Rossotrudnichestvo—a "plausibly deniable" place to meet with Kremlin officials. Cohen allegedly held talks with Oleg Solodukhin, a Russian official operating under Rossotrudnichestvo cover.

The dossier further alleged that Cohen turned up at the meeting with three "colleagues." Who they were was unclear. The agenda: how to make "deniable cash payments" to hackers who "worked in Europe under Kremlin direction against the Clinton campaign." And "various contingencies for covering up these operations and Moscow's secret liaison with the Trump team more generally."

Cohen vehemently denied Steele's claims. The lawyer said he'd never visited Prague. There was no evidence he was there. If Prague was wrong, could the meeting have taken place somewhere else? Cohen—who has a Ukrainian wife—tweeted the cover of his US passport and showed off the visa stamps inside.

According to intelligence sources in Washington and London, the FBI was sceptical of Cohen's denials. It examined Cohen's movements and considered whether he might have got to Europe on a private jet. I asked Chernitsyn if Rybolovlev and Cohen had met.

Chernitsyn's reply: "As to Michael Cohen—maybe, he [Rybolovlev] meets a lot of people. I myself have never been present on a meeting with this person—so I can't say you definitely."

Rybolovlev did know some politicians and public figures, including former French president Nicolas Sarkozy. They watched soccer in Paris. And Prince Albert of Monaco. But not Trump, Chernitsyn said.

With little hard information, reporters were left chasing phantoms. In mid-August 2016 Ivanka and Jared Kushner visited Dubrovnik in Croatia. Rybolovlev's yacht, *My Anna*, was spotted in Dubrovnik on the same dates. Was this perhaps planned? Or, as Cohen insisted, was it the musings of a deranged liberal media determined to besmirch the president?

Finding out more was made difficult by the fact that Rybolovlev managed his business affairs offshore. Many of his companies were registered in the British Virgin Islands, an impenetrable tax haven. Rybolovlev used a Panama-based law firm, Mossack Fonseca. It was known for asking few questions of its rich customers. One of them was the wife of Dmitry Peskov, Putin's press spokesman. The firm's leaked database became the Panama Papers.

Rybolovlev also used another major offshore centre, Cyprus. In 2010 he sold most of his stake in Uralkali, held via a Cypriot company, to a consortium of Russian oligarchs, reportedly for more than $5 billion. Soon after he bought nearly 10 per-cent of the Bank of Cyprus, the island's biggest lender. Many of its depositors were Russian. Meanwhile, back in Moscow Rybolovlev's old friend Trutnev was promoted and became an assistant to Putin.

Cyprus was a haven for billions of dollars in Russian capital, much of it of suspect origin. The cash typically went into shell companies. Some of this "investment" was then returned to Russia as foreign revenue. The island was also a significant hub for Russian espionage and intelligence operations.

Rybolovlev's fellow investors in the Bank of Cyprus were an interesting bunch. After a bailout in 2013 the bank got a new vice chair: Vladimir Strzhalkovsky. Strzhalkovsky was a former KGB agent and long-time Putin associate who served on the boards of Russian state enterprises. Another board member was Viktor Vekselberg, a Russian oligarch on good terms with the Kremlin.

There was one other major investor, an American. His name was Wilbur Ross.

In 2014 Ross became the bank's chief shareholder. He gained the position of vice chairman, attended board meetings with the ex-KGB agent, and restructured the bank's debts. Ross is said to have curbed rather than increased Kremlin influence and to have improved corporate governance. He brought in Josef Ackermann, the former chief executive of Deutsche Bank, as chairman. According to Chernitsyn, Rybolovlev never contacted Ross or the other Russians and his stake in the bank got smaller.

Even so, it was a curious picture. Like his oligarch contacts, Manafort used Cypriot vehicles for his business affairs, and at one point had at least fifteen bank accounts on the island. Trump set up two companies in Cyprus. One of them, Trump Construction Co. Ltd, was registered in September 2008, two months after he sold Maison de l'Amitié. What the company did, the scale of its activities, its annual filings—all were secret.

So in the months leading up to Trump's election campaign Ross, an American venture capitalist, was working closely with a group of Putin-connected Russians. All of this in a jurisdiction that the US State Department said was prone to "money-laundering." And where "international criminal networks" were active.

Ross resigned from the Bank of Cyprus in 2017 when he got a new job.

It was a good one.

Trump made him US secretary of commerce.

Rybolovlev wasn't the only Russian to acquire a Trump property. In fact, Russian and Eurasian buyers had been purchasing real estate from him for a long time, ever since the building of Trump Tower began in 1980.

Some were legitimate. Others, though, were intimately involved with Russian organized crime. At key moments in Trump's career, when Western banks were reluctant to lend and credit evaporated, income originating from the former Soviet Union appears to have rescued Trump from financial ruin.

The Russians came in waves. Some arrived with the tide of Soviet refugees who emigrated to the United States in the 1970s, many of them Jewish. Most of the money that left Russia during this late communist period came from the mafia. This meant moving cash, lots of it, sometimes using Israeli contacts as conduits, but more often via banks in Luxembourg and Switzerland. They deposited gold bullion and precious stones.

Trump Tower opened in 1983. Among the new tenants were East European incomers with considerable cash resources.

In 1984 Trump sold five apartments on the fifty-third floor to David Bogatin, an alleged Mogilevich associate. The price was $6 million. Bogatin then used his Trump properties to carry out a gasoline bootlegging scam and, as prosecutors put it, to "launder money and shelter assets." In 1987 a court sentenced him to two years in jail for tax evasion. Bogatin pleaded guilty but skipped bail and fled to Poland. He was eventually extradited back to the United States and prison.

There was a second Russian influx in the early 1990s, prompted by the end of the USSR. Inside Russia, there was widespread looting of property and assets that had previously belonged to the Party or state. These new immigrants fuelled mafia activity in New York, in particular in Brighton Beach and other parts of Brooklyn.

One of them was Vyacheslav Ivankov, a well-known Moscow felon. Ivankov—known as Yaponchik, or the Little Japanese—was a crime boss, or *vor*. His criminal career was extensive—forgery, firearms, drug trafficking, extortion, punctuated by long spells inside Soviet penal institutions. In spring 1992 Ivankov moved from Russia to New York.

There, he and a group of gang members took over mafia operations in Brighton Beach, moving into gambling, prostitution, and arms smuggling. Ivankov was a superior kind of villain. He nurtured connections—with Mogilevich's powerful organization in Hungary and central Europe; with the Solntsevskaya Bratva in Moscow, the world's number one mafia group; and with Russian former intelligence.

Federal agents were keen to arrest Ivankov. There was only one problem—where was he? The bureau found it easy to wiretap and prosecute Italian American mobsters, who were fond of walking and talking. But Ivankov was elusive.

FBI agent James Moody was tasked with hunting him down. Moody told Robert Friedman, author of *Red Mafiya*, a book about the US-based Russian mob, that Ivankov's hideout was a surprise. It took three years to find it.

"At first all we had was a name. We were looking around and had to go out and really beat the bushes," Moody said. "And then we found out that he was in a luxury condo in Trump Tower."

Before he could be arrested Ivankov vanished from Manhattan. A special investigator with New York State's Organized Crime Task Force, Gregory Stasiuk, followed the clues. According to Friedman, Ivankov went to the Taj Mahal in Atlantic City, New Jersey, the casino owned by Trump that was later fined nearly half a million dollars for money laundering. The casino was popular with Russians, who spent large sums at Trump's gaming tables.

The FBI eventually caught up with Ivankov at his mistress's flat in Brighton Beach. They found $75,000 in cash and a gun wrapped in a sock. It had been tossed into the bushes outside. Agents recovered a copy of Ivankov's personal telephone directory. In it, they found a number for Trump Tower and the fax of the Trump Organization's office.

How much of this could be related to Trump? Like any other successful real estate developer, Trump had sold a lot of properties during his career. He could scarcely be blamed for the nefarious activities of some of his Russian customers. Or the fact that a few of them turned out to be swindlers and professional crooks.

The reality, though, was that Russian clients were a core part of Trump's business. This was true from his early years as a developer to his later arm's-length ventures in which he licensed his brand to foreign investors, from Panama to Baku in Azerbaijan and Toronto in Canada.

Trump's links to the underworld were multifarious. As were those of his nearest business partners.

At the same time that the FBI was looking for Ivankov, another Moscow-born immigrant was sitting in jail. This was Felix Sater. Sater's family was Jewish. In 1974, when Sater was eight, his parents emigrated from the Soviet Union to Israel. From there they moved to Baltimore and then to Brighton Beach.

According to court documents, Sater's father—originally called Mikhail Sheferofsky—was a Mogilevich crime syndicate boss who headed the Russian mafia in Brooklyn. He served prison time in Britain for counterfeiting and fraud. In the US Sater Sr ran an extortion scheme in Brighton Beach. The charge sheet accused him of terrorizing restaurants, food stores, and a local medical clinic. This took place during the

1990s and involved the "wrongful use of actual or threatened force, violence and fear."

Felix Sater had a criminal record, too. He began his career selling stocks on Wall Street. In 1991, aged twenty-five, he stabbed another man after work during a bar-room brawl, attacking his victim with the stem of a margarita glass. Sater spent 15 months in jail. His conviction meant that he lost his securities licence and could no longer work in finance.

At least not legally. Broke, married, and with a four-month-old baby daughter, Sater got involved in a pump-and-dump stock market fraud. His fellow conspirators came from leading New York Italian mafia families. They defrauded investors of $40 million. During this period Sater travelled frequently to Moscow. His involvement in crime—as Sater tells it—ended in 1996.

Normally Sater might have expected another jail term. It was at this point that he cut a deal with the FBI. The bureau said it was struggling to penetrate stock market frauds, including one carried out by Mogilevich using a Philadelphia-based shell company.

The FBI recruited Sater as an informant. He was now a co-operating witness. He pleaded guilty to racketeering and fraud. In return for his services Sater got federal immunity.

There were two ways of interpreting what happened next. One, that Sater's life entered a new redemptive phase, in which he effaced his past sins by returning from Moscow and working diligently for the FBI. Two, that Sater exploited the fact that his fraud record was under seal, and therefore not public, to make a lot of money.

Not just for him but for his new associate—Donald Trump. At the turn of the new millennium Sater began working for a real estate development company. Its name was Bayrock LLC. The firm had begun in Moscow during the tail end of communism. Its founder was Tevfik Arif. Born to a Turkish family in Soviet Kazakhstan, he was a former bureaucrat who had worked in the USSR's commerce and trade department.

Arif landed in New York from Russia and Turkey, his operations base for much of the 1990s. He hired Sater to manage the company. In 2003 Bayrock moved into offices in Trump Tower on the twenty-fourth floor, two floors below Trump's own premises. Sater, Arif, and Trump became associates.

Over the next five years Sater worked on various licensing deals for Trump properties, including a trip with Donald Jr to Phoenix. He had a Trump Organization business card, which said his role was "senior adviser to Donald Trump." At Trump's request Sater met with Donald Jr and Ivanka in Russia in 2006 and showed them around the capital, and arranged for Ivanka to "sit in Putin's private chair at his desk and office in the Kremlin." (Ivanka said she couldn't recall this.) Overall, Sater said that he had a "friendly" relationship with Trump. He dropped into his office "numerous times" to pitch ideas.

One topic of conversation was Trump's latest Manhattan project, Trump SoHo.

Trump unveiled plans for the new forty-six-storey glass tower and hotel during an episode of his show, *The Apprentice*. He failed to mention the fact that other people would be paying for the Spring Street building. One investor was Bayrock. Bayrock in turn teamed up with an Icelandic hedge fund, the FL Group, which contributed $50 million. Another associate was Tamir Sapir, a businessman from Soviet Georgia.

These equity cash flows into Trump's newest branded property were mysterious. Bayrock had an opaque corporate structure. There were several tiers. The FL Group was based in the British Virgin Islands.

In common with Cyprus, Icelandic banks were a favoured destination for Russian capital. There was speculation that Moscow interests might be behind the FL Group. Proving this—or disproving it—was difficult. The group was linked to a maze of shell companies whose ultimate owners were unknown. The FL Group financed two other large Trump projects, in Queens and Fort Lauderdale.

How much did Trump know about his Russian American business associates? The official answer, it turned out, was not a great deal. Trump insisted that he had no idea about Sater's background. Actually, he scarcely knew the guy. . . .

In September 2007 Trump, Arif, and Sater attended the launch party for Trump SoHo. A photo shows the three of them together, grinning. Two and a half months later the *New York Times* published an article revealing Sater's colourful criminal past.

Asked for comment, Trump said the news surprised him: "We never knew that." He added: "We do as much of a background check as we can on the principals. I didn't really know him very well."

Sater left Bayrock soon after the embarrassing piece was published. In 2009 he was sentenced for his role in the original stock scam. Sater told the judge he had "built a very successful real estate company, a Trump project," and was sad to leave it. Sater's long years of service to the FBI paid off. Instead of getting twenty years in jail, the usual tariff, Sater received a $25,000 fine.

While Trump was suffering from selective memory loss, Bayrock's former finance director, Jody Kriss, was preparing a devastating complaint, the first of several in what would turn out to be years of bitter litigation. It alleged that Bayrock had funnelled money from the FL Group to people outside the company.

The writ added: "For most of its existence it [Bayrock] was substantially and covertly mob owned and operated." Arif and Sater had carried out "a pattern" of crimes, including fraud, tax evasion, money laundering, and embezzlement, it said. Sater and Arif denied this.

The writ didn't suggest Trump was complicit. But its key allegation was clear: that post-Soviet speculators invested in Trump licensing deals primarily in order to launder money. Arif faced further difficulties when the Turkish police arrested him on a yacht in the company of several young women and charged him with running a prostitution ring. He was later acquitted.

In New York, financial disputes played out in courtrooms, with judges, attorneys, and multi-page affidavits. They were measured in years and sometimes decades.

In Moscow, business feuds were fixed more bluntly. Ivankov, the celebrated *vor*, was deported in 2004 from the United States and extradited to Russia. Back home, he was acquitted of murder charges. He kept a low profile.

In July 2009 he went for lunch in a Thai restaurant. After an enjoyable meal he walked back to his car. From a neighbouring rooftop an unknown person shot him in the stomach. The weapon was a sniper's rifle.

Ivankov was laid to rest in Moscow's Vagankovskoye Cemetery, plot 26, in a funeral attended by old-time members of Russia's waning gangster brotherhood. He was buried next to his mother.

*

It was 2011, the era of Barack Obama, and FBI agents were applying for a court warrant. They wanted to listen in on a suspect's phone calls. Their target was Vadim Trincher, a poker player who was suspected of running an illegal gambling ring from his upscale New York apartment.

That Trincher was wealthy wasn't in doubt. He had bought the suite in 2009 from another well-off Russian, Oleg Boiko, paying $5 million in cash. Trincher had filled his home with expensive furniture and a valuable silk rug. The question for the bureau was whether Trincher's regular card-playing sessions constituted a federal crime.

Using information obtained from wiretaps the FBI sketched out a plan of Trincher's contacts. One person he called was Alimzhan Tokhtakhounov, an ethnic Uzbek crime lord from Tashkent. Another was Helly Nahmad, a Lebanese American art dealer who owned a major New York gallery, founded by his father.

The FBI spent two years monitoring the activities inside Trincher's luxury apartment—number 63A. Its location? The fifty-first floor of Trump Tower.

Trump Tower was now a significant crime scene. Trump lived just three floors above Trincher, in a lavish triplex penthouse. Nahmad had purchased the entire fifty-first floor of the building, at a cost of $20 million, and funded gambling operations run by Trincher's son, Ilya.

Federal agents weren't seeking to eavesdrop on Trump. Rather, their probe was directed at the Russian mob, who happened to be Trump's almost next-door neighbours.

In April 2013 the FBI raided Trump Tower in an operation

in which thirty people were arrested. Trincher got five years in jail. A court heard that he laundered the profits of his gambling operation—some $100 million—through shell companies in Cyprus. Cash allegedly travelled via the Bank of Cyprus. Nahmad served five months in jail, as did another Russian, Anatoly Golubchik.

The only person who managed to escape the net was Tokhtakhounov, whom the FBI termed a major authority inside Russian organized crime. He disappeared.

Tokhtakhounov led a picaresque life. He had spent time in various Soviet prisons, and one in Venice, and had lived in Germany and Paris. The United States accused him of bribing judges to fix the ice-skating competition during the 2002 Winter Olympics in Salt Lake City. He was on good terms with his fellow mafia bosses. He liked Putin. Of the late Ivankov, a friend for more than forty years, he said: "A legendary man. Very well-read. Interesting."

Tokhtakhounov's whereabouts were unknown until November 2013, when he was spotted in Moscow. According to *Kommersant*, Tokhtakhounov was seen at a major international event—the Miss Universe competition. He was sitting in the ground-floor auditorium, in the area reserved for VIPs, not far from Agalarov and Trump. The mobster was part of a big crowd including Steven Tyler, the lead singer of Aerosmith, who performed that night.

The FBI raid had a postscript. The lawyer who approved the arrests in connection with Trump Tower gambling was Preet Bharara, US attorney for the Southern District Court of New York. Bharara was Punjab-born, Harvard-educated, and a graduate of Columbia Law School. He would make numerous enemies in a starry career, including the presidents of the United States and Russia.

Obama nominated Bharara to the post in 2009. Bharara immediately embarked on a high-profile crusade against corruption. He pursued banks, hedge funds, crooked traders, and politicians from both sides of the divide. And Russians. One signal feature of his attorneyship was a willingness to pursue suspects who lived far away, in foreign jurisdictions.

Bharara examined the $230 million allegedly stolen in the Magnitsky case. Some of the money, it transpired, had been spent on New York real estate, including on a luxury condominium at 20 Pine Street, just a few blocks from Wall Street. The money had gone from Moscow via shell companies in Moldova to a holding company in Cyprus.

The company was called Prevezon and its owner was Denis Katsyv. It was Katsyv who hired Veselnitskaya to contest the case in New York. As the *Guardian* reported, there was also a Trump connection. Prevezon bought the Pine Street apartment from Lev Leviev, a billionaire tycoon and diamond mogul. In 2015 Leviev sold several floors of the old New York Times Building at 43rd Street in Manhattan for $295 million. The buyer was Jared Kushner.

Bharara's investigations displeased the Kremlin. In April 2013 it barred him, together with seventeen other Americans, from visiting Russia. Bharara carried on as before. The next month he closed down the Rasputin restaurant in Brooklyn, a popular gathering spot with alleged Russian mafia bosses. Its owner was arrested for fraud.

It seemed unlikely that Bharara could prosper under Trump. In November 2016 the president-elect summoned him to

Trump Tower. The meeting was apparently warm. Speaking afterwards in the lobby, Bharara told reporters that Trump had asked him to stay on as attorney for Manhattan. He said he had agreed and had promised to work independently and without fear and favour, as before.

This concord lasted until March, when Sessions requested that all forty-six US attorneys appointed during the Obama era resign. Bharara refused. He was fired. Two months later his successor settled the Prevezon case on the eve of trial. The firm paid a $5.9 million fine. Veselnitskaya claimed victory. The sum was so slight "it looked like an apology from the [US] government," she said.

The deal seemed fishy, at least to sixteen Democratic senators who wrote to the Justice Department asking for an explanation. They wanted to know if the White House had interfered in an agreement described by one constitutional expert as "frankly outrageous."

Felix Sater and Michael Cohen, Trump's lawyer, were old friends. They had known each other as teenagers. In 2015, in the early stages of his campaign, Trump had said of Sater: "I'm not that familiar with him." Sater, it appeared, had disappeared from view.

Emails released to Congress, however, suggest that Sater was still in the thick of things. Not only was he plotting to get his old boss elected president, he was also working to make Trump Tower in Moscow a reality. Sater's playbook: Trump could use Moscow's support to his political advantage, showing off his skills as negotiator and deal-maker.

Sater was confident he could arrange everything. On November 3, 2015, he wrote to Cohen:

I will get Putin on this program and we will get Donald elected. We both know that no one else knows how to pull this off without stupidity or greed getting in the way. I know how to play it and we will get this done. Buddy our boy can become President of the USA and we can engineer it. I will get all of Putins team to buy in on this, I will manage this process.

We don't have Cohen's reply. But the emails lay out Sater's plan for glory—a ribbon-cutting ceremony in Moscow and praise from Putin of Trump's peerless business skills. To achieve this, Sater said he could show video clips to his Russian contacts of Trump speaking glowingly of Russia: "If he [Putin] says it, we own this election. America's most difficult adversary agreeing that Donald was a good guy to negotiate."

Okay, but who was going to put up the cash for Trump's Moscow tower? Sater had a plan here, too. VTB, Russia's state-run bank, had agreed to provide finance, Sater wrote. VTB was an eyebrow-raising choice. First, it was under US sanctions. Second, it had interesting connections to Russian intelligence.

Sater added that it would be "pretty cool to get a USA president elected." His anticipated reward for bringing off this great deed would be modest. He wished to be ambassador to the Bahamas. He told Cohen: "That my friend is the home run I want out of all this."

So while Trump was out on the campaign stump speaking sweetly of Putin, his aides were seeking to win Russian government support for Trump's long-cherished Moscow real estate project. Without it, Sater correctly understood, the tower would never get built.

All of this was happening in private. US electors knew nothing of Sater's Kremlin outreach scheme. Trump did, though.

So did Cohen. Cohen said he talked to Trump about the Moscow tower three times. When it appeared that the project was faltering, despite a letter of intent, Cohen took a bold step. He sent an email to someone big: Putin's press secretary, Dmitry Peskov. The email was a petition, a meekly phrased plea for help. The date was mid-January 2016.

Cohen wrote:

> Over the past few months I have been working with a company based in Russia regarding the development of a Trump Tower-Moscow project in Moscow City. Without getting into lengthy specifics, the communication between our two sides has stalled.
>
> As this project is too important, I am hereby requesting your assistance. I respectfully request someone, preferably you, contact me so that I might discuss the specifics as well as arranging meetings with the appropriate individuals. I thank you in advance for your assistance and look forward to hearing from you soon.

Cohen dispatched the email to a generic address, rather than to Peskov's personal account. Nonetheless, the email would have been found and closely examined. The email's recipient, Peskov, wasn't only Putin's long-serving mouthpiece, he was also in charge of the operation to compromise Clinton, according to the Steele dossier, and someone who saw Russia's president practically every day.

Cohen insisted there was no collusion. And yet this is precisely what his email looked like: a direct (and covert) request for assistance from Team Trump to Team Putin. Was this politics or business or both? As always with Trump, it was hard to tell.

In evidence to Congress Cohen said that Peskov didn't answer—or at least that he couldn't recall a reply. The tower plan was shelved, he said. As for Sater's emails? They were salesmanship and "puffery."

A year later, in January 2017, Sater and Cohen were involved in another clandestine joint endeavour, this time involving Ukraine. Cohen went to see Trump in the White House. He hand-delivered the plan to Michael Flynn, shortly before Flynn resigned as national security adviser, the *New York Times* reported. It envisaged Russia obtaining a lease on Crimea, for fifty or one hundred years. Sater drafted the document with the assistance of a Ukrainian deputy, Andriy Artemenko. The Cohen–Sater proposal didn't come off. Had it done so, it would have pleased the Kremlin.

For four decades Trump's property empire effectively functioned as a laundromat for Moscow money. Funds from the former Soviet Union poured into condominiums and Trump apartments. Even as Trump was campaigning in Iowa and New Hampshire, his associates were chasing Kremlin permission—and cash—for the candidate's elusive Moscow tower.

A Reuters investigation found that at least sixty-three individuals with Russian passports or addresses bought $98.4 million worth of property from seven Trump-branded towers in Florida. The true figure was probably higher. Nearly one-third of all units were sold to limited liability companies, whose buyers were unidentified.

Trump Tower even offered a refugium for Russian gangsters. Back home, the population of old-school *vors* was declining, not unlike the woolly mammoths that once roamed the

Siberian plains, as Putin's bureaucratic state took over their territory. New York, by contrast, provided a place of safety and a base for international operations.

Russian money undoubtedly helped Trump's bottom line. But it was another source of revenue that kept Trump's finances afloat at a time when the global financial crash threatened to drown him.

This money was respectable. It came from a bank. It came from Germany. Or did it?

11

The Strange Case of the German Bank

2011–2017
Moscow–New York–Frankfurt

Woah, party now
Too much money in the bank account
Hands in the air make you scream and shout
—TIMATI (Russian rap star), "Welcome to St. Tropez"

The tone was weary exasperation. The sort of exasperation you might deploy when faced with a capricious and badly behaved child. One who agrees to do something but who then reneges on the promise, big-time, and blames everyone else, while screaming and throwing toys from his pram.

The man-child in this case was Trump. The fed-up reproving parent was Deutsche Bank, Trump's New York creditor. At issue was a very large sum of money that Trump borrowed from the German bank in 2005 to fund the construction of the Trump International Hotel & Tower in Chicago. Trump had personally guaranteed to repay the $640 million debt.

Since then, a global financial crash had arrived. In late

November 2008, the bank's attorney, Steven F. Molo, wrote a motion for summary judgement. Against the backdrop of crisis Trump had defaulted on payment, with $330 million still outstanding. Deutsche was seeking an immediate $40 million from the tycoon, plus interest, legal fees, and costs.

One had to be a little awed by Trump's nose-thumbing response. Even by his sophistical and treacherous standards it was quite something. Instead of paying up, he counter-sued. In a complaint to the Supreme Court of New York, in the county of Queens, Trump wrote that he had no intention of giving back the outstanding loan. He described the world crisis as a "once-in-a-century credit tsunami" and an "unforeseen situation."

According to Trump, the crash was a *force majeure* event. He argued that Deutsche Bank had co-created the financial downturn. Or as he put it: "Deutsche Bank is one of the banks primarily responsible for the economic dysfunction we are currently facing."

Therefore, he was not obliged to pay back any money.

Therefore, Deutsche Bank owed *him* money.

He wanted $3 billion in damages from Deutsche.

The German bank's next move was an affidavit. Molo drew up a withering document, which was filed in New York. In a section ironically titled "Trump: The Guarantor," the attorney contrasted Trump's frivolous writ with his long career of boasting about how rich he was.

It began:

Trump proclaims himself "the archetypal businessman, a deal-maker without peer." Trump has stated in court he is worth billions of dollars. In addition to substantial cash, personal investments and various other tangible assets, he maintains substantial interests in numerous extraordinary properties in New York and around the country.

These assets included hotel projects in seven US cities, as well as in Mexico, the Dominican Republic, Dubai, Canada, and Panama, the lawyer noted. There were casinos and golf courses. These, too, were scattered all over the world, including Trump's latest golf course development project in Scotland.

In fact, the same day he argued that the depression meant he was off the hook, Trump gave an interview to *The Scotsman* newspaper. After a two-year fight, he had succeeded in getting approval from the Scottish government for a new Trump golf resort near Balmedie in Aberdeenshire. The decision thrilled Trump. (It outraged environmentalists, who believed the course would wreck sand dunes and damage coastline ecology.) Trump was in carefree mood.

"The world has changed financially and the banks are all in such trouble, but the good news is that we are doing very well as a company and we are in a very, very strong cash position," Trump told the paper.

Trump said he didn't have any exposure to the stock market, had bought the Scottish land for cash, and was now well placed to build "the world's greatest golf course." Two weeks later George Sorial, a Trump organization executive, assured *The Scotsman* that the tycoon had a billion dollars earmarked for the course. Sorial was vague as to where this fortune was, bankwise, but said: "The money is there, ready to be wired any time."

If this weren't damning enough, Molo's affidavit cited Trump's own literary works, which summarized Trump's insouciant attitude towards paying back other people's money—something he didn't feel greatly obliged to do.

The attorney observed:

> Trump provides extensive advice on how to do business through at least half a dozen books he has authored. In *How to Get Rich* Trump advised readers to use the courts to "be strategically dramatic." In *Think Big and Kick Ass in Business and in Life*, he boasts of how he "love(s) to crush the other side and take the benefits."

Trump strategy—honed during terrible struggles and shouting matches with lenders during the 1990s—"was to turn it back on the banks. . . . I figured it was the bank's problem, not mine," Molo quoted Trump as saying, in connection with unpaid debt.

Molo concluded his petition by arguing that Trump must now settle his outstanding balance. "To date, he has failed to pay," he wrote.

Trump's outrageous behaviour vis-à-vis Deutsche Bank might have been anticipated. He was, after all, someone who had been through a slew of corporate bankruptcies. His Taj Mahal casino, his other casinos in Atlantic City, his Plaza Hotel in NYC all filed for chapter 11 bankruptcy in the early 1990s.

After those failures, US banks that had previously advanced the capital to Trump for building projects, believing them to be sound investments, stopped lending. Chase Manhattan, Citibank, and other burned Wall Street houses declined further credit and refused his calls.

The one institution willing to advance him loans in the new century was Deutsche Bank.

Now Trump had shafted Deutsche, too. Trump was a litigious client, slippery, untruthful, loud, wily, and knavish. He was prepared to use vexatious and underhanded tactics that toppled into absurdity. He had sued the bank for $3 billion. A judge had sensibly thrown out Trump's suit. Evidently Deutsche would have nothing further to do with him. It would reclaim its investment and rip up its client file.

There was a certain symmetry to the fact that Trump would do business with a bank whose American headquarters were at 60 Wall Street. A century earlier, Donald's German grandfather, Friedrich Trump, had worked at the same address. Friedrich was born in 1869 in Kallstadt, a small village in southwest Germany. He emigrated to New York aged sixteen. He opened hotels in Seattle and the Yukon, cashing in on the gold rush, before returning to lower Manhattan.

On Wall Street Friedrich didn't work as the proprietor of another food and drink establishment. He went back to the profession he had learned as a teenager: barber. While his wife Elizabeth looked after their young son, Fred—Trump's father—Friedrich snipped the hair of brokers and speculators. He later became a hotel manager. He died in the flu pandemic of 1918.

Friedrich's Wall Street barber's shop no longer exists. In its place is the US headquarters of Deutsche Bank, a fifty-storey skyscraper built in the late 1980s in giant postmodern style. Next door is a public atrium with fake palm trees and a Starbucks. There's a shoe repair store, "while u wait." The East River—a shimmer of silver-grey water—is visible as one exits the grand lobby of the Deutsche building.

In 2010 Trump settled his feud with Deutsche. This was done, extraordinarily, by borrowing more money from . . . Deutsche Bank.

Shut out from its real estate division, Trump turned to another part of the same institution—Deutsche's private wealth division, which typically deals with high-net-worth individuals. It doesn't normally do property. Still, the unit lent him the money. And later gave him another $25 to $50 million in credit.

This was Trump's route back to corporate solvency.

The decision to keep lending to Trump was unusual, bizarre even. Deutsche Bank employees in New York were surprised. Asked whether it was normal to give more money to a customer who was a bad credit risk and a litigant, one former senior Deutsche staff member said: "Are you fucking kidding me?"

The banker—who didn't want to be named—told me that only the private wealth division accepted personal guarantees. "Real estate refused to lend to him [Trump]," the banker said. Still, senior risk managers and the compliance department straddled divisions and would likely have approved the move.

Remarkably, Trump was able to borrow even bigger sums. He took out two mortgages against his Trump National Doral resort in Miami. And a $170 million loan to finish his hotel in Washington in the old post office tower. These loans flowed from the private-wealth wing. There was also the outstanding Chicago loan.

According to an analysis by Bloomberg, by the time he became the forty-fifth president Trump owed Deutsche Bank around $300 million. All four debts were due in 2023 and 2024.

This was an unprecedented sum for an incoming president and one that raised awkward questions about conflict of interest. If Deutsche Bank were to get into regulatory difficulty, one of the bodies that would investigate was the Department of Justice. Which reported to Trump. It was hard to see how the department could work dispassionately. Or how Deutsche might take legal action against a sitting president if he defaulted again.

During the same period Deutsche was doing something abnormal—something that would provoke the interest of regulators, and in turn lead to punishment. The bank was laundering money. Russian money. Not small amounts but many billions of dollars. This dubious tide flowed from Moscow to London, and from London to New York, enveloping the spot where Friedrich Trump had once worked, setting his descendants on a path to greater affluence.

In 2005 Deutsche bought UFG, a boutique investment bank already well established in Moscow. UFG's co-founder and chairman was Charlie Ryan, a charming American banker with libertarian views. Ryan's partner was Boris Fyodorov, a former Yeltsin finance minister. The bank neatly straddled West and East. It was international and localized. It would be Deutsche's beachhead into Moscow.

The man behind Deutsche's aggressive expansion was Anshu Jain, its future co-CEO. He persuaded Ryan to stay on and head up Deutsche's new Moscow office. Jain came up with a controversial strategy: to tap into potentially huge Russian profits, he decided to forge relationships with state partners.

He desired, in effect, to become best friends with the Kremlin.

One way of doing this was to hire people with connections. Russia's most powerful banker was Andrey Kostin. Kostin had served in Sydney and London as a Soviet diplomat. Intelligence sources think he was a KGB spy. In the 1990s, he became head of Vnesheconombank—VEB—a state development bank described by one former CIA analyst as the "Kremlin's cookie jar." Then Putin made Kostin head of Vneshtorgbank, or VTB, also state-run. After which Kostin expanded VTB to operate in nineteen countries. It worked in jurisdictions with minimal oversight. This flexibility meant the Kremlin could use VTB for sensitive international operations. In 2005 VTB absorbed two banks traditionally used in Soviet times for espionage and for shifting currency to Western communist parties. These were the Moscow Narodny Bank, based in London, and Eurobank, in Paris.

Jain and Deutsche Bank recruited Kostin's twenty-something son, also called Andrei, with an *i*. In spring 2007 Kostin Jr moved from a posting in London to Deutsche Bank in Moscow. Suddenly, Kostin got massive flows of business. It appeared Dad may have helped. Deutsche did a series of lucrative trades with VTB.

According to one estimate, the German bank's Moscow subsidiary began notching up profits of $500 million to $1 billion a year, with VTB generating somewhere between 50 and 80 percent of all revenue. This picture was pieced together from interviews with Deutsche Bank staff looking for jobs elsewhere. Other investment banks based in Moscow were chagrined. And a little suspicious.

"They were doing some very curious things. Nobody could make sense of their business," said Chris Barter, the CEO of Goldman Sachs Moscow at the time. He added: "We found the nature and concentration of their business with VTB quite galling. Nobody else could touch VTB."

Clearly Deutsche Bank owed its success to its newfound alliance with Russian state interests. As everyone in Moscow understood, VTB was more than a bank. It had ties to Russian intelligence. Putin's FSB spy chief, Nikolai Patrushev—and Patrushev's successor, Alexander Bortnikov—both sent their sons to work at VTB. The bank's deputy chief executive, Vasily Titov, chaired the FSB's public council. According to Trump's business associate, Felix Sater, writing in his email to Michael Cohen, VTB had agreed to bankroll Trump Tower Moscow.

So some well-connected people were helping Deutsche Bank, or at least aiding the office of their Moscow affiliate. And possibly Trump, too.

Maybe they were doing so out of kindness, as a favour. Or perhaps they wanted something in return.

Moscow was an alluring destination for Western expatriates. Especially for young single males.

There were the *devushki*—attractive long-legged Russian girls, some from Moscow, some newly arrived from the provinces—who were keen to meet foreigners and practise their English. There were the nightclubs, the parties, fuelled by toasts and endless vodka shots. And the friendships, always more intense and philosophical than those at home.

In the new millennium the Russian capital was awash with petrodollars and opportunity. There was a dark side, too—as one of those attracted by its offer of riches discovered. Tim Wiswell grew up in Old Saybrook, Connecticut, one hundred miles northeast of New York. He was more of a "repatriate" than an expat: his father had worked in oil and gas in Russia. At the age of seventeen Wiswell spent a year at the

Anglo-American School in Moscow and then returned to the United States to study.

In his mid-twenties, Wiswell went back to Moscow and got a job with Alfa, the private bank owned by oligarch Mikhail Fridman. From there he moved to Deutsche Bank. By twenty-nine he was head of Russian equities. He found a Russian girlfriend—Natalia Makosiy, an art historian whom he met at a Moscow dinner party.

In the wake of the 2008 crash, profits from the bank's Russian business line were reduced by half. Traders were now under pressure to increase revenue. According to Barter, it was evident that "something nefarious" was going on at Deutsche during the Wiswell period.

Barter recalled how he was approached by "broker types, not very senior," seeking to do large, unexplained volumes of trade with Goldman Sachs. These were on behalf of major Russian clients. The brokers declined to identify their counterparties. Their names were concealed beneath "shell company after shell company," Barter said, making a due diligence process impossible. He turned this business down "in five seconds."

Seemingly, the same entities approached Wiswell. There they got better results. Over five years, between 2011 and February 2015, Wiswell presided over a money-laundering scheme run from the equities desk of Deutsche's Moscow office. According to the New York State Department of Financial Services (DFS), more than $10 billion was shifted from Russia to the West.

The method was simple—and effective. In Moscow, a Russian client bought blue chip Russian stocks from Deutsche Bank Moscow in companies like Gazprom or Sberbank. The payment was in roubles. The size of a typical order was $2 to $3 million. Shortly afterwards a non-Russian "customer" sold exactly the same number of securities to Deutsche Bank in London, paying in dollars.

These "mirror trades" were fake and had no economic logic. The selling parties were based in offshore territories like Cyprus or the British Virgin Islands. The buyers and sellers were linked, with related owners and agents. At least twelve different entities used the scheme to surreptitiously convert roubles into dollars. The money was interred in offshore accounts.

Thus, billions were moved out of one Deutsche Bank, from its modern glass office at Building 2, 82 Sadovnicheskaya Street, to another Deutsche Bank, at 60 Wall Street. There were nearly six thousand transactions. Nobody in New York or London or Frankfurt or any of the international financial centres really noticed.

When concerns were raised—by an unnamed European bank, for example—Wiswell swatted them aside. According to the New York regulator, he told the European bank that "there was no reason for concern." Wiswell approved, or "on-boarded," the Russian parties. He "threatened" and browbeat his colleagues on several occasions "when it appeared they had not moved quickly enough to facilitate transactions."

In Moscow, Wiswell's twenty-person equities desk was made up of Russians and Americans. One of its duties was to keep clients happy. That might mean extravagant skiing trips, visits to elite nightclubs, or weekends away. Sometimes clients repaid the favour. One of Wiswell's business and skiing partners was Dmitry Perevalov, owner of a Moscow fund called Lanturno.

For his fortieth birthday, Perevalov flew a group of people on a private jet to Mauritius. The jet belonged to Russian Orthodoxy's most important bishop: Patriarch Kirill of

Moscow. Perevalov chartered it for the occasion. One of his guests was Wiswell. The weekend was designated "for wives," and Wiswell brought Natalia.

One fellow guest who met Wiswell at the party described him as charismatic and charming. He was a tall, handsome, all-American guy. At the same time, the person said, Wiswell came across as a "major lightweight" in terms of banking and finance.

"He had nothing special going for him. I remember him speaking pretty poor Russian. We wondered whether he was doing kosher business," the guest said, adding that Wiswell's wife was "quite aloof and spent the weekend with her friends."

Guests stayed at the luxurious Four Seasons hotel at Anahita, on the east coast of the Indian Ocean island.

Perevalov flew in a famous name to crown his birthday celebrations—the Russian rapper Timati. Timati gave a concert. Under a starry sky, and against a view of sea and mangroves, guests danced and twirled to Timati's foot-stomping hit, "Welcome to St. Tropez."

Woah, party now
Too much money in the bank account
Hands in the air make you scream and shout

Drinks, private villas, waterskiing out in the lagoon . . . everything was taken care of. "I was wondering: who the fuck is paying for all this? It was crazy," the guest told me. Some invitees scarcely knew Perevalov, a former bartender. Those who were his actual friends—including Wiswell—called him Dima.

Lightweight or not, Wiswell was getting rich. In 2010 he had married Natalia at a ceremony in Newport, Rhode Island. While the mirror trades were occurring, Natalia became the beneficial owner of two offshore companies—one in the British Virgin Islands, one in Cyprus. In 2015 a counterparty paid $250,000 into her account. This was for "financial consulting." Similar payments totalling $3.8 million were made through two companies in Belize.

These payments were "undisclosed compensation," the Department of Financial Services found—"a bribe." Which bank cleared these bribes? Deutsche in New York.

According to Ed Caesar, author of a *New Yorker* long-read on the Deutsche scandal, there were further payments made to the Wiswells. These arrived as cash, in a bag. The idea of the money was "to hook you, so you are not going to do unexpected things," one Moscow broker told Caesar. "Guys always pay something."

The end came in August 2015, when Deutsche Bank suspended Wiswell and then fired him. After that, he disappeared. There were Facebook postings from Southeast Asia and Bali, where the Wiswells went with their two small children. He appeared to be on the run from US authorities and is now allegedly back in Moscow. One friend described him to *The New Yorker* as "finance's Edward Snowden." His lawyer, Ekaterina Dukhina, refused my request for comment. In a wrongful-dismissal suit Wiswell said he'd been scapegoated. Around twenty colleagues, including two senior managers in London, knew all about the trades, he said.

The affair was a grievous blow to Deutsche Bank's reputation. And an expensive one. The DFS—which has the power to suspend any bank with a branch in New York—fined Deutsche $475 million. London's Financial Conduct Authority imposed a £163 million penalty. The bank carried out an internal review, Project Square.

The review did not identify the Russians behind the scheme. We don't know who they were or where the billions went. Or where the money came from in the first place. Effectively, Deutsche Bank facilitated the illegal flight of capital by a number of well-connected superusers and Kremlin insiders.

These fines were imposed ten days after Trump's inauguration. The larger picture was disturbing. A Kremlin bank, VTB, run by proxies of the FSB, had seemingly captured Deutsche Bank's Moscow outpost. Deutsche's London and New York divisions were economic beneficiaries of this arrangement. While this was going on, Deutsche Bank in New York lent hundreds of millions of dollars to the future president.

What Democratic senators and representatives wanted to know was this: Was there a connection?

It was a good question.

My attempts to get information from Deutsche Bank over its lending to Trump were unsuccessful. House and Senate Democrats fared no better.

There were legitimate things to ask. Such as:

Had Deutsche sold any part of Trump's debt to foreign entities?

Plus, what meetings had the bank held with the Trump administration? Had Trump or his family received preferential treatment? Who decided to carry on lending to Trump after he defaulted in 2008? Had Russia or Russian entities underwritten any aspect of these loans? Was Deutsche shielding POTUS because of the Justice Department's ongoing investigation into mirror trades?

Every inquiry, question, and query came up against a wall.

Deutsche Bank's press offices in London and Frankfurt refused to comment. The policy was to say nothing about the president, whose tax filings remained a mystery. It was difficult to interpret the bank's non-cooperative approach. A cover-up? Or the actions of an institution terrified of what the Trump White House might do to it, given the motivation?

Meanwhile, I was piecing together another Russian money-laundering scheme, also involving Deutsche Bank. A group of Moscow bankers were sending cash out of the country via a different route, nicknamed the Global Laundromat. Putin's cousin, Igor Putin, sat on the board of one such bank. The Laundromat ran between 2010 and 2014. It processed at least $20 billion. The true figure may have been $80 billion.

It was this investigation that had led me and my *Guardian* colleague Nick Hopkins, in December 2016, to the Shakespeare pub and our meeting with Christopher Steele.

The scheme involved shell companies set up in the United Kingdom. These companies "lent" money to one another, at least on paper. Russian businesses underwrote these "loans." Company A would default on paying back Company B. Typically, a Moldovan citizen was involved. The companies would obtain a court judgement in Moldova, asking the Russian firms to settle the debt.

And *voilà*! The Russian businesses would legally transfer hundreds of millions of dollars to a bank in Moldova's capital, Chişinău. From Chişinău the money went to a bank in Latvia, Trasta Komercbanka. From Latvia, the cash went everywhere, to ninety-two countries, much of it vanishing offshore. The use of Moldovan judges was an imaginative ruse.

The Latvian bank required a corresponding Western bank to process its dollar-denominated transactions. Most US banks, including JP Morgan Chase, refused to offer banking services to Trasta, given Riga's notorious reputation as a European money-laundering hub. Only two Western banks agreed. Both were German. They were Deutsche and Commerzbank.

Once again, Deutsche was the entry point for criminal Russian money into the global financial system. (Deutsche severed its relationship with Trasta shortly before Latvian officials shut down the bank in 2016 for money laundering.) According to the DFS, Deutsche was reluctant to classify Russia as "high-risk," doing so only after other "peer banks" improved checks.

Overall, Germany's largest bank was in trouble. Its staff was demoralized. It was clocking up vast losses. And record fines. In 2005 the DFS reprimanded the bank for rigging the LIBOR, the main interbank lending rate. There was a further fine for sanctions busting—processing dollar transactions on behalf of entities in Iran, Libya, Syria, Myanmar, and Sudan. And another $7.2 billion for selling high-risk mortgage-backed securities before the 2008 slump.

Since our forward approach to Deutsche's corporate office was rebuffed, we tried other routes. We talked to current and former Deutsche Bank staff. According to one senior ex-employee, who worked in equities in Asia and New York, the bank's problems went way beyond these scams.

The 2008 crash hit Deutsche badly, the employee said. In order to paper over holes in the balance sheet, a few members of staff conducted deals with "hair"—complex, creative, and possibly illegitimate—forms of finance. These dark-arts practices were extensive, he alleged. They might involve innovative and opaque ways of getting outside parties to underwrite risky loans, he added, using structures "out of the cookbook."

Did Trump accept Russian sources of funding during these

times? Richard Dearlove, the former head of MI6, said this question hangs over the president. Dearlove told the magazine *Prospect*: "What lingers for Trump may be what deals—on what terms—he did after the financial crisis of 2008 to borrow Russian money when others in the West would not lend to him." (Dearlove said allegations of illegal contact between Trump's staff and Moscow were "unprecedented.")

It wasn't just Donald Trump who maintained a warm relationship with Deutsche. The German bank looked after his entire family. Jared Kushner, Ivanka, and Kushner's mother Seryl Stadtmauer were all Deutsche clients. Kushner's relationship with Deutsche emerged in 2013, when he ordered a flattering profile of Trump's wealth manager, Rosemary Vrablic. It appeared in the *Commercial Observer*, which Kushner owned.

Vrablic was a former Citibank employee who joined Deutsche in 2006. In 2014 she attended a society dinner with Kushner at the Frick museum in New York, held against a backdrop of Vermeers and Goyas. Trump described her (wrongly) to reporters as Deutsche Bank's "boss." And invited her to his inauguration, the *New York Times* reported.

According to our sources inside Deutsche, Trump's bid to become president made him a politically exposed person, or PEP. Banks were obliged to scrutinize PEPs carefully. Deutsche reviewed its lending to Trump and his relatives, and the review was sensitive. Its goal was to discover if there was a Russian connection to Trump's loans. The DFS also requested information.

The sources insist that the answer was negative. No trail to Moscow was ever discovered, they told us. Deutsche, however, refused to make public comment. Nor would it provide details of its private review to Capitol Hill. Senators wrote letters; the bank stonewalled, citing privacy rules. Congress showed interest in mirror trades. It got the same evasive *nein*.

In a letter to Bill Woodley, Deutsche's US CEO, Senator Chris Van Hollen expressed concerns about the bank's lending to Kushner. Kushner had a $25 million line of credit with Deutsche. Additionally, in October 2016, it loaned him $285 million. The cash was used to replace an existing loan on the old New York Times Building, the retail property Kushner bought the previous year from the Russian Lev Leviev.

The loan was made around the time when Kremlin representatives were eagerly seeking Kushner's ear. Kushner first met Sergey Kislyak in April, when Trump gave his foreign policy speech at DC's Mayflower Hotel—just a handshake and pleasantries, Kushner said. Next came the meeting with Natalia Veselnitskaya. Then, on November 16, Kislyak got in touch again. By this point it was clear that Kushner would become senior adviser to the president.

The Kushner–Kislyak meeting on December 1 took place at Trump Tower. Michael Flynn was present, too. Kushner made an unusual proposal. He asked Kislyak if it would be possible to set up a secret and secure communications channel between the Trump transition team and the Kremlin. The purpose, seemingly, was to keep any conversations hidden from the outgoing Obama government and US intelligence. A backchannel, in effect.

Could this be done, Kushner wondered, by using Russian diplomatic facilities in the United States?

The inquiry was staggeringly naïve. If Kushner or Flynn were to drop by the Russian embassy, then US intelligence would certainly notice.

The FBI didn't bug the conversation but learned of it

afterwards, when Kislyak reported to his superiors back in Moscow. According to FBI intercepts of Russian communications, Kislyak was taken aback by Kushner's unusual request. It was unlikely Moscow would allow any American to use its encrypted networks. The Trump transition team said nothing about these secret negotiations. One person who knew the details was so alarmed he sent the *Washington Post* an anonymous note.

Russia, it seemed, didn't need to expend much effort to get close to Trump's aides. Kislyak came up with a suggestion of his own. Perhaps Kushner would like to meet with another person from Moscow, someone with "a direct relationship" to President Putin?

The details were agreed during a meeting on December 12 between Kislyak and Kushner's assistant, Avi Berkowitz. Putin's emissary turned out to be a banker, or more accurately, a banker-spy. His name was Sergei Gorkov. He was the head of VEB, the state development bank, which Kostin had run, and whose board Putin had chaired during his four years as prime minister.

It was VEB that had played a role in the story of Russian intelligence and Carter Page. VEB's office in Manhattan was an espionage front. The two SVR officers who had discussed Carter Page—calling him a "bit of an idiot"—had been working with an undercover colleague based at the bank, Evgeny Buryakov. (It was the unfortunate Buryakov who was jailed in 2015 for acting as an unregistered foreign agent.)

Gorkov was a cut above Buryakov and his two US-based SVR colleagues, all of whom were mid-level intelligence operatives. His path was shinier. He had trained in the 1990s at the FSB's academy, before joining Yukos and the state-run

Sberbank. Like VTB, Sberbank performed certain Kremlin functions. It was the official sponsor of the 2013 Miss Universe contest in Moscow, attended by Trump and hosted by Agalarov. Eight days after the contest Sberbank announced it was lending Agalarov 55 billion roubles ($1.3 billion) to finance new projects. One of those under consideration was Trump's Moscow tower. In February 2016 Putin promoted Gorkov to VEB chief.

VEB's mission was to support Moscow's political programmes. It provided capital to build facilities at the Sochi Olympics and cash to secessionist rebels in eastern Ukraine. These top-down ventures lost money. VEB had large debts. The United States had included VEB, VTB, and Sberbank in its 2014 sanctions package. This came two years after Putin first banned US couples from adopting Russian children. Gorkov's job was to restore the bank's fortunes.

Gorkov was well prepared for his meeting with Kushner, as befits a graduate of what was known in KGB times as the Dzerzhinsky Higher School. He flew in from Moscow. On his plane were gifts. These were a piece of art and some earth carefully dug up and transported from the town of Novogrudok in northwest Belarus.

The town was where Kushner's paternal grandmother Rae Kushner grew up. In 1941 the German army arrived. The town's Jewish inhabitants were rounded up and forced to live and work in an agricultural college. Around half were executed. The survivors dug a tunnel, and in September 1943 they crawled out, fleeing into the forest.

This and much else would have been included in the FSB's bulging Kushner file. Gorkov's presents were chosen to remind Kushner of his origins in a part of the world that once belonged to the Soviet imperium, and of his spiritual roots. This subtlety was wasted. In evidence, Kushner said Putin's messenger had given him a "bag of dirt." It came from "Nvgorod," he wrote, spelling his grandmother's birthplace incorrectly.

This meeting took place on December 13. According to Kushner, Gorkov introduced himself and "made some statements about the Russian economy." The banker said he was friendly with Putin and expressed disappointment about the state of US–Russian relations under Obama and "his hopes for a better relationship" in the future, Kushner told congressional committees.

There was no discussion of lifting sanctions, Kushner said. Nor was he offered any commercial deals.

Kushner characterized the encounter as brief, meaningless. Without an official note this was hard to verify. After all, it was difficult to discuss the Russian economy without mentioning its depressed state. Next Gorkov flew directly from New York to Japan, where Putin was attending a summit. The banker would have certainly reported to his boss.

Kushner's official account of his dealings with Kremlin representatives runs to eleven pages. It's a flat, sterile document, clearly reviewed by other hands. In his version there was no wrongdoing. What happened was a series of inconsequential meetings during a hectic campaign. Kushner says he forgot Kislyak's name. There was no secret channel. Nor did he rely on "Russian funds" to finance his business. In short, a nothing burger.

Despite these protestations, it's clear that Russian intelligence found it remarkably easy to gain access to Trump's inner circle. Ambassadors, lawyers, bankers bearing bags of dirt . . . all found their way to Trump Tower in 2016, all were welcomed and listened to. Gorkov was one part of a multiperson penetration exercise. The cast included Kislyak, Veselnitskaya, the Agalarovs, and other unknown actors working behind the scenes.

Targeting Kushner was logical. He was soon to become a federal employee. His portfolio included tax, banking policy, the military, and international affairs. In a protean White House—where anyone could be fired—Kushner's status as the president's son-in-law made him unsackable.

During his meetings with Russians, Kushner said nothing about Moscow's attack on US democracy.

Afterwards, he kept quiet about the encounters. So did the Trump administration. In his security clearance form Kushner didn't mention Gorkov or Kislyak. (Kushner said this was an administrative mistake, made by an underling, and that he left off details of all foreign contacts.) The American public only found out because of leaks.

By autumn 2017 the questions that led us to meet with Steele had acquired greater definition.

Was Moscow *blackmailing* Trump? And if yes, *how exactly?*

As a candidate, Trump's praise of Putin had been a steady theme. In the White House, his fidelity to Russia's president had continued, even as he lambasted other world leaders, turned on aides and allies, fired the head of the FBI, bawled out his attorney general, and defenestrated his chief ideologue, Steve Bannon.

It was Steele's dossier that offered a compelling explanation for Trump's unusual constancy vis-à-vis Russia. First, there was Moscow's *kompromat* operation against Trump going back three decades, to the Kryuchkov era. If Trump had indulged in compromising behaviour, Putin knew of it.

Second, there was the money: the cash from Russia that had gone into Trump's real estate ventures. The prospect of a lucrative deal in Moscow to build a hotel and tower, a project that was still being negotiated as candidate Trump addressed adoring crowds.

And then there were the loans. These had helped rescue Trump after 2008. They had come from a bank that was simultaneously laundering billions of dollars of Russian money.

Finally, there was the possibility that the president had other financial connections to Moscow, as yet undisclosed, but perhaps hinted at by his missing tax returns.

Together, these factors appeared to place Trump under some sort of obligation. One possible manifestation of this was the president's courting of Putin in Hamburg. Another was the composition of his campaign team and government, especially in its first iteration. Wherever you looked there was a Russian trace.

Trump's pick for secretary of state? Rex Tillerson, a figure known and trusted in Moscow, and recipient of the Order of Friendship. National security adviser? Michael Flynn, Putin's dinner companion and beneficiary of undeclared Russian fees. Campaign manager? Paul Manafort, long-time confidant to ex-Soviet oligarchs. Foreign policy adviser? Carter Page, an alleged Moscow asset who gave documents to Putin's spies. Commerce secretary? Wilbur Ross, an entrepreneur with Russia-connected investments. Personal lawyer? Michael Cohen, who sent emails to Putin's press secretary. Business associate? Felix Sater, son of a Russian American mafia boss. And other personalities, too.

It was almost as if Putin had played a role in naming Trump's cabinet. The US president, of course, had done the choosing. But the constellation of individuals, and their immaculate alignment with Russian interests, formed a discernible pattern, like stars against a clear night sky. A pattern of collusion.

If Trump had been telling the truth—about his visits to Moscow, his dealings with Russian and Soviet emissaries, his financial entanglements—he had nothing to fear. It was a big if.

If he had been lying, the situation was grave. Sooner or later, the truth might engulf him and sweep away his presidency.

EPILOGUE

2017–?
Washington–Moscow

Jerk-off artists, playing jerk-off games, thinking you're
the biggest fucking wise guys in the universe.
You're nothings, hear me!
—JOHN LE CARRÉ, *A Legacy of Spies*

On the eve of his first anniversary in office, Trump's achievements were few. In fact, it was hard to think of any. There was plenty of noise: tweets on immigration and tax reform, speeches to his loyal base, and personal insults thrown at North Korea's dictator, Kim Jong-un, whom Trump would later embrace at a summit. But nothing that might heal America, restore common values, or soothe the country's pained racial and cultural divide.

His White House was beset by problems. Most were self-created. Even Trump's natural allies were struggling. Relations between Trump and Senator Mitch McConnell, the Republican majority leader, were so bad that they were no longer speaking. The president repeatedly berated Congress, too.

Trump's Republicans controlled both houses, but he was surely the weakest president of modern times. Much of his personal energy went into fighting gratuitous battles. He was at odds with his staff, big business, the National Football League, the US intelligence community, and the FBI.

It was this last institution that posed a mortal threat to Trump. Mueller's investigation was moving aggressively forward. The bureau leaks that characterized the first half of 2017 had pretty much dried up. It was difficult to be sure, but Mueller seemed to be proceeding with a determination, a ruthlessness even, that boded ill for the president. Nothing less than the FBI's credibility was at stake.

Certainly, it looked bad for Trump's lieutenants. It was clear that both Manafort and Flynn were now major targets. Mueller's strategy seemed designed to unnerve them both. The special prosecutor had reportedly targeted Flynn's son and former chief of staff, Michael Flynn Jr, with a subpoena. This was a classic bare-knuckle prosecutorial tactic—go after the son to step up pressure on Dad.

Seemingly, the goal was to get Flynn to co-operate. For Flynn to receive immunity, he would have to provide information that materially advanced the case against people higher up the chain of command. That meant Trump. Of course, Trump might pardon Flynn for any reason or none. But, as constitutional lawyers noted, Trump could not issue a pardon for an improper reason or to frustrate justice. Flynn would go on to plead guilty. And agree to work with Mueller.

Meanwhile, Manafort's woes piled up. Further subpoenas were issued covering his lawyer and prominent DC lobbying firms with which he had worked on the Ukraine brief. Further humiliating details emerged of the FBI's pre-dawn raid on his home. The agents picked the locks, burst in with weapons drawn, and even patted down Manafort's bleary-eyed wife, Kathleen, CNN reported. This physical roughness was normally reserved for cases of organized crime or treason.

Another Mueller target, Carter Page, announced that he would plead the Fifth Amendment. His desire not to self-incriminate was understandable. Were he to testify before Congress he might say something at odds with the records of his private conversations, bugged by the FBI and now in the hands of the government.

Trump's lawmaking achievements, meanwhile, were scant. There was one piece of significant legislation, but one that Trump had bitterly opposed. On August 2, 2017, he had been forced to sign into law the new sanctions against Moscow, after a near-unanimous vote in the Senate and House. The act could be revoked only with Congress's approval. The prospect of a Trump administration lifting sanctions on Russia receded.

For Putin, this was a profound setback. The Kremlin's campaign to help Trump win the White House had a primary goal: to bring about an end to America's economic embargo. (The secondary aim was to shove a finger in the United States' pre-existing social and ideological wounds. This had succeeded well enough.)

Putin's operation was bold, cocky even. It involved cyber hacking, fake Facebook accounts, and classic KGB techniques of deceit and cultivation. But it had backfired, you might argue. Kremlin officials often imagined America to be a mirror copy of Russia. They had a poor understanding of US institutional politics. They failed to appreciate the separation of powers or the constraints on a president—any president.

Wiser voices inside the Russian administration—sacked

chief of staff Sergei Ivanov and US ambassador Sergey Kislyak, now recalled to Moscow—had been right. As with Putin's 2014 invasion of Ukraine, intervening in the 2016 US presidential election had been a tactical triumph and a strategic disaster. The consequences for Russia's economy were lasting. It remained shut out from cheap Western credit.

Were it not for his dossier, Trump would have lifted sanctions and created a new alliance with Russia, Steele believed. As one friend put it: "Chris stole a great strategic victory from right under Putin's nose." Steele's motivations weren't connected to politics or ego. Rather, it was about uncovering the truth and public service, the friend said. At some point Steele may want to tell his own story.

It was an open question as to when the dossier would be "proven up," Steele added to friends. The Kremlin had had a year to cover up all traces of its operation. It had done this successfully. In contrast to DC, Russian officials didn't leak; journalists based in Moscow had struggled to find original material. There were quite a few people "still alive and kicking" who knew significant things, but they were not likely to come forward "anytime soon," Steele thought.

These people included ex-KGB officers with knowledge of historic plots. There were paper records, too: typically looseleaf folders with documents arranged in chronological order. Does the Trump file still exist? The chatter in Moscow is that Putin has grown so paranoid that any incriminating material will have been destroyed or hidden in his safe. Certainly, the Soviet-era file on Steele, compiled when he was a junior embassy spy, will now be much enhanced.

Inside Russia, change looks unlikely. In 2017 Putin's stint in power (including his spell as prime minister, when he remained in charge) surpassed that of Leonid Brezhnev. His victory in the 2018 presidential election surprised nobody. Six more years takes him to 2024. He will probably outlast Trump. Even without Putin, Putinism may survive in new form.

Even so, details of Moscow's Trump project may eventually trickle out. A change of regime, a defector, a loose cannon—all could see well-buried secrets emerge. After the collapse of Soviet communism, Stalin's spy chief wrote a memoir. The KGB lost control of its foreign intelligence archive detailing secret post-war operations. It ended up in the hands of MI6. It can be read in Cambridge.

For now, the Russian half of the collusion story lies beyond Mueller's grasp.

Mueller's focus is the American half. That is more gettable. And what we know there is bad enough.

The first indictments were no surprise—those of Manafort and Manafort's associate, Rick Gates. When Manafort was the Trump campaign chairman Gates served as his deputy. The charges dated from the period between 2006 and 2016, mostly from when both men worked for Yanukovych in Ukraine.

Their alleged crimes were stunning. There were twelve counts in all. They included conspiracy against the US, money laundering, failing to declare foreign bank accounts, and not registering as a foreign agent. Plus, making "false, fraudulent, and fictitious" statements. The pair were said to have run a "multi-million-dollar lobbying campaign" inside the US on behalf of the Yanukovych regime. They tried to hide this, the indictment claimed.

It was known that Manafort was richly rewarded for his activities in Kiev. Even so, the alleged sums discovered by the FBI were dizzying. The bureau said that more than $75 million had flowed through offshore accounts belonging to Manafort.

He had set up a series of foreign front companies run by nominees. These in turn controlled numerous bank accounts—in Cyprus, St Vincent and the Grenadines, and the Seychelles.

What had Manafort done with all this cash? The bureau claimed that he had laundered much of it, "more than $18 million." The money had funded an oligarch-like splurge. Manafort had bought luxury goods such as antique rugs, clothes, works of art, and cars, including a Mercedes and three Range Rovers. And the properties in New York. (One of them, the SoHo condo, was let out on Airbnb for "thousands of dollars a week.")

In better times Manafort was arguably the most articulate member of Trump's campaign team. As news of the indictment broke, he went silent. He and Gates turned themselves over to the FBI and appeared in a federal court in Washington. They pleaded not guilty to all charges, and Manafort was freed on a $10 million bond. He was now under "home confinement," his fate uncertain ahead of a trial.

Trump's response to his ex-aide's troubles? Minimal, just a couple of tweets. It was left to Manafort's attorney to defend his client. Speaking outside court, Kevin Downing dismissed the charges as ridiculous. He said there was no evidence that Manafort or the Trump campaign had ever colluded with the Russians. As the White House noted, the charges pre-dated Manafort's work for Trump.

Still, the accusations kept coming. There were dozens of further indictments for money laundering and bank fraud. Gates changed his plea, agreed to cooperate with Mueller and told what he knew. Meanwhile, Manafort ended up in jail, his bail revoked, after allegedly trying to interfere with witnesses. Manafort and Gates would face off against each other in a courtroom in Alexandria, Virginia—a brutal battle between two erstwhile friends. The verdict, when it came, was devastating. Manafort was found guilty of eight counts, including tax and bank fraud, with the jury unable to agree on another ten. Ahead of him lay the prospect of years in federal jail.

The sense of foreboding engulfing the Trump administration was real. There was another unexpected development: a third indictment of someone from Trump's team. This was George Papadopoulos, a young Greek American who lived in London. He had joined the campaign, aged twenty-nine, in March 2016—an "excellent guy," as Trump put it later that same month, unveiling Papadopoulos as his foreign policy adviser.

The FBI's indictment laid out a secret plot. Much of it took place on Steele's doorstep. The characters involved seemed to have come straight out of the board game Cluedo: a mysterious "professor" based in the UK; a female Russian national; and an "individual" in Moscow with impeccable connections to Russia's foreign ministry.

The bureau's fourteen-page "statement of offense" was unsealed the same day Manafort and Gates appeared in court. It set out in calm, logical tones an attempt by Papadopoulos to arrange a high-level meeting between Putin and Trump. Discussions with Moscow took place behind the scenes throughout the spring and summer of 2016. Trump knew about them. So did his senior team.

The statement revealed Papadopoulos learned in late April 2016 that the Kremlin had stolen Democratic Party emails. At this point the Democrats had no idea of the hack. It was made public six weeks later. Seemingly, the timeline shed fresh light on why Donald Trump Jr was so eager to meet Veselnitskaya, and on Trump's public appeal to Moscow to locate Hillary's "missing" 30,000 emails.

Papadopoulos first met the professor in March 2016, during a trip to Italy. The professor—identified by the *Washington Post* as Joseph Mifsud—showed little interest in him. Until, that is, Mifsud discovered Papadopoulos's Trump connection. In London, Mifsud introduced Papadopoulos to a "female Russian national." Papadopoulos wrongly called her "Putin's niece" in emails sent back to the campaign. (Mifsud denies any connection with the Russian government.)

What did they discuss? According to the FBI, how to improve US–Russian ties. And, more concretely, arranging a meeting between "us"—the Trump campaign—and the Russian leadership. A week later Papadopoulos flew to Washington, DC. He was photographed sitting around a table with Trump and the candidate's national security team. Papadopoulos introduced himself and made a bold offer: using his "connections," he could engineer a Trump–Putin meeting.

Next, Papadopoulos worked with his new friends to make this happen. He sent emails to the Russian woman, who replied in enthusiastic terms. The professor got in touch from Moscow, and introduced Papadopoulos to an influential "individual" with links to Russia's foreign ministry and its North America desk. Meanwhile, Papadopoulos kept the campaign apprised of his activities and Kremlin contacts. One "campaign supervisor" replied: "Great work."

And so it went on. There was a breakfast with Mifsud in a London hotel. The professor had just returned from Moscow, where he met "high-level Russian government officials." He brought intriguing news: the Russians had obtained valuable "dirt" on Clinton. "They have thousands of [her] emails," the professor said. After this conversation, Papadopoulos continued to "communicate with Trump campaign officials." Might

London work, he wondered, as a venue for a Russia–Trump get-together?

No one could fault Papadopoulos's enthusiasm. Throughout May, June, and August 2016 there were further emails and updates, plus messages relayed to the Trump campaign with the unambiguous subject line: "Request from Russia to meet Mr Trump." Some of these missives reached Manafort and Gates. Papadopoulos even offered to fly to Moscow himself, if the candidate couldn't make it. Despite his best efforts, the trip never happened.

All of this went to the heart of the FBI's collusion inquiry. In January 2017, a week after Trump's inauguration, federal agents interviewed Papadopoulos for the first time. He lied—about when he knew of the email hack and his multiple engagements with Moscow and its intermediaries. The agents reinterviewed him in February. A day later he deleted his Facebook account and changed his cell phone number.

Papadopoulos was a lousy conspirator. In July 2017, the FBI arrested him at Dulles International Airport. Seemingly, they had retrieved his wiped data. From this point on, he began co-operating. He met with the government on "numerous occasions," answered questions, and provided information. In October, he pleaded guilty to lying to the FBI.

These three indictments were the first. Others would surely follow. Trump's claim that there had been no collusion sounded increasingly hollow and fake. Now there was evidence of collusion. It was impossible to read the legal documents—with their cold, empirical facts—in any other way.

Mueller's investigation was far from over. The agony of Donald J. Trump was just beginning.

*

Throughout 2018, Trump's fidelity to Putin was painfully visible. Indeed, it often seemed that the president was more loyal to Russia and its leader than he was to his own country. Or to America's traditional European friends, including the UK.

That March, a retired Russian spy, Sergei Skripal, was found collapsed on a park bench in the English city of Salisbury, together with his daughter Yulia. They had been poisoned. The weapon was a nerve agent, Novichok, made by the late Soviet Union. The plot was crude. And chilling. Someone had smeared it on the front-door handle of Skripal's semi-detached home.

The evidence pointed to Russia, and the British government blamed Moscow for this blatant near murder (both Skripals survived). There were several theories as to motive. The most obvious was revenge: Skripal is a former GRU intelligence officer who spied for MI6, got caught, served jail time, and landed in Britain and exile after a 2010 spy swap.

Two weeks after the attempted hit, Trump rang Putin. The commander in chief spoke from the White House. Did Trump, as might have been expected, express outrage over the incident? Or solidarity with Britain, seemingly once again a playground for Russian undercover special operations?

No. Rather, Trump congratulated Putin on his recent victory in Russia's presidential election—this despite the fact that aides had given him a briefing note that read in capitals: "DO NOT CONGRATULATE." The same national security advisers had told the president to raise the case of the Skripals, at that point gravely ill in intensive care. He ignored them.

Instead, Trump floated the idea of a grand diplomatic summit with Putin, to take place in Washington or some other location. Trump explained his beneficent treatment of Putin via Twitter. Getting on with Russia was "a good thing," he wrote.

True, the US did expel fifty Russian diplomats as part of a response coordinated by Britain and its allies over the Novichok affair. The UK had supplied "persuasive information" about the plot, a senior State Department official said. But, as ever, it was hard to discern a coherent or unitary policy towards Moscow from the Trump White House. Trump's own public comments were never less than ingratiating.

The Trump–Putin meeting was agreed for July. The venue was the Finnish capital, Helsinki, but first Trump embarked on a wrecking-ball tour through Europe. In Brussels, he blasted fellow NATO members for alleged military underspending. He described the EU as a "foe." And he criticized Theresa May's Brexit strategy in an interview with the *Sun* newspaper.

Trump's apparent gripe was trade—the EU and others were "taking advantage" of America, he stated. But this seemed largely a pretext. His real goal, it appeared, was to turn post-war Western relations inside out, to confound and dismay the countries that had stood by America's side throughout the Cold War. The beneficiary of this new disorder was Russia.

After Brussels came Britain. Trump flew in for a four-day visit. There was a banquet at Blenheim Palace in Oxfordshire, talks with the prime minister, and a meeting with the Queen at Windsor Castle. There, Trump appeared to walk in front of the ninety-two-year-old monarch—a diminutive figure dressed in blue—as they inspected a ceremonial guard of honour.

Meanwhile, in Washington, deputy attorney general Rod Rosenstein announced a new set of indictments from the special prosecutor. Mueller's latest charges named twelve Russian career intelligence officers working for the GRU in Moscow. These were the Russian spies who carried out the 2016 DNC hack.

The facts were set out with startling clarity. One centre of operations was a GRU building nicknamed the "Tower" in Moscow's Khimki district. It was from here and a second GRU facility that the group broke into the email accounts of Clinton volunteers and campaign employees. The operation's masterminds were military officers: Viktor Borisovich Netyksho and Major Boris Alekseyevich Antonov. Not so much a witch hunt as a "vich" hunt, as Twitter put it.

The indictments built on the preliminary assessment made in early 2017 by the Obama White House. It added fascinating detail. The hack was a textbook "*maskirovka*," or deception operation. It featured spear phishing, fake persons, hidden crypto-currency payments, and a special piece of GRU malware called "X-Agent." The hack ran from March to November 2016.

The platforms used to release the stolen material—Guccifer 2.0 and DCleaks.com—were GRU fronts. Or, as the indictment put it, "fictitious online personas." The GRU used "Guccifer" to relay the DNC material to WikiLeaks, sending Julian Assange an email. Later, the Russians tried to cover their tracks, deleting traces of the Democratic Congressional Campaign Committee from the network.

The indictment on the eve of the Helsinki summit created a dilemma for Trump. He could dismiss it, but then he would once again look like Putin's poodle. If he accepted its accuracy, this would mean finally acknowledging that Russia had interfered in 2016. And admitting he owed his historic victory to the Kremlin, at least in part.

The two leaders met for more than two hours. As in Hamburg, there were no aides present, only interpreters. What was discussed is secret. In a joint press conference afterwards, Trump made no mention of Russia's cyber-interference. Nor did he demand the extradition of the twelve GRU officers fingered by Mueller.

And so, with Putin, a physically smaller figure, at the president's side and the world watching, it was left to the press to ask Trump the obvious question: would he now condemn Moscow's interference in US democracy? Trump couldn't bring himself to do so. "They said they think it's Russia; I have President Putin, he just said it's not Russia," Trump replied.

He continued: "I will say this: I don't see any reason why it would be. I have great confidence in my intelligence people, but I will tell you that President Putin was extremely strong and powerful in his denial today." Trump then changed the subject to the DNC's "missing" servers, and how Hillary blew an election she should have won.

It was an abject performance, and the single worst moment in Trump's presidency to date. Even leading Republicans had to acknowledge that Trump had failed to stand up for his own nation, preferring instead to side with Russia's president. Underlying Trump's slavish behaviour was something irrational and primal. It appeared Putin terrified America's president.

In Washington, there was a firestorm. The former CIA director John Brennan, a notable Trump critic, summed up the mood of outrage: "Donald Trump's press conference performance in Helsinki rises to & exceeds the threshold of 'high crimes & misdemeanors.' It was nothing short of treasonous," he tweeted.

Brennan added: "Not only were Trump's comments imbecilic, he is wholly in the pocket of Putin."

It was difficult to disagree. The debate about collusion, and the degree to which Trump and his team may have cheated using Russian assistance, now had a harder dimension. There was elemental clarity. It seemed wholly possible that the president of the United States was a traitor. The best explanation for Trump's fear vis-à-vis Putin was that laid out by the dossier—*kompromat*, both sexual and financial.

Since Hamburg, Trump had insisted that the meeting between Veselnitskaya and Donald Trump Jr was "primarily" about the adoption of Russian children. In August 2018, troubled as usual by the Mueller inquiry, he tweeted something different. "This was a meeting to get information on an opponent, totally legal and done all the time in politics—and it went nowhere," Trump wrote. He added: "I did not know about it!"

Here, then, was the president seemingly admitting attempted collusion. His earlier statement dictated from Air Force One was a lie. The president's new defence was unconvincing, a little desperate, and amounted to this: *Yes, it happened. But I didn't know about it, and it didn't go anywhere.*

In fact, Mueller's investigation was going somewhere—somewhere uncomfortable for Trump. Over in Virginia a jury convicted Manafort of various frauds. Meanwhile, in a Manhattan court Michael Cohen—the president's lawyer and long-term fixer—admitted a string of serious crimes. They included breaking campaign finance laws and paying off Trump's alleged mistresses, including an adult-movie actress and a former *Playboy* Playmate. The first featured a $130,000 payout to the actress Stephanie Clifford, aka Stormy Daniels, during the 2016 election campaign.

Sure, none of this was directly related to collusion. However, Cohen testified under oath that someone else had directed him to commit these illegal acts—Trump. As Cohen's lawyer Lanny Davis noted, if the payments made by Cohen were a crime, then the president had surely committed the same crime. In short, Trump's personal attorney was accusing Trump of criminal behaviour. Cohen also indicated he might be ready to cooperate with Mueller in return for leniency. The fixer held the answers to some intriguing questions. Did Trump have advance knowledge of the DNC hack and the meeting in Trump Tower? And did he collude with Russian officials who were trying to subvert the 2016 vote?

The accusations against Trump were moving from abstract to concrete, from the stuff of partisan politics to the unforgiving realm of the courtroom. The president's fervent supporters remained loyal. So did his Republican allies. And yet it was becoming easier to imagine a world in which Donald Trump was no longer in the White House and fading slowly into history.

NOTES ON SOURCES

I spoke to many sources. These conversations took place in a variety of places. In no particular order, the back of a London taxi; a bar in downtown Washington, DC; a park bench overlooking the River Thames (yes, touches of John le Carré here); and a participants' dinner at an East Coast university faculty.

Other contacts happened in coffee bars (multiple times); pubs (quite a few of those); a restaurant belonging to a celebrity chef (repeat lunches); the New York green room of a major TV network; and a well-known five-star hotel. Plus, an upstairs room that has featured in some of this century's biggest international news stories.

Over time, the number of people willing to supply me confidential information grew. I saw a few sources regularly. Others I never met. We swapped messages mostly via encrypted channels. One person got in touch offering useful Soviet-era background. They were in a faraway time zone. Our exchanges were staggered. My *Guardian* colleagues Stephanie Kirchgaessner and Nick Hopkins were generous in sharing sources.

After four years living in Moscow and a decade writing about Vladimir Putin's Kremlin, I have many Russian friends and colleagues. They helped shape this book. So did notes. I keep a score of old reporters' notepads smuggled out of

Moscow. My interviews with Aras Agalarov and Paul Manafort emerged from a forgotten lodging place on top of a cupboard, like treasure from a dusty vault.

My interlocutors were mostly men—the world of security and intelligence is still overwhelmingly male. They included former senior advisers to the National Security Council, under two US presidents; an ex-head of the CIA and NSA; retired intelligence officers; defectors; historians; law lecturers; ex-diplomats; and a taxi-sized number of emeritus professors. I spoke to a lot of journalists, too.

It is this last group that has made the greatest contribution to investigating the story of collusion. The *Washington Post* and *New York Times*, as well as other US newspaper titles and websites, have done some bravura reporting in the face of unceasing hostility from this president. They deserve great credit. Where possible, I have attributed investigation done by others.

Luke Harding

THANKS

I would like to thank the sources, anonymous and not so anonymous, who helped with this book. You know who you are.

INDEX

Abe, Shinzo, 135
Abramson, Jill, 74
Ackermann, Josef, 283
Adams, John, 183
Afghanistan, 116, 218, 263
Agalarov, Aras, 229–34, 236, 237, 239, 241, 318
Agalarov, Emin, 230, 236, 240, 241, 242–3
Agalarov, Heydar, 230
Agalarov, Irina, 232
Agalarov, Sheila, 232
Akhmetov, Rinat, 146, 148, 149
Akhmetshin, Rinat, 244–5, 246
Albert, Prince, of Monaco, 281
Aleksashenko, Sergei, 47
Alexei, Tsar, 17
Alexseyev, Vladimir, 105
Aliyev, Ilham, 230
Allbeury, Ted, 6
Ames, Aldrich, 227
Andres, Greg, 269
Andrew, Christopher, 119, 120, 121, 214, 218, 225
Andropov, Yuri, 212–13
Antonov, Boris, 334
Anikeev, Vladimir, 93–4, 96
The Apprentice, 236, 288
Arif, Tevfik, 288, 289, 290
The Art of the Deal (Trump), 218, 220, 223
Artemenko, Andriy, 297
Ashcroft, John, 175
Assad, Bashar al-, 194
Assange, Julian, 93, 109, 124, 173, 334
Awada, Juliana, 255

Baker, Howard, 131
Baltic states, 17, 82
Bannon, Stephen, 160, 188, 263, 271, 320
Baquet, Dean, 71
Baron, Marty, 72
Barrack, Thomas Jr, 157
Barrow, Tim, 22
Barter, Chris, 52, 53, 306, 308
Bayrock, 288–9, 290
Berezovsky, Boris, 77, 119
Berkowitz, Avi, 317
Bernstein, Carl, 67
Beyrle, John, 78
Bharara, Preet, 292–4
Bildt, Carl, 85
Bishop, Maurice, 131
Blair, Tony: and Putin, 21
Blake, George, 120–1
Blokhin, Oleh, 18
Blow, Charles M., 137
Blumenthal, Richard, 184
Bogatin, David, 284
Boiko, Oleg, 291
Borger, Julian, 64, 197, 208, 270
Bork, Robert, 190
Bortnikov, Alexander, 106, 307
Boston Globe, 224
bots, Russia's use of, 111
Bowcott, Owen, 239–40
Bremmer, Ian, 46, 255
Brennan, John, 34, 106, 335
Brexit, 6, 38, 86, 173, 333
Brezhnev, Leonid, 327
Browder, Bill, 234, 244, 245
Burgess, Guy, 120

INDEX

Burr, Richard, 210
Burrows, Christopher, 5, 20
Buryakov, Evgeny, 43–4, 49, 317
Bush, George H. W., 226
Bush, George W., 145, 175; and Putin, 21
Bush, Jeb, 26–7
BuzzFeed, 67–70, 86, 87, 101

Caesar, Ed, 311
Calandra, Lisa, 222
Cambridge University, and spying, 16, 120
Carter, Jimmy, 123, 213
Chacon, Bobby, 189
Chaika, Yuri, 234, 242
Chapman, Anna, 43
Charlottesville, 262
Cheney, Dick, 175
Chernitsyn, Sergey, 279–80, 281
Chevron, 155
Christie, Chris, 129, 159
Churchill, Winston, 147
Churkin, Vitaly, 101, 222
CIA, 9, 12, 25, 92, 106, 155, 194, 216; slow to grasp Trump–Russia connections, 34; and Page, 60; hackers accused of being a front organization for, 92; report from FBI, NSA, and, 107–10
Clapper, James, 34, 57, 122–3, 204
Clifford, Stephanie, 336
climate change, 250, 258, 263
Clinton, Hillary: and emails, 7, 36, 70, 84, 126, 176, 187, 188, 329, 330; Trump's lambasting of, 7; Russian dossier on, 29, 55, 75; hacking operations against, 31; and State Department, 47, 261; compromising material on, 75; as secretary of state, 105; assumption of victory by, 106; in CIA–FBI–NSA report, 108; Trump voters' anger towards, 111; and use of bots, 111; Flynn's strident criticism of, 126–7; Putin happy with operation against, 128; "hated and feared" by Putin, 161; FBI office's hatred of, 174; early post-election appearance by, 182–3; Comey on probe into, 183–4; Trump calls for jailing of, 194; documents to "incriminate" offered to Trump, 241–2; and diplomatic cables, 261; Trump accuses of criminal conduct, 279
CNN, 36, 74; and dossier, 66–7
Cohen, Michael, 65, 69, 280–1, 294–5, 296–7, 321, 336–7
Cohen, Roger, 263
Cold War, 16, 19, 21, 62–3, 78, 88, 108, 120, 196, 216
Comey, James, 35, 36, 37, 40, 60, 170, 174–6, 178–82, 197–201, 268; and Trump's "nut job" accusation, 171, 193; confirms probe into Russian interference, 178; on Clinton investigation, 183–4; and Judiciary Committee, 183–4; on Trump–Russia evidence, 184; Trump fires, 185–92, 196; Steele's recommendation for, 185; memos written by, 197, 198–9, 200; post-firing dinner with Trump, 199–200; and Trump's plea re. Flynn, 200–1; out-intrigues Trump, 202–3; and Senate Committee, 203–4, 207–11; briefs Trump on dossier, 204–5; on encounters with Trump, 204–7; Trump demands loyalty of, 206; *see also* FBI
Commercial Observer, 315
Condon, Richard, 6
Conway, Kellyanne, 189, 190
Corn, David, 27, 36, 65
Costa, Robert, 73
Cox, Archibald, 190
Crimea: and US sanctions, 47, 54; undercover troops in, 81; Russia annexes, 121; Yalta conference in, 147; and Ukrainian revolution, 152; Cohen–Sater proposal for, 297
Crocker, Lizzie, 210
Cruz, Ted, 26, 83
cyber espionage, *see* hacking
Cyprus, Bank of, 168, 282, 292
Czechoslovakia, intelligence service in, 216, 217

Daily Beast, 74, 210
Daily Mail, 85
Daniels, Stormy, *see* Clifford, Stephanie
Davis, Lanny, 336–7
de Gaulle, Charles, 219

Dearlove, Richard, 119, 121, 315
Defense Intelligence Agency (DIA), 116, 121–3
Democratic National Committee (DNC), 9, 97, 103, 106, 152, 161; and Steele's probing of Trump, 27; Russians hack HQ of, 171–2; *see also* Democratic Party
Democratic Party: emails of, 7, 35, 70, 84, 93, 329; and information on Trump, 27; National Convention, 35; and Gang of Eight, 66; seen as weak and beaten, 72; and hacking, 93, 102, 103; and Sessions, 187; calls for special counsel, 201
Denman, Diana, 83–4
Department for Homeland Security, 109; and "GRIZZLY STEPPE", 102
Department of Financial Services (DFS), 308, 311, 314
Deripaska, Oleg, 145–6, 157, 163
Deutsche Bank, 73–4, 300, 302–7, 308–9, 311–16; money laundering by, 305, 308–9, 313–14; unsuccessful questions to re. Trump, 312–13
Diveykin, Igor, 53, 55
Dodon, Igor, 80
Dokuchaev, Dmitry, 91–2, 97
Dole, Bob, 83, 145
Donnelly, Brian, 56
Doughnut, 33
Downing, Kevin, 328
Dreeben, Michael, 268
Dreiser, Theodore, 276
Dubinin, Yuri, 218, 219–20, 222
Dubinina, Irina, 220
Dubinina, Natalia, 218–20
Dukhina, Ekaterina, 311
Dunbar, Mike, 226
Dvorkovich, Arkady, 96
Dzerzhinsky, Felix, 89–90

Ehrlichman, John, 195
Elias, Marc E., 27
Erdoğan, Recep, 129; at G20, 249
Erovinkin, Oleg, 99–100
Estonia, and hacking, 260
Eurasia Group, 46
Exxon, 53, 155, 251

Facebook, 110

Falwell, Jerry, 197
Farage, Nigel, 173
FBI, 9, 23, 25, 35, 71, 88, 106, 166, 170, 216; slow to grasp Trump–Russia connections, 34; and lack of conclusive Trump–Russia link, 36; and Buryakov, 43; and Page, 59–60; and dossier's accuracy, 82; and "GRIZZLY STEPPE", 102; report from CIA, NSA, and, 107–10; and Flynn, 133, 134; HQ of, 172–3; and Trump's patriotism, 174; and domestic surveillance, 175; confirms Russian interference, 178; and wiretapping allegations, 179–80; Trump reacts to probe by, 182; and first subpoenas, 185; Flynn probe by, 201; and Manafort raid, 269–70; and Ivankov, 285–6; and Sater, 287; and Trump Tower, 291–2; and Trincher, 291; Manafort raid by, 324–5; and first indictments, 328–9; statement of offence of, 329; *see also* Comey, James; Mueller, Robert
Fedun, Leonid, 237
Feinstein, Dianne, 183
Felt, Mark, 181
The Field of Fight (Flynn, Ledeen), 123–4, 131
FIFA, corruption within, 25
Financial Times, 74, 86–7, 244
Firtash, Dmytro, 148, 169
Five Eyes, 33
FL Group, 288–9, 290
Flynn, Michael Jr, 324
Flynn, Michael "Misha", 114, 116–19, 120–7, 128–37, 193, 200–1, 264, 267, 297, 316, 321, 324; Trump briefs, 129; Trump appoints, 130; Trump fires, 136, 200; Trump defends, 139, 200; perjury probe into, 201; and Mueller probe, 270, 271; and being "flipped", 271
Foch, Ferdinand, 3
Foer, Franklin, 65
Ford, Gerald, 145, 213
Fox News, 73, 160, 179
France: election in, 260; and hacking, 260
Fridman, Mikhail, 308
Friedman, Robert, 285

INDEX

Frum, David, 256
FSB, 89–92, 104, 229; takes over from KGB, 19; Putin becomes chief of, 21, 89–90; and Mogilevich, 23; and World Cup, 24–5; sexual encounters filmed by, 76–9; author's apartment entered by, 76; CIA–MI6–Steele entity viewed by, 87; Steele's understanding of, 88; HQ of, 89–90; "new nobility", 90; and Shaltai-Boltai, 95; and hacking, 96; leading cyber-ops role of, 96; and Erovinkin, 100; and "harassment" of US diplomats, 111–12
Fukuyama, Francis, 21
Fusion GPS, 24, 27, 35, 39, 52, 96, 127, 234, 244
Fyodorov, Boris, 305

García Márquez, Gabriel, 223
Gates, Rick, 146, 158, 166–7; and first indictments, 327; not-guilty plea of, 328
Gates, Robert, 227
Gazprom, 44, 47, 308
GCHQ, 33–4, 41, 179
German Democratic Republic, 222
Germany: BND in, 34, 259; Trump criticizes, 258; and hacking, 259; Trump unpopular in, 259; plan to influence elections in, 260
Gessen, Masha, 222
Gingrich, Newt, 159
Giuliani, Rudi, 83, 228
Gizmodo, 198
Gizunov, Sergey, 105
global financial crash, 298, 299, 308, 314–15
Global Policy, 47–8, 52
Goldfarb, Alex, 244–5
Goldman Sachs, 52, 306, 308
Goldstone, Rob, 239–44, 246
Golubchik, Anatoly, 292
Gorbachev, Mikhail, 15, 213, 217, 226–7; and failed coup, 18; KGB coup against, 227
Gorbachev, Raisa, 226–7
Gordievsky, Oleg, 120, 214, 218, 225
Gordon, J. D., 84
Gorkov, Sergei, 317–20
Gowdy, Trey, 181

Graff, Rhona, 241
grand juries, 185, 270
Grassley, Chuck, 184
Greenwald, Glenn, 70
Gref, Herman, 238
Griffin, Phil, 164
"GRIZZLY STEPPE", 102
Gromov, Alexander, 124
Group of 7 (G7), 258
Group of 20 (G20), 248–58, 266; protests at, 248–9, 253, 254–5
GRU, 102, 104, 107, 109, 115–18, 121, 152, 164, 193, 220, 221, 244, 334
Gryshchenko, Kostyantin, 142
Guardian, 173, 189, 197, 293; and blackmail rumours, 8; leads pursued by, 73–4; Moscow office of, 228
Gubarev, Aleksej, 87
Guerin, Richard, 46

hacking, 9, 92, 93–7 *passim*, 102–11 *passim*, 325; and Trump–Russia co-ordination, 31; and Democrats, 93, 102–3; and "bear" sobriquets, 102–3; and "weaponized" data, 104; and CIA–FBI–NSA report, 107–10; and local and state electoral boards, 109; and US–Russia working group, 252–3; Trump threatens more sanctions over, 252; and EU institutions, 260
Haldeman, Bob, 135
Halifax International Security Forum, 38
Hamilton, Alexander, 111
Hannigan, Robert, 34
Hannity, Sean, 246
Hanssen, Robert, 227
Harding, Warren, 208
Harrison, Geoffrey, 77
Hatcher, Kyle, 78
Hayden, Michael, 40, 103–4, 111, 188–9, 202, 257
Heck, Joe, 181–2
Hill, Fiona, 251–2
Holt, Lester, 191–2
Hoover, J. Edgar, 202
Hopkins, Nick, 10, 69, 313
Horton, Scott, 268
House Intelligence Committee, 66, 172, 176–82

INDEX

Huckabee Sanders, Sarah, 190
Hudson, James, 78

Ignatius, David, 132
Igumnov, Gennady, 276
Inkster, Nigel, 70
Isikoff, Michael, 263
ISIS, 117, 123, 194
Islamic Republic of Iran, 117
Isler, Maria Gabriela, 237
Ivan the Terrible, 98
Ivankov, Vyacheslav, 284–6, 290, 292
Ivanov, Sergei, 124, 127, 128, 326;
   Putin fires, 128
Ivanova, Galya, 77

Jackson, Andrew, 111
Jain, Anshu, 305, 306
Jefferson, Thomas, 183
Johnson, Larry, 179
JP Morgan Chase, 13, 314

Kadakin, Alexander, 101
Kara-Murza, Vladimir, 119
Kasowitz, Marc, 266
Kasparov, Garry, 196, 256
Kasyanov, Mikhail, 79
Katsyv, Denis, 234, 293
Katsyv, Pyotr, 234
Kaveladze, Ike, 244
Kerry, John, 26
KGB, 15–16, 18, 76, 90, 193, 212–24
   passim, 327; FSB takes over from,
   19; Trump file of, 216, 223–4; and
   Intourist, 221, 223, 229; "global
   priorities" of, 225; and Gorbachev
   coup, 227; US moles of, 227; and
   aggravating disagreements, 256; and
   historic plots, 326
Khodorkovsky, Mikhail, 145, 277
Khrushchev, Nikita, 219
Kilimnik, Konstantin, 163–6
Kim Jong-un, 323
Kirill, Patriarch, 309–10
Kislyak, Ivan Petrovich, 57–9
Kislyak, Sergey, 55–9, 83, 114, 118,
   127, 130, 132, 171, 177, 187,
   192–5, 197, 316–17, 320, 326
Kislyak, Sergey (junior), 58
Kissinger, Henry, 195–6
Klitschko, Vitali, 151

Kommersant, 227, 237, 292
Korobov, Igor, 104–5
Kostin, Andrei, 306, 317
Kostin, Andrey, 305–6
Kostyukov, Igor, 105
Kovalev, Andrei, 56, 220
Kovtun, Dmitry, 12
Kozhin, Vladimir, 237
Kramer, David, 39
Kremlin: Trump's relationship with,
   6–7, 29, 82; Clinton dossier of, 55;
   cautious faction within, 59; dossier in
   possession of, 92; and major foreign
   targets, 96; protests against, 109; and
   expelled diplomats, 112; evasive and
   opaque, 138; and DNC emails, 158,
   329; actively cultivating Trump, 236;
   interference of, 252, 253, 259; and
   sensitive Clinton material, 267; and
   "regular" information exchange, 278;
   and Bharara, 293; *see also* mafia/mob;
   Russia
Kriss, Jody, 289–90
Krivov, Sergei, 100–1
Kryuchkov, Gen. Vladimir, 212–14,
   218–19, 222, 225, 227, 256
Kurkov, Andrey, 148
Kushner, Jared, 9, 130, 157, 159, 173,
   188, 193, 243, 246, 254, 266, 267,
   281, 293, 316–17; and Deutsche
   Bank, 315, 316; and Gorkov, 318–20
Kushner, Rae, 318
Kusturica, Emir, 124
Kuzmin, Maj. Andrei, 98

Lacovara, Philip Allen, 190–1
Larouche, Lyndon, 128
Lauder, Leonard, 218
Lavrov, Sergei, 112, 113, 171, 192–5,
   197, 248, 251, 253
Le Pen, Marine, 260–1
Ledeen, Michael, 123
Lefortovo, 97
Lenin, Vladimir, 81, 222–3
Leshchenko, Serhiy, 149–50, 159, 160
Lesnoy, Anatoly, 58
Leviev, Lev, 293, 316
Lewandowski, Corey, 83, 158, 163
Lewis, Sinclair, 64
Litvinenko, Alexander, 12, 21–2, 70,
   81, 97, 113, 117, 119, 138

Logan Act, 132
Lokhova, Svetlana, 121
Lorber, Howard, 228
Lugovoi, Andrei, 12, 113
Lyovochkin, Serhiy, 144, 154

McCain, John, 7, 38–40, 66, 174, 203
McChrystal, Gen. Stanley, 122
McCloskey, Pete, 156
McFaul, Mike, 125
McGahn, Don, 133–5, 188, 202
Maclean, Donald, 120
McMaster, Lt Gen. H. R., 194, 251
Macron, Emmanuel, 249, 255, 258
mafia/mob, 12, 145, 146, 268, 284–7, 290, 291–2
Magnitsky Act, 234–5, 244–5
The Magnitsky Act, 245
Magnitsky, Sergei, 234, 245, 293
Maison de l'Amitié, 274, 283
Makosiy, Natalia, *see* Wiswell, Natalia
Malanin, Andrey, 101
Male-1, *see* Page, Carter
Malofeev, Konstantin, 91
Manafort, Paul, 83, 140, 142–50 *passim*, 151, 153–69, 243, 246, 266, 267, 280, 321, 324; Ukraine election campaigns run by, 15; scrutiny of, 27; and Party of Regions, 146, 154, 156, 159; and Ukraine disaster, 153; Trump's relationship with, 156–60; becomes Trump campaign manager, 158; and WikiLeaks emails, 158; and "secret ledger", 159–60, 167–8; and Steele dossier, 160–3; quits, 160; and DNC emails, 161; and Kilimnik, 163–5; and Deripaska, 163; centre of various investigations, 166; and cash routing, 167–9; NY properties bought by, 168; Tymoshenko sues, 169; FBI raids apartment of, 269–70; and being "flipped", 271; and FBI raid, 324–5; and first indictments, 327–8; and money laundering, 328; not-guilty plea of, 328
Manchin, Joe, 211
The Manchurian Candidate (Condon), 6
Manning, David, 22
Marković, Duško, 258
Marlowe, Christopher, 120

May, Theresa: and Steele, 86
Medvedev, Dmitry, 49, 93, 105, 127, 264
Merkel, Angela, 193, 249, 258–9, 260
Messner, Tom, 226
MI6: and Litvinenko, 12; and Cold War spies, 16; government acknowledges existence of, 19; Steele leaves, 22
Mifsud, Joseph, 329–30
Mikhailov, Col. Sergei, 91–3, 94–5, 97
Mirzoyan, Gari, 97
Miss Universe, 236, 237, 240, 292, 318
Mitrofanov, Alexsey, 237
Mitrokhin, Vasili, 120
Mitusov, Alexander, 234
Mogilevich, Semion, 23, 169, 268
Molo, Steven F., 300, 301–2
AS Monaco, 275
Monaghan, Gregory, 59
money laundering, 13, 168, 169, 283, 285, 290, 292, 327, 328; and Deutsche Bank, 305, 308–9, 313–14
Montenegro, 258
Moody, James, 285
Mother Jones, 27, 65, 74, 173
Mueller, Robert, 175, 202–3, 210, 246, 266, 327; probe by, 267–70; grand juries used by, 270; determination of, 324; and first indictments, 327–8; indicts Russian intelligence officers, 333

Nahmad, Helly, 291, 292
Nalobin, Sergey, 166
Napolitano, Andrew, 179
National Football League, 324
National Security Agency (NSA), 70, 84, 106; and GCHQ, 33; report from CIA, FBI, and, 107–10
NATO, 82–3, 84, 85, 155, 217, 256–8; Putin reviles, 85; Trump undermines, 85; KGB's priority, 225
Nayyem, Mustafa, 147, 151, 154, 166
Nekrasov, Andrei, 245
Nemtsov, Boris, 82
Netyksho, Viktor, 334
New York Times, 8, 71, 74, 114, 135, 137, 159–60, 171–2, 188, 193, 197, 200, 224, 246, 263, 266, 315; and Trump–Russia link, 36; and bots, 111; and Manafort, 157; on

Comey–Trump dinner, 199; and Rosenstein, 201; on Trump early presidential ambition, 224; on Trump Russia visit, 226; and Trump Jr, 246; and Flynn, 270; and Sater, 289

The New Yorker, 36, 71, 176, 199, 311

Niebuhr, Reinhold, 197–8

Nixon, Richard, 5, 37, 75, 135, 181, 190, 202

North Korea, missile tests by, 135

Norwich House, 102

Novichok, 332

Nuland, Victoria, 26

Nunes, Devin, 181

Obama, Barack, 30, 102, 291, 293; Trump's lambasting of, 7; and Steele dossier, 40; New Economics School talk of, 49–50; Medvedev's talks with, 49; and Russian spy agencies, 104–5; criticizes "Russia's actions", 105; confronts Putin over cyber op, 106; Flynn criticizes, 123, 126; Putin's dim view of, 125; and Flynn, 130; and wiretapping allegations, 179–80; citizenship of, 236; and diplomatic compounds, 263

Obama, Michelle, 30

Oliver, John, 190

Oltermann, Philip, 254

Olympic Games, 236, 318

Onassis, Aristotle, 275

Orbis Business Intelligence, 4–5, 24, 32, 88; spying status of, 4; Steele establishes, 22; possibility of litigation against, 87

Page, Carter (Male-1), 44–55 *passim*, 100, 128, 161, 193, 280, 317, 321; Russian media praise, 50; suspicions grow concerning, 59–60; and Trump–Kislyak meeting, 59; disavowed by Trump campaign, 60; becomes liability, 62; and Trump nomination, 83; and Fifth Amendment, 325

Page, Lisa, 268

Panama Papers, 109–10, 282

Papadopoulos, George, 329–31

Patrushev, Nikolai, 90, 307

Pelevine, Natalia, 79

Pence, Mike, 83, 133, 134, 136, 188; Trump chooses, 158–9

Perevalov, Dmitry, 309–10

Peskov, Dmitry, 29, 62, 75, 124, 127, 282, 296–7

Philby, Kim, 120

Pioneer Point, 101–2

Podesta, John, 182

Podhoretz, John, 70

Podobnyy, Victor, 42–5

Politburo, 90, 220

Politico, 47, 163, 164–5, 182

Politkovskaya, Anna, 70

Polshikov, Petr, 101

Powell, Colin, 122

Prelogar, Elizabeth, 268

Priebus, Reince, 133, 271

Priest, Dana, 125

Putin, Igor, 313

Putin, Lyudmila, 222

Putin, Maria, 222

Putin, Vladimir: Trump's flattering praise of, 7–8; Trump seen as puppet of, 7; and blackmail rumours, 8; author's unflattering reports on, 10; and Litvinenko, 12; USSR's loss mourned by, 19; becomes FSB chief, 21; "black box" description of, 21; and World Cup, 25; and Ukraine, 47; Obama's breakfast meeting with, 49; as prime minister, 49, 105, 317; and Sechin, 51; and Rosneft sale, 61; and Skuratov, 77; hacking allegations against, 93; Shaltai's view of, 94–5; "without human emotions", 94; Obama confronts over cyber op, 106; said to have personally directed cyber op, 106; and CIA–FBI–NSA report, 107–8; grudges said to be harboured by, 109; Ivanov fired by, 128; and Erdoğan, 129; calls Trump after presidential victory, 135; and Ukraine's gas bill, 150; and Ukraine revolution, 152; and Kissinger, 196; in GDR, 222; and Magnitsky Act, 234–5; and Agalarov, 237; Trump meets at G20, 250; and Tillerson, 251; and martial arts, 276; intention to continue of, 327; Trump meets in Helsinki, 334–5; at G20, *see* G20; and Steele dossier, *see* Steele dossier;

and Yanukovych, *see* Yanukovych, Viktor

Quarles, James, 268
Quayle, Dan, 226

Raffel, Josh, 266
Ramsey, Arnaud, 274–5
Reagan, Ronald, 84, 131, 145, 213
Red Mafiya (Friedmann), 285
Reid, Harry, 36–7, 60, 69
Republican National Committee (RNC), 7, 126; HQ of, 172
Republican Party: Committee emails of, 7; and information on Trump, 27; Kislyak at events of, 58–9; and Gang of Eight, 66; Trump nominated by, 83
Rezun, Vladimir, *see* Suvorov, Viktor
Richardson, Elliot, 190
Richman, Daniel, 200
Robinson, Eugene, 210
Rogers, Mike, 176, 180, 181, 182
Roldugin, Sergei, 110
Romanovich, Nikita, 98
Romanovna, Anastasia, 98
Romney, Mitt, 73, 174
Roosevelt, Franklin D., 147
Rosenstein, Rod, 186, 187, 190–1, 333; and special counsel, 201–2
Rosneft, 51, 52, 53–4, 61–2, 99, 251, 276–7
Ross, Wilbur, 282–3, 321
Rostropovich, Mstislav, 120
RosUkrEnergo (RUE), 23
RT (Russia Today), 82, 124–6, 179
Rubio, Marco, 26, 158
Ruckelshaus, William, 190
Ruffin, Phil, 237
Russia: Trump seen as candidate of, 6–7; author deported by, 10, 138; author's time in, 10; and alleged financing of Trump, 13; failed coup in, 18; Federation, birth of, 19; hostile agents of, in UK, 21; and World Cup, 24–5, 54, 233; US sanctions on, 47, 53, 54–5, 83–4, 104, 114, 133, 135, 235, 256, 326; Obama's praise for, 49–50; allegations concerning Trump and, 64; first suspicious interactions between Trump campaign and, 73; and Pioneer Point, 101–2; and sport doping, 109; and Facebook, 110; and bots, 111; and restraint on US diplomats, 113–14, 132; House Intelligence Committee investigates, 176–82; crashed economy of, 228; wealthy residents of, 229; and "adoption", 234–5, 246; and cyber-crime working group, 252–3; and NATO divisions, 256–7; US attempts to "normalize" relations with, 263–4; mass expulsions from, 264–5; reacts to US's new sanctions, 264; post-USSR looting in, 284; and Crimea, *see* Crimea; and CIA–FBI–NSA report, *see* hacking; and hacking, *see* hacking; and mafia, *see* mafia/mob; and Mueller probe, *see* Mueller, Robert; and Steele dossier, *see* Steele dossier; and Ukraine, *see* Ukraine; *see also* USSR; *individual leaders*
Russia Today (RT), *see* RT (Russia Today)
Ryan, Charlie, 305
Ryan, Paul, 195
Rybolovlev, Dmitry, 272–7, 278–80, 281–3; Trump mansion bought by, 273–4; jailed, 273; AS Monaco bought by, 275
Rybolovlev, Elena, 272–3, 274
Rybolovlev, Evgeny, 273
Rybolovlev, Katya, 273, 275, 278

Saakashvili, Mikheil, 50
Safra, Edmond, 275
Samochornov, Anatoli, 244
Sapir, Tamir, 288
Sarkozy, Nicolas, 281
Sater, Felix, 286–8, 289, 290, 294–5, 297, 307, 321
Saturday Night Live, 7
Saudi Arabia, 225
Sberbank, 238, 308, 318
Schiff, Adam, 177, 179
Schiller, Keith, 186, 188
Schmidt, Michael, 200
Schwarzer Block, 248–9, 253
Scott, Rick, 173
Sechin, Igor, 51–4, 60, 62, 99, 251, 276; US bans, 53
Senate Intelligence Committee, 66, 172, 185, 203–4, 207–11

Senate Judiciary Committee, 183, 269
Sendgikoski, Anna-Catherine, 278
Sergun, Igor, 118
Sessions, Jeff, 186, 187, 190, 193, 201, 269, 294
Shaltai-Boltai, 93–5, 96–7
Shaltai (of Shaltai-Boltai), 94–5
Shevardnadze, Sophie, 124
Simonyan, Margarita, 124
Simpson, Glenn, 23–4, 27, 35, 39, 64–5, 67–8, 244
Singer, Mark, 71–2, 228
Singer, Paul, 26–7
Skripal, Sergei, 332
Skripal, Yulia, 332
Skuratov, Yuri, 77
Smith, Ben, 67, 69, 70
Smith, David, 189
Snowden, Edward, 33, 70
Sokolov, Sergei, 52, 54
Soldatov, Andrei, 97
Solodukhin, Oleg, 280
Solzhenitsyn, Alexander, 113
Sorial, George, 301
Spayd, Liz, 71
Spicer, Sean, 133, 179, 189–90, 271
Sporyshev, Igor, 43–4
Stadtmauer, Seryl, 315
Stafford, Andrew, 20
Stalin, Joseph, 18, 57, 90, 147, 221
Stasiuk, Gregory, 285
Steele, Christopher: investigation requested of, 5–6; Orbis office of, 5; journalists' interview with, 10–11, 12–14; author interviews, 10–14, 138–9; and Litvinenko, 12, 21–2; background of, 16–17; at Cambridge, 16–17, 20; as Moscow diplomat, 16–18; recruitment of, 17; sent to Soviet Union, 17; in Stalin's bunker, 18; leaves Moscow, 19; and leaked MI6 officers' names, 20; Paris posting of, 20; schooling of, 20; Russia desk posting of, 21; Orbis set up by, 22; and Simpson, 24, 27; and soccer, 24; Russia, Ukraine reports authored by, 26; and Fusion, 28–9, 35, 52, 96, 127–8; FBI contact briefed by, 35; US journalists' meeting with, 36; *NYT* reporters meet, 71; vanishes, 85–6; *FT*'s view of, 86–7; May

distances UK government from, 86; journalists avoided by, 87; fugitive status of, 88, 138; on FSB's cyber-ops role, 96; and Erovinkin, 100; Fusion memos of, 127; and return to normal life, 138, 139, 184; on Comey and dossier, 185; Moscow residence of, 228–9; and Mueller probe, 270; and sanctions on Russia, 326; Soviet-era file on, 326; Russia dossier of, *see* Steele dossier
Steele dossier, 5–6, 27–32, 36–7, 38–41, 51, 53, 64–7, 160–3, 195, 236, 238–9, 326; and Kislyak, 59; news breaks concerning, 66–7; *BuzzFeed* publishes, 67–70, 87; fake-news accusation against, 68, 69; Trump's reaction to, 68; Steele outed as author of, 70; growing readership of, 75; Peskov denounces, 75; Putin's reaction to, 79–80; Trump, Putin united in repudiating, 80–2; FBI establishes some accuracy in, 82, 210; FBI looks at truth of, 82; Kremlin's possession of, 92; Russia cyber-ops summarized in, 96; and deaths of government insiders, 100; and Flynn, 118–19; and Manafort, 160–2; and Yanukovych, 162; Schiff cites, before House Intelligence Committee, 177; Comey briefs Trump on, 204–5; on information exchange, 278; and Cohen, 280–1; compelling explanations in, 320–1
Steele, Janet, 20
Steele, Perris, 20
Stein, Jill, 124, 128
Stone, Roger, 108, 156
Stoyanov, Ruslan, 91–3, 97
Streep Meryl, 8
Strzhalkovsky, Vladimir, 282
Sullivan, Margaret, 70
Sunday Times, 25, 121
Suvorov, Viktor, 115, 117–18, 221
SVR, 42–3, 63, 95
Syria, 116, 129, 130

Tantum, Geoffrey, 20
Tass, 193
Thatcher, Margaret, 17
Tillerson, Rex, 251, 252, 262, 265, 321

Timati, 299, 310

Titov, Vasily, 307

Tokhtakhounov, Alimzhan, 291, 292

Trincher, Ilya, 291

Trincher, Vadim, 291–2

Trudeau, Justin: at G20, 249

Trump Construction Co., 283

Trump, Donald J.: presidential campaign of, 6–7; seen as Russia's candidate, 6–7; presidency won by, 6, 37; Putin praised by, 7–8; and missing emails, 7, 66; seen as Putin's puppet, 7, 334; and blackmail rumours, 8; finances of, 9; Florida mansion of, 13–14; Russia's alleged covert financing of, 13; and sexual activities, 14, 65; swift political rise of, 26–7; Steele probes on DNC's behalf, 27; and sexual proclivities, 30–1; Russia talking to associates of, 33–4; and Page, 48; Russia's damaging material on, 55; Kislyak meets, 59; tweets by, 68, 72, 80–1, 114, 138, 179, 180, 194, 200, 203, 237, 238, 257; mainstream media hated by, 71–2; media accessibility of, 73; Republicans nominate, 83; and meeting with May, 86; presidency of, and "weaponized" data, 104; "Russia's actions" set to help, says Obama, 105; in CIA–FBI–NSA report, 108, 110; agrees to meet intelligence community, 112; Obama's Oval Office meeting with, 130; Flynn fired by, 135; Putin calls after presidential victory, 135; *Metro* story on, 137–8, 139; assumption of defeat of, 173–4; FBI questions patriotism of, 174; rebuked over collusion, 178; and wiretapping allegations, 179–80; reacts to FBI probe, 182; and lack of loyalty to staff, 191; meets Lavrov, Kislyak, 192–5, 197; and ISIS intelligence leak, 194; and special counsel, 202–3; and talk of impeachment, 203; and marriage to Zelnickova, 216–17; KGB file on, 216, 223–4; early interest in politics by, 217; first Moscow trip by, 218, 222–3; and Russia hotels, 218, 220, 223, 226, 227; meets Dubinins, 219, 220; ads taken out by, 224–5; early presidential ambition of, 224–5; Russia reappearance of, 227–8; end of first marriage of, 227; and Gorbachevs' US visit, 227; virtually bankrupt, 227; further Russian business attempts by, 235–6; Kremlin said to be cultivating, 236; and Miss Universe, 236, 237; Putin meets at G20, 250; and company of autocrats, 257; first European trip of, as president, 257; and climate change, 258, 263; and BND, 259; on Charlottesville, 262; inward-looking worldview of, 263; and troops in Afghanistan, 263; and use of torture, 263; on Russian expulsions, 265; Palm Beach mansion of, 273–4; and Rybolovlev's plane, 278–80; Clinton accused of criminality by, 279; Cyprus companies set up by, 283; casinos of, 285, 301, 302; and Sater, 288, 289, 294–5; FBI raids, 291–2; Scottish golf course of, 301; worldwide projects of, 301; first anniversary in office, 323; and Moscow sanctions, 325; congratulates Putin after presidential victory, 332; tours Europe, 333; meets the Queen, 333; and Comey, *see* Comey, James; and Flynn, *see* Flynn, Michael "Misha"; at G7, *see* G7; at G20, *see* G20; and Manafort, *see* Manafort, Paul; and Mueller probe, *see* Mueller, Robert; allegations concerning Russia and, *see* Steele dossier; Russia's alleged covert financing of, *see* Steele dossier; treason allegation against, *see* Steele dossier; and Deutsche Bank, *see* Deutsche Bank

Trump, Donald Jr, 160, 217, 240–3, 245–6, 256, 266–7, 272, 288, 329, 336

Trump, Fred, 303

Trump, Friedrich, 303

Trump, Ivana, *see* Zelnickova, Ivana

Trump, Ivanka, 157, 159, 173, 240, 254, 266, 281, 288, 315

Trump, Melania, 252, 255

Trump Revealed, 73

Trump SoHo, 288, 289

Trump Tower, 45–6, 107, 129, 130,

157, 168, 179, 204, 218, 219, 227, 235, 261, 283, 288; Moscow plan for, 238, 295–7, 307, 318; opening of, 284; mafioso found in, 285; seen as crime scene, 291; and Trincher, 291

Trutnev, Yuri, 276–7, 282

Tsargrad, 91, 92, 97

Tsereteli, Zurab, 228

Turkey, "Putinization" of, 129

The Twentieth Day of January (Allbeury), 6

25th Amendment, 203

Tyahnybok, Oleh, 151

Tyler, Steven, 292

Tymoshenko, Yulia, 141, 148, 150, 167; sues Manafort, 169

UFG, 305

UK: and trade with US, 86; expels Russian diplomats, 113; circumvention claim concerning, 160

Ukraine: and natural gas, 23; and Canada, 38; and 2014 conflict, 47; and US–Russian tension, 82; Russian military in, 83; Moscow's part in unrest in, 93; elections in, 141–4, 146–9 *passim*; and Orange Revolution, 141, 150; and Party of Regions, 141, 142, 146–50 *passim*, 154, 155, 156, 159; Yanukovych becomes president of, 149–50; discounted gas bill for, 150; revolution in, 151–3; and disappearances, 151; Putin's covert war in, 152; and "secret ledger", 159–60, 167–8; and Crimea, Cohen–Sater proposal for, 297; and Manafort, *see* Manafort, Paul

UPDK, 229

Uralkali, 273, 277, 282

USA: porous banking system of, 13; State Department in, 26, 47, 111, 147, 261–2, 263; Russian immigrants in, 50; Moscow spies based in, 57; and Ukraine, 82; expels Russian diplomats, 104, 111–12, 132; and "harassment" of diplomats of, 111–12; deep-running divisions in, 111; Congress building in, 172; USSR perceives nuclear plot of, 213;

and nuclear reduction, 227; and cyber-crime working group, 252–3; and attempt to "normalize" relations, 263–4; seen as mirror of Russia, 325; and sanctions on Russia, *see* Russia; 2016 presidential election in, *see* Trump, Donald J.; *see also* Obama, Barack; Trump, Donald J.

USSR, 18, 19, 212, 213, 215, 217, 218, 223; break-up of, 56, 284; and nuclear reduction, 227; *see also* Russia

Van Hollen, Chris, 316

VEB, 43, 306, 317, 318

Vekselberg, Viktor, 282

Veselnitskaya, Natalia, 233–5, 243–5, 246, 256, 266, 270, 293, 294, 316, 320, 329, 336

Voloshin, Oleg, 155–6

Vrablic, Rosemary, 315

VTB, 61, 295, 306–7, 312, 318

Walker, Shaun, 50–1, 94–5, 237–8

Wall Street Journal, 23, 70

Washington Examiner, 182

Washington Post, 36, 60, 72–3, 74, 106, 132, 135, 156, 158, 163, 181, 188, 189, 210, 266, 317; and Trump early presidential ambition, 224

Watergate, 5, 9, 14, 37, 67, 73, 131, 135, 156, 172, 181, 190, 195–6, 203

Weissmann, Andrew, 268

Wells Fargo, 13

Westminster, Duke of, 3–4

Whitehouse, Sheldon, 135

WikiLeaks, 93, 109, 260, 334; and emails, 7, 35, 158, 161; moves hosting to Moscow, 109

Wilson, Duncan, 120

Wilson, Woodrow, 111

Wimmer, Willy, 124

Wiswell (née Makosiy), Natalia, 308, 310–11

Wiswell, Tim, 307–11

Wood, Andrew, 38

Woodley, Bill, 316

Woodward, Bob, 67

World Cup, 24–5, 30, 54, 108, 233

Yahoo! News, 36, 60

Yanukovych, Viktor, 141–4, 147–8, 149–52, 153, 154, 166, 327; and Moscow loan, 150–1; flees Ukraine, 152; death of, 156; Putin's dim view of, 162; and secret Putin meeting, 162
Yates, Sally, 133–5
Yatsenko, Sergei, 47
Yatsenyuk, Arseniy, 151

Yeltsin, Boris, 17, 77, 228; and failed coup, 18
Yushchenko, Viktor, 141, 143, 146

Zakaria, Fareed, 74
Zakharova, Maria, 112
Zelnickova, Ivana, 216–17, 222, 227
Zelnickova, Milos, 217
Zuckerberg, Mark, 110

ALSO BY LUKE HARDING

ff

A Very Expensive Poison

1st November 2006: Alexander Litvinenko is brazenly poisoned in central London. Twenty-two days later he dies, killed from the inside by polonium—a rare, lethal and highly radioactive substance. His crime? He had made some powerful enemies in Russia.

This is the inside story of the life and death of Litvinenko and of Russia's new cold war with the West. Harding traces the journey of the nuclear poison across London, from hotel room to nightclub, assassin to victim. It's a deadly trail that leads back to Vladimir Putin, and to a regime exposed by the Panama Papers.

"An expert chronicle of a sensational but opaque crime, and of the terrifying lawlessness it epitomised. Enthralling." A. D. Miller, author of *Snowdrops*

"Harding, a former Moscow correspondent for the *Guardian*, tells this ghastly tale with real authority, wit and panache . . . This book is as 'definitive' as it claims." *The Times*

"Gripping . . . Harding doesn't overcook the metaphor, but Mayfair and all it represents is portrayed here as something potentially, maybe inherently toxic." Peter Pomerantsev, *London Review of Books*

ff

The Snowden Files: The Inside Story of the World's Most Wanted Man

Edward Snowden, a young computer genius working for America's National Security Agency, blew the whistle on the way this frighteningly powerful organisation uses new technology to spy on the entire planet. The consequences have shaken the leaders of nations worldwide. This is the inside story of Snowden's deeds and the journalists who faced down pressure from the US and UK governments to break a remarkable scoop. From the day he left his glamorous girlfriend in Hawaii, carrying a hard drive full of secrets, to the weeks of secret-spilling in Hong Kong and his battle for asylum, Snowden's story reads like a globe-trotting thriller.

"Reads like a le Carré novel crossed with something by Kafka . . . A fast-paced, novelistic narrative. Leaves readers with an acute understanding of the serious issues involved." *New York Times*

"A super-readable, thrillerish . . . exciting account." *London Review of Books*

"Harding captures nicely the moment when the *Guardian* pushes the button on its first Snowden story, an intense, adrenalin-filled cocktail of high-minded journalistic zeal and the sheer thrill of publishing sensitive information." *Financial Times*

ff

WikiLeaks: Inside Julian Assange's War on Secrecy

It was the biggest leak in history. WikiLeaks infuriated the world's greatest superpower, embarrassed the British royal family and helped cause a revolution in North Africa. The man behind it was Julian Assange, one of the strangest figures ever to become a worldwide celebrity. Internet messiah or cyber-terrorist? Information freedom fighter or sex criminal?

Award-winning *Guardian* journalists David Leigh and Luke Harding follow the story as it takes on ever-weirder twists and turns. In London, Assange went to ground in the back bedroom of the Ecuadorian embassy. Meanwhile, in a courtroom near Washington, the fate of the US army whistleblower Bradley Manning hung in the balance. And in Hawaii, a young man named Edward Snowden, working as a contractor for the National Security Agency, was about to take WikiLeaks into even darker territory.

"A rip-roaring narrative of secrets, tantrums, technological wizardry, personal betrayal and vengeance." *Irish Independent*

"A behind-the-scenes adrenalin rush of secret meetings, encrypted websites and passwords written on hotel napkins." *Metro*

"Excellent." *Sunday Times*

ff

Mafia State: How One Reporter Became an Enemy of the Brutal New Russia

In 2007 Luke Harding arrived in Moscow to take up a new job as a correspondent for the *Guardian*. Within months, mysterious agents from Russia's Federal Security Service—the successor to the KGB—had broken into his flat. He found himself tailed by men in cheap leather jackets, bugged, and even summoned to Lefortovo, the KGB's notorious prison.

The break-in was the beginning of an extraordinary psychological war against the journalist and his family. Putin's spies used tactics developed by the KGB and perfected in the 1970s by the Stasi. This clandestine campaign burst into the open in 2011, when the Kremlin expelled Harding from Moscow—the first Western reporter to be deported from Russia since the days of the Cold War.

Mafia State is a brilliant and haunting account of the insidious methods used by a resurgent Kremlin against its so-called "enemies"—human rights workers, Western diplomats, journalists and opposition activists. Harding gives a unique, personal and compelling portrait of today's Russia, two decades after the end of communism, that reads like a spy thriller.

"A courageous and explosive exposé." Orlando Figes

"Russia laid bare in an absorbing account of four years spent as head of the *Guardian*'s Moscow bureau . . . An essential read." David Clark, *New Statesman*